DATE DUE

DE 19 '97			

DEMCO 38-296

KNOWLEDGE AND POWER

This book is dedicated to the victims of the war in the former Yugoslavia.

Knowledge and Power
The Changing Role of European Intellectuals

Edited by
PHILIP K. LAWRENCE
and
MATHIAS DÖBLER

Ashgate

Aldershot • Brookfield USA • Singapore • Sydney

© Philip K. Lawrence and Mathias Döbler 1996

Ashgate Publishing Limited
Gower House
Croft Road
Aldershot
Hants GU11 3HR
England

Ashgate Publishing Company
Old Post Road
Brookfield
Vermont 05036
USA

British Library Cataloguing in Publication Data
Knowledge and power : the changing role of European
    intellectuals. - (Perspectives on Europe)
    1.Intellectuals - Europe - Political activity 2.Europe -
    Politics and government - 1945-
    I.Lawrence, Philip K., 1953- . II.Mathias Döbler
    305.5'52'094

Library of Congress Catalog Card Number: 96-084798

ISBN 1 85972 266 0

Printed and bound by Athenaeum Press, Ltd.,
Gateshead, Tyne & Wear.

Contents

v

Contributors

András Bozóki is Associate Professor of Political Science at the Central European University, Budapest, Hungary.

Lena Dominelli is Professor of Social Administration at the University of Sheffield, UK.

Ankie Hoogvelt is Professor of Sociology at the University of Sheffield, UK.

Philip K. Lawrence is Professor of Politics at the University of the West of England, Bristol, UK.

Steven Longstaff is Associate Professor in Sociology at Atkinson College, York University, Toronto, Canada.

Lennart Ollauson is Associate Professor of the History of Science and Ideas and Director of Research in Humanities at the University of Göteborg, Sweden.

M'hammed Sabour is Associate Professor of Sociology at the University of Joensuu, Finland.

Avizier Tucker is Lecturer in Philosophy at Palacky University, Oloumouc, The Czech Republic.

Ido Wiejers is Associate Professor in Education at the Catholic University, Nijmegen, Netherlands.

Acknowledgements

These are not pleasant times in the world of British university intellectuals. The academic press is full of tales concerning the low state to which the profession has fallen. The current state of affairs is one that leads to highly competitive impulses. We are all looking over our shoulder worried about whether our research output is sufficient.

Bearing these comments in mind it has been a particularly pleasant and contrasting experience to work and liaise with colleagues in Europe whose approach is more relaxed and less competitive than that found in the UK. I thank all of the contributors here for making the editing of this book a very rewarding experience. I would also like to thank my friends David Coates, Jack Spence, Steve Giles, and David Boucher, as well as my new colleagues at the University of the West of England, who reveal that not all of us have succumbed to the logic of hyper-competition.

Thanks are due to the secretarial staff at BAe Airbus Filton and Professor John McDermid, of the Department of Computer Science, University of York, who kindly provided an office for me while I was researching at York University. A major debt is also owed to Mathias Döbler who organized the original workshop at the ISSEI in Graz where most of the contributors to this book were first brought together.

Finally, profound gratitude is due to my wife, Benita, who has given her time generously to me even though she has her own intellectual projects to complete. She is a tower of strength.

Philip Lawrence, Bristol, May, 1996

1. Introduction

PHILIP K. LAWRENCE

The collection of essays brought together here does not represent an attempt to articulate a unified and homogeneous account of the role of intellectuals in Western society today. Indeed, the variety of perspectives presented in this book reveals the difficulty in developing a straightforward model of the modern intellectual. The fragmented and disjointed spirit of the times at this fin de siècle makes such a task unworkable.

Despite these problems the introduction to these texts can illuminate some interesting points of comparison between the various contributions. One thing that is certain is that in the period since the Second World War the nature of the intellectual's identity and role has undergone profound changes. In the West the death of the Keynesian economic paradigm and the assault of the market on social democracy has profoundly altered the relationship of the state to the university based academic. The inclusion of intellectuals in the post-war renewal of Enlightenment projects is over. The managed, corporate, welfare state did much to bring a new generation of intellectuals into the domain of state sponsored social engineering. But now the paradigm is one of private sector business rationale, linked, as Garnham has shown in the British case, to a critique of the role of intellectuals in fostering an anti-entrepreneurial spirit.[1]

In the East the collapse of the USSR and East European communism has similarly pulled the rug from under the feet of a differently inclined group of social engineers. Thus the Marxist-Leninist version of Modernity is clearly more discredited than its Western counterpart. Western liberal democratic narratives of social progress may be problematic, if not absurd, but not quite as ludicrous as the notion that what was going on behind the Iron Curtain was a form of worker's paradise. But even so I am inclined to agree with Meštrović that both the East's and the West's variants of

1

Enlightenment narratives may be in trouble.[2]

The difficulties inherent in the role of intellectuals in bringing social democracy to fruition are apparent in the essays in this volume by Ollauson and Dominelli and Hoogvelt. Ollauson's chapter on Gunnar Myrdal shows how the Swedish economist wrestled with the contradictions inherent in unifying the role of intellectual and social engineer. For Myrdal the problems were overcome by clarifying the ends of social science research in terms of enlightenment, rationality and social welfare. Myrdal appealed to the arbitration of powerful groups in society, a tactic reinforced by the political hegemony of social democracy in Sweden after 1945, but ultimately the grounds of justification for Myrdal, as Ollauson shows, are a set of Enlightenment assumptions concerning rationality and progress. But what happens when historical processes undermine the credibility of a social democratic vision of social progress?

Today the prosetylisers of Keynesian welfare economics are voices crying in the wilderness. Myrdal argued, that contrary to the views of von Hayek, the mixed economy and managed social welfare were inevitable consequences of the development of the capitalist economy.[3] But now the resurrection of the free market and the critique of state intervention also appear as the inevitable consequence of the intensification of capitalism in the form of globalization. Moreover, the neo-conservative mobilization of protest against the state indicates that the cultural experience of state managed welfare programmes has not been positive. Thus while the model of the command economy applied in Eastern Europe is completely moribund, the economic model of social democracy is also virtually a corpse. Historical transformations show that trans-cultural and trans-historical models of social progress now seem utterly ridiculous.

The consequences of capitalist globalization for intellectuals are explored here in the chapter by Dominelli and Hoogvelt, which examines recent events in Britain. They show how universities in Britain benefited from the expansion of the welfare state and the need of the mixed economy for a cadre of experts drawn from the social sciences. With hindsight I would argue that an extraordinary feature of this process was that university based intellectuals were able to effect contempt for the society which funded their affluent and highly autonomous lifestyle. 'Counter hegemonic' intellectuals could preach on the evils of their society with impunity.

In the early 1970s these themes were taken up by theorists exploring the idea of a legitimation crisis in Western society. From a left perspective Jürgen Habermas explained how the Keynesian inspired welfare state had spawned a set of institutions which were undermining traditional capitalist value systems.[4] Planning, anti-market welfare programmes, extended and expanded higher education and new cultural initiatives - often funded by the state - were depicted as hostile to the belief systems essential to capitalist legitimation. Certainly here the university would occupy a central place. It is no accident that exponents of critical theory, tired of waiting for the proletariat to stir itself, indulged in the whimsy of believing that students could be a revolutionary agent in the West. These expectations were overblown, but it was true that in the late 1960s and early 70s many universities were environments hostile to the other established institutions of society. Perhaps I might mention, though, that what no one seemed to notice was that in societies that were deemed to be superior to the West, the same freedom to protest and articulate critical views was entirely lacking.

As Dominelli and Hoogvelt show these times are long gone. In the 1980s in Britain a series of reforms have expanded the system, while denying the resources necessary for traditional patterns of teaching and research to continue. Through installing mechanisms of competition in teaching and research performance, and redefining higher education via a market inspired discourse of product delivery and efficiency, the British state has effectively destroyed the autonomy of intellectuals who might articulate a 'counter hegemonic' ideology. Today in Britain career success for academics, defined in terms of pecuniary reward and status, exists in the realm of providing research and consultancy for the private sector or in occupying the senior management roles which define and enforce the new regime. We have here, then, a dramatic new form of structuration in the Academy. Those who are of use to private capital or the state's new regime of deregulation are often removed from traditional intellectual activities altogether, those left behind are stymied by the bureacracy implicit in the highly interventionist practices of deregulation, while at the bottom an army of teaching assistants, temporary and part-time lecturers and contract researchers earn salaries often lower than those of menial occupations.

This characterization of British academia, which I believe is substantially correct, reveals the weakness of new class theories which were so persuasive two decades ago. In the post-industrial era the university intellectual had supposedly come of age. The corporate state needed the skills and the hegemonic discourse of the new intellectuals. Gouldner argued that modern states required ideological support more than any previous political forms. Intellectuals were the 'purveyors of the regime of truth'.[5] But the regime of truth characteristic of the 1970s has melted away. The new right militancy of the 1980s, with its strident proclamation of the market, and reinvigorated possessive individualism, was conceived and articulated in think tanks, largely outside the domains of established academia. When these ideas were actualized in the governance of the Reagan/Thatcher era, the liberal arts

3

academic establishment was simply sidelined.

Bearing this in mind, we might ask where the 'cultural capital' of the last fifteen years has been produced? In Britain not only has the output of scholars and intellectuals been made socially irrelevant, the traditional values of the British arts and cultural establishment have been undermined as well. Following a trend already well established in the United States the form of art available in museums, galleries and displayed in public places, as well as the music performed at major concert venues, is increasingly determined by its capacity to attract corporate funding.[6] In other words the selection of which elements of modern culture to promote, is driven increasingly by its symbiotic relationship with the meaning systems of large business corporations. What we deem to be of universal value may simply reflect a configuration that power and money has made universally present. I mean by this something more than Adorno's notion of the culture industry. It is not just that there is a huge media, entertainment/information industry churning out a standardized product to promote 'fun culture', the residual aesthetics explicit in this production come increasingly from a deregulated private corporate sector, whose values are regarded as self evident common sense and are rarely investigated.

Assuming that my remarks above have some validity I wonder if the time may have come to speak of a post-literate society in some Western countries. It is often reported that in the United States ninety percent of what is read is consumed by ten percent of the population. Thus if we can still speak of a transmission belt for culture, we must concede that intellectuals have little to do with its character and direction. But of course this observation needs to be qualified. If the traditional function of intellectuals in promoting argument and reflection through the medium of writing and speech is moribund, new functions are very much alive in the activities of the media intellectuals. Thus as Garnham shows we can make a sharp distinction between media intellectuals and the traditional intelligentsia.[7] This distinction is taken up here in the chapter by Sabour who speaks of the distinction between employee intellectuals and propagators/vulgarisors. In terms of influence there is no contest. Intellectuals who sell their services to television and the popular press reach a much wider audience and attain a far greater power to shape images and beliefs than their traditional counterparts. In Britain a top academic journal may have a global circulation of 3000. In essence publication in such journals is a form of peer group communication. Similarly many published monographs sell less than 1000 copies. In comparison the ideas of mediatic intellectuals reach mass audiences numbered in millions. This difference in impact also corresponds to differences in prestige. While the status of the traditional employee

4

intellectual continues to decline, a fact reinforced by a traditional antagonism to intellectuals in Anglo Saxon culture, mediatic intellectuals can attain the status of major celebrities. But is the role of the media intellectuals problematic?

In Britain in the 1980s the intellectuals who came to prominence in the media did not enhance the reputation of their colleagues. Rather media performances and press output were geared to undermining and lambasting their peers.[8] Highly visible media intellectuals joined the populist assault on the liberal arts image of the university. In France Pierre Bourdieu has attacked the mediatics as vulgarisors who have cheapened the integrity of the intellectual's vocation.[9] On the other hand it is more than likely that those in traditional guise will resent the fame and fortune of media intellectuals. However, there does seem to be a point of serious criticism here. Prime-time television is unlikely to want analysis or commentary of a deep or serious nature. Interviews on current affairs programmes are short and often reduced to a soundbite, while editors and programme managers for talk shows usually insist that issues are sensationalized and trivialized. Many articles by academics in mass circulation newspapers in Britain are often just populist hot air and reveal a transparent lack of integrity. In addition there is a clear political agenda. In the Gulf War of 1991 armies of academic pundits apppeared on US television to debate the unfolding drama. But as Kellner has shown virtually no air time was given to those who were sceptical about US policy.[10] Similarly academics in the West have made little headway in correcting the clichés that have characterized commentary on the war in Bosnia.[11] Thus as Bourdieu indicates there may well be grounds to see the absorbtion of intellectuals into the media as a form of prostitution and vulgarization. Ultimately, as Sabour argues, the media exposure may serve to discredit intellectuals and to further erode their autonomy.

These difficulties have been posed for intellectuals in Western countries. But those in Eastern Europe were also included in the new class analysis of the 1970s. The bureaucratic and technocratic structures of state socialism were regarded as the perfect architecture for the social engineers of the command economy. Here at least the class identity of intellectuals was clear. The majority were tools of the regime, their function really was to disseminate a regime of truth couched in a modernist socialist narrative. On the other hand Poland, Hungary, Czechoslovakia and the USSR had a handful of intellectuals who would surface occasionally to cause the authorities a headache. Here, though, the obvious point is that the party intellectuals failed to ground their states' practices in a regime of truth. The political authority of the Polish United Workers Party or the SED in the DDR rested on force and the threat of Soviet invasion if political disorder threatened, not political legitimacy. In the whole of Eastern Europe the modernist strategy of replacing local and national forms of identity with the credo of international socialism failed. History, culture, religion and ethnicity have all outlived the experiment of state socialism.

The death of state socialism left intellectuals in the former communist countries in a double bind. One group were simply discredited and in some cases criminalized. But the groups who fought to end these regimes have also found the changed times difficult. The experience in Poland of Solidarity showed that unity could disintegrate almost immediately. As the chapter by Bozóki reveals, former opponents of the communist authorities in Hungary found themselves at loggerheads in 1991 over the character of the coalition led by the MDF. His analysis of the rise of the Charter movement shows how a group of intellectuals came to see the new regime as quasi totalitarian. These intellectuals founded a movement which sought to protect a minimum standard of democracy in Hungary.

Opinions about the Charter movement will probably be split. It is certainly possible that Charter intellectuals exaggerated the authoritarian tendencies of the new regime. However, it is also feasible to maintain that the Charter movement helped to develop and sustain a form of civil society in Hungary that would tolerate no other political form but democracy. Its activities impress me because the movement seemed to be asking questions about the nature of democracy which we are not asking in the West. The Charter movement also helped to ward off the tendencies to fragmentation I mentioned above. But in the long term a movement like the Charter cannot remove the crisis that is implicit in the new situation in Eastern Europe. To put it bluntly, intellectuals in the former communist countries are caught in the crossfire between resurgent nationalism and the forces of globalizing capitalism. If state socialism was a huge experiment, so too is transforming industrial command economies into capitalist market forms. It was obvious in the 1980s that many groups in the East were envious of the seeming lifestyle of Westerners. But what is clear now is that their cultures were unprepared for the contigency, ambiguity and vicissitudes of the capitalist market. In the West the negative consequences of market driven social systems have been offset by a hundred and fifty years of reform and reaction to periods of crisis. In Eastern Europe and Russia citizens have received an unprecedented and sharp education in the realities of capitalist accumulation overnight. In many cases intellectuals who invited their countrymen to this party are now discredited. Thus it is not really surprising that we now see former communist leaders regaining crediblity in Eastern Europe, while reinventing themselves as ardent nationalists. Many citizens in the former communist countries now seem to believe they have been sold a false prospectus. The ultimate outlook for these countries is far from clear.

The chapter in this collection by Avi Tucker contains a powerful argument against this contention. Tucker attacks Vaclav Havel for his utopian critique of modernism and his belief that communist totalitarianism and capitalist democracy are just two different sides of modernity. Havel's theory of human authenticity, which is based on the philosophy of Heidegger, is hyper critical of capitalist consumerism and the technological imperative of the Western economy. According to Tucker Havel is also dismissive of the formal institutions of Western democracy, in particular political parties. In addition Havel favours a morality of conviction, as opposed to a morality of social responsibility.

Tucker's key point is not to critique Havel as a thinker, but rather to show how his beliefs emasculated him politically after the Velvet Revolution. From a Western point of view there is a huge irony in this. The logic of the collapse of communism was supposed to come from the superiority of capitalist democracy and the desire of the citizens of the former communist countries to convert to the gospel of liberal democracy. Thus to discover that leaders of the anti-communist revolutions were not very keen on capitalism either, may have come as a shock. Perhaps, though, it is merely our narcissism which induces us to see the issues in this way. While it is undoubtedly the case that Western capitalism is more productive, provides greater consumer choice and guarantees a higher degree of personal freedom than existed in Eastern European communism, this is not to say that the system does not have serious and growing problems. In Canada and Italy political volatility has reached new heights, in other Western countries political cynicism is eating away at democratic culture and producing serious political alienation. Surveys in America reveal an astounding degree of distrust amongst citizens towards their government. In the past critiques of the Western way of life, especially post-war, have been little more than the malaise of intellectuals. Marcuse and others sought to show that citizens were merely happy in their unfreedom. But the symptoms of chronic discontent are now more palpable. In Europe's and America's middle classes a new sense of economic insecurity permeates groups which were previously secure, or believed they were. At the end of the century there is certainly no vision of a new arcadia for the next millenium.

None of this is meant as a critique of the arguments advanced by Tucker. I merely seek to suggest that the jury is still out on the experiment going on in Eastern Europe because the future of the West itself is unclear. This brings me to the contribution of Weijers. His chapter laments the sick condition of Western democracy and he cites a pressing need for some spiritual and intellectual inspiration. Yet he challenges the right of intellectuals to provide this and he suggests that in democracies there is no need for intellectuals to testify in the manner of Benda, Satre or Said. My view of this is that we no longer know what condition our democracies are really in. A habit developed in the heyday of pluralism has been to see the quality of democracy as evident in the existence of certain formal institutions.[12] But institutions need vision, action and cultural habits to deliver the promise of their formal charters. Today are our 'habits of the heart' compatible with a tolerant and vital democracy? This is debatable and I would contend that there may well be the need for civil movements, such as the Charter movement, to stir up new enthusiasm for democracy in the West. If intellectuals are not to speak then from where can reinvigorated beliefs come? In the media the excited voices of some postmodern intellectuals are heard, offering in my view an ecstatic vision of despair. In contrast some of the rest of us may seek to testify about the values of our civilization and whether they offer some hope for the future. Postmodern despair is after all a theory; it is not an essential construct inscribed into our being.

The final two contributions in this collection harp back to earlier times. Longstaff reveals how American intellectuals, after World War Two, were at the forefront of the CIA's ideological attack against the cultural edifice of communism in Western Europe. The battle was for the hearts and minds of European intellectuals who might sympathize with Soviet political aims. Thus the target was Paris, rather than Moscow. Longstaff's chapter reveals how art, literature and music came to be manipulated as variables in the Cold War. In terms of the general post-war debate about the role of intellectuals his chapter indicates how critical the logic of the Cold War was in organizing the class allegiance of certain intellectuals, and in revealing the true nature of intellectuals' interests in the United States. What I believe is often not understood in Europe, where debate has often centred on the rival claims of normative versus sociological views of the intellectual, is that intellectuals have been pivotal in providing the American Security State with a discourse about Western interests and the rationality of US Cold War policy. Intellectuals have 'written security'. Arguments about the declining possibility of the universal or hegemonic intellectual must contend with the unprecedented power of the mandarins of US foreign policy. After all in the US a Harvard academic became Secretary of State, and he certainly was not smitten with Havel's morality of conviction.

My own chapter deals with this issue as well, against the background of traditional assumptions concerning the intellectual's vocation. I seek to show how the security arm of the state co-opted specific academics to disentangle the contradictions of a nuclear security policy, and to provide a security discourse which removed the palpable anxiety, which some members of the political elite felt concerning nuclear weapons. I further show how the discourse shifted focus towards the issue of counter insurgency and Vietnam. Thus, to use an allusion of Sabour's, men of the pen and men of the sword walked hand in hand.

I contend that in the US the greatest influence on the output of orthodox social science research is the question, broadly conceived, of American security interests. When intellectual output makes a telling point in relation to this issue it can propel the author to unprecedented fame. Thus Paul Kennedy's *Rise and Fall of the Great Powers*, published in 1988, had a huge impact on intellectual reflection concerning US power. Similarly the ideas of former State department official Francis Fukuyama served to frame much of the debate concerning America's post-Cold War mission. Even the manic outpourings of Alvin Toffler now apparently inform the reforming zeal of politicians such as Newt Gingrich.

Little about the future role of the intellectual is clear, but obituaries for the universal intellectual may be premature. As we stand transfixed by the fashionable pessimism of postmodern discourse, the states of East Asia will have no trouble in locating narratives to justify their claim to hegemony in the next century.

Notes and references

1. Garnham, Nicholas (1995), 'The Media and Narratives of the Intellectual', *Media, Culture and Society*, vol. 17, no. 3, p. 375.
2. See, Meštrović, Stjepan, G. (1994), *The Balkanization of the West*, Routledge, London.
3. This view is also taken by Habermas. See, Habermas, Jürgen (1973), *Legitimation Crisis*, Heinemann, London, 1976.
4. Ibid, Ch. 1.
5. Goulner, Alvin (1978), *The Dialectic of Ideology and Technology*, Heinemann, London.
6. See, Schiller, Herbert (1989), *Culture Inc.*, Oxford University Press, New York and Oxford, Ch. 1.
7. Garnham, 'Narratives of the Intellectual', p. 362.
8. Ibid, p. 375.
9. Bourdieu, Pierre (1994), 'L'emprise du Journalismey', *Actes de la Recherche en Sciences Sociales*, no. 101. pp. 3-9.
10. Kellner, Douglas (1992), *The Persian Gulf TV War*, Westview, Boulder.
11. For an account of the way in which the Bosnian conflict has been misrepresented see my 'European Security: a New Era of Crisis?', in Bideleux, R. and Taylor, R. (eds) (1996), *European Integration and Disintegration: East and West*, Routledge, London, pp. 45-64.
12. See my, (1990) *Democracy and the Liberal State*, Dartmouth, Aldershot, Ch. 3.

2. Between Patronage and Autonomy: the Position of Intellectuals in Modern Society

M'HAMMED SABOUR

The deepest structure in the culture and ideology of intellectuals is their pride in their own autonomy, which they understand as based on their own reflection, and their ability to decide their course in the light of this reflection. Thus any authority that demands obedience or any tradition that demands conformity without reflection and decision is experienced as a tyrannical violation of self. (Gouldner 1979: pp. 33-34)

L'intellectuel est un personnage bidimensionnel qui n'existe et ne subsiste comme tel que si (et seulement si) il est investi d'une autorité spécifique, conférée par un monde intellectuel autonome (c'est-à-dire indépendant des pouvoirs religieux, politiques, économiques) dont il respecte les lois spécifiques, et si (et seulement si) il engage cette autorité spécifique dans des luttes politiques. (Bourdieu 1992: p. 462)

Position and Dependency of Intellectuals in Society

Creating, elaborating, evaluating, interpreting and disseminating ideas have been some of the main tasks of intellectuals. As mythmakers, masters of words and symbols, and cultural workers they have since ancient times constantly held a prominent position in society. This can be seen in the eminent status philosophers have had in Greek culture, the ulama (learned men) in Islamic civilization and the hommes de lettres and scholars in European history.

From this perspective, the position of intellectuals in society is regulated by the interplay of at least five factors: (i) The relations which link intellectuals to like-minded people, men of ideas and learning. (ii) The relations which link them to the cultural market and to those who consume their product (the educated and the laity). (iii) Their position in the

11

dominant political paradigm or official Establishment (e.g. academic institutions, political parties, etc.). (iv) The stance they adopt in relation to the prevailing currents of thought and ideas. (v) Their position in the social structure and their cultural disposition and habitus. Above all, their livelihood and freedom are primordial factors in these dimensions and prerequisite to a definition of their activity. According to Andreski an intellectual 'who has a private and earned income, on which he can maintain himself at a customary standard and defer expenses connected with his work, is completely immune from economic restraints on his freedom' (1965: p. 211). The economic factors thus represent a significant element in the autonomy or dependency of intellectuals. In this regard, Andreski classifies intellectuals according to the way they obtain their livelihood and the freedom they enjoy in their work. For some a livelihood is earned by the intellectual work they do, for others it is not. In addition, Andreski divides them into professional and non-professional. For the latter, intellectual activity may be a hobby or time-filler, while the professionals include the employees and the freelancers who live from the sale of their products. The employee-intellectuals are therefore classified according to 'their security of tenure, and the extent to which they are directed and supervised in their work' (1965 p. 202). On this basis, Andreski differentiates four sets of employee-intellectuals: (i) Those who have insecure tenure and supervised work (e.g. research fellows); (ii) those with secure tenure and supervised work (e.g. pemanently appointed researchers); (iii) the academics in the European university sector who have a secure tenure but are free of any supervision of their activity; and (iv) those with insecure tenure and whose work is not supervised (e.g. in classical times when intellectuals depended on kings and the nobility for their livelihood). Let us deal with this last group first.

Historically speaking, in spite of the importance of intellectuals their position was relatively unstable and fluctuating because it depended on the recognition of others (e.g. the rulers, like-minded intellectuals and the laity). Because of their insecure income, they were obliged by force of circumstances to seek protection. As those who were culturally and artistically oriented and sensitive, and who were likely to be ready to understand and consume their art, ideas and intellectual support came from influential social groups and the upper ranks, the intellectuals found refuge within their sphere. Often, these 'lovers of ideas and knowledge' also had political and economic power. The price of this protection often involved dependency and submission. But at that time intellectuals were almost by vocation oriented towards this kind of patronage.[1] In fact, only the most talented and distinguished intellectuals were fortunate enough to find a patron. Sometimes, the patronage they found took the form of benefaction.[2]

The Enlightenment in Europe with its whole intellectual, humanistic, artistic and cultural project brought a striking change to the ontology of intellectuals. This is evidenced by the foundation of numerous literary and scientific academies and institutions in different parts of Europe between the 14th and 17th centuries. Moreover, their position was endorsed and empowered by the attention paid to them by the educated strata in society. Until the 17th century their protectors were usually kings, princes, the high nobility and members of the aristocracy. The 18th century saw the flourishing of 'salon-culture' in Europe, and especially, as described by Coser (1965: pp. 11-18), in France. Maintained mainly by wealthy and culturally-inspired ladies (e.g. Mme. Geoffrin, Mme. Necker) from the upper class, these literary salons constituted a forum where the intellectuals (e.g. hommes de lettres, poets and savants) could exhibit their knowledge and talent, and receive criticism, appreciation and feedback for their creativity. Moreover, for these dilettante ladies the salon was a place for showing the sense of their cultural distinction, taste and generous maecena by attracting famous men of art and ideas. For the latter, on the other hand, entertaining their benefactors and assuaging their artistic and literary fantasy and curiosity, was rewarded by recognition and a pension.

The role played directly or indirectly in the French Revolution by the writings of some intellectual-philosophers has, to some extent, shed the light on their power and their impact on change in society; they were the disseminators of the seeds of this Revolution. The reaction of the leaders of Revolution against the works of some intellectuals (e.g. Pascal, Beaumarchais, Diderot) was not based only on the fact that their thinking was a menace to the Revolution but also on their social origins or their courtship of the upper class and nobility. The intellectuals were relatively hated or admired by the different educated strata and by the laity, but the powerholders looked often at them with an eye of suspicion. Napoleon named them vermin and imbecile bacause they demanded more freedom of the press and freedom of speech (Nettl, 1969, pp. 71-80). A few decades after Napoleon, thanks to the changes in the social, economic and cultural fields, which consisted largely of a movement of l'art pour l'art (art for art's sake) led by T. Gautier and G. Flaubert, this type of patronage of the intellectuals came to an end (Bourdieu 1992).

The Patronage of Intellectuals

From what has been presented above we can deduce that the position of intellectuals depended on the recognition of others, and that their status in society was marked by uncertainty and fragility. The importance and the strength of this position was in proportion to the degree of acceptance of their knowledge and its symbolic significance in the eyes of those who consumed their ideas in oral or written form, that is, their cultural and symbolic product (e.g. the rulers, the reading public, like-minded intellectuals). This fluctuating situation made an impact on their existence and ontology. Because of the instability linked to the political and economic structure intellectuals were often relatively insecure and dependent.

In order to survive, the search for a culturally-enlightened, comprehensive and generous protector was an important concern for intellectuals. They were obliged to struggle for their social utility and indispensability. If some intellectuals embarked on challenging the prevailing mode of thought (e.g. Rousseau), others were more compromising and directed their intellectual activities according to the goals, the interests, and the expectations of the reading public and the tastes of their sponsors.[3] It goes without saying that those intellectuals who were economically independent and from distinguished social origins (e.g. Montaigne, Voltaire, Goethe), and for whom intellectual activity was more of a hobby than a bread-earner, practised their activities without having to conform to material restrictions or patrons' requirements. There are cases, however, where hommes de lettres from the upper classes and well-to-do origins were active in acquiring recognition from the members of their own class or the nobility, not only for economic success but also for their intellectual and cultural creativity and talent (e.g. Montesquieu).

We can, therefore, outline different forms of patronage. There was a patronage of endorsement, where an individual, a family or an institution sponsored the activities of intellectuals for the sake of intellectual and scientific curiosity alone (e.g. Mme de Lambert endorsed Montesqieu to have a chair in the Academy). There was a patronage inspired by admiration and concretized in the support and dissemination of another person's ideas, a mode of patronage which was widely common during the period of 'salon culture' in the 18th century (e.g. the relationship between Diderot and Mme. Geoffrin).

Then there was also a patronage of identification. Individuals or institutions identified themselves with intellectuals' work and sponsored it because it served their interests and the purposes of their ideology. Thirdly, intellectuals were also involved in Machiavellian patronage. This patronage aimed at integrating and chaining the intellectuals to a certain range of social and cultural action, and at profiting from their knowledge about and influence over others, especially the laity (e.g. Napoleon took advantage of

14

intellectuals' support in gaining access to power, and then rejected them). But, whatever the type of patronage, it often existed at the expense of intellectuals' freedom and autonomy.

The Autonomy of the Intellectual and the Emergence of the Universal

During the second half of the 19th century, and the beginning of the 20th century, the growth of industrialization, the relative universalization of formal education, the development of printing and publication techniques, and the increasing consumption of newspapers have all had a tremendous impact on the status of intellectuals. The active involvement of many intellectuals (e.g. E. Zola, M. Proust, A. Gide, A. France) in the Dreyfus Affair[4] and the intelligentsia in the Bolshevik Revolution has made them visible as a self-conscious group and as agents who, from their particular standpoints, can directly intervene and influence the political field. The strengthening of civil society (in the 1910s and 1920s), of which the intellectuals were the initiators and ideologists, was positively reflected in their position in society, and this has prepared the ground for the formation of new types of intellectuals; those who are economically and politically 'autonomous'.

The 'autonomy' of intellectuals means that they are free in their intellectual and artistic actions, choices and appreciation, and their activity is not predetermined by any political interference, economic pressure or bureaucratic supervision (Lindley 1986, Bourdieu 1992). In other words, the autonomy of intellectuals can be divided into four fields: (i) economic autonomy, (ii) intellectual-scientific autonomy, (iii) political-expressive autonomy and (iv) existential-ontological autonomy. The aim of every intellectual is to obtain all of these forms of autonomy. Nevertheless, owing to historical, contextual and cultural factors this autonomy is the privilege of a happy few. Moreover, for some intellectuals this autonomy is restricted to one field or another, and others are deficient of them all (heteronomous).

Even though the autonomy of intellectuals is constituted by intercausally overlapping elements, its economic and political-expressive dimensions have been constantly subjected to debate and conflict. Historically, the relationship between intellectuals and political power (between men of the pen and men of the sword) has often been characterized by conflict and confrontation (Ibn Khaldun 1958, Popiel & Mohan 1987). In confrontation with men of the sword, intellectuals have been able to rely upon the recognition they have gained amongst their likeminded fellows and the reading public in order to preserve their freedom and autonomy. The symbolic power and intellectual

15

reputation linked to this recognition can be a source of immunity against harrassment and interference from men of the sword (Sabour 1993).

There are contexts however, where the intellectuals are obliged to negotiate their autonomy. In order to avoid being constricted (or worse), intellectuals try to negotiate a relationship of 'coexistence' with the holders of political power (Roniger 1994). They are often asked either to become a sort of mandarinated intelligentsia, integrated as civil servants or in extreme instances, to run the risk of being marginalized and pushed into misery. Therefore, when intellectuals are confronted by a situation where their 'self-groundedness', to use Gouldner's (1979) concept, can be jeopardized, a compromise with the paradigm becomes inevitable. They are forced to build up some kinds of relationship with the political powerholders and subsequently to accept a relative autonomy.[5] In this regard, Saad Eddine Ibrahim (1989:213-245) suggests that in order to avoid conflicts and marginalization intellectuals should accept a compromise with those who embody political power (e.g. State, 'modern prince', party, etc.) and bridge the gap of mistrust and mutual rejection which separates them from this power. Ibrahim metaphorically proposes three kinds of bridges: (i) The golden bridge, where there is mutual recognition and endorsement. The intellectuals advise the prince and in return the latter respects their freedom and the autonomy. Their relationship is based on democratic and open dialogue and coexistence. (ii) The silver bridge which, in spite of their disagreements and different vocation, the interests of society oblige them to develop a common ground for understanding, where the intellectuals can criticize the prince without undermining his power and the latter can refuse the former's appreciation and criticism without harming his position. (iii) This gap could be bridged by a wooden bridge. In this situation, although there is mutual rejection there is nevertheless no intention to undermine the existence of the other. In this conflictual situation, mutual acceptance requires tacit recognition by the prince of a minimum vital autonomy and also recognition by the intellectuals of a minimum admissible legitimacy. It is the minimal form of coexistence. Unfortunately, many historical examples show that in their coexistence rarely the intellectuals have been on the same footing with the prince. The latter managed, in one way or another, to manipulate this relationship to his advantage.

This kind of explicitly or implicitly negotiated freedom and autonomy may seem strange in the European context of today, and more typical of Third World societies. However, when we look back at what was happening in Eastern Europe just a decade ago we can say that the political context has played a determinant role in the autonomy of intellectuals. In fact, in Eastern European societies intellectuals were given freedom in their activities, but at the same time they were under continual supervision and obliged to comply with the dominant paradigm in one way or another. In other circumstances, where this freedom was denied, intellectuals were required to follow a pre-established way of behaving and thinking (Janson 1991: pp. 99-130). As a result, they had to practise some sort of self-censorship and self-direction to meet the expectations of the then dominant ideology. Sometimes it was comprehensive and even acceptable for intellectuals to regulate their intellectual appreciation and criticisms in order to endorse, strengthen and even justify the paradigm in power. This was done in exchange for economic autonomy and ideological allegiances (see Shlapentokh, 1990).

The various social changes during the opening decades of this century reinforced autonomy of intellectuals, which became an established right that was taken for granted. What is more important, however, is not only the reinforcement of intellectuals' autonomy but their awareness of this autonomy (Pels 1995). This awareness crystallized with the ending of dependence on patrons and maecenas and the growth of freelance intellectual activity, which has enabled its practitioners to live and survive on the sale of their cultural and symbolic products.

As a consequence of the fragmentation of knowledge and the rise of new fields of specialization and professionalization, the status and image of intellectuals also became diffuse and specialized. This metamorphosis was amplified by the foundation of academic institutions, the bureaucratization of society and the development of the mass-media. It gave rise to various different groups of intellectuals: (i) Men of letters, writers; (ii) employee-intellectuals (e.g. academics, intellocrats); and (iii) propagators, vulgarisors (e.g. journalists). As a result of changes occurring in society, these three groups found themselves in different positions in the field of cultural and symbolic goods in relation to the State, to the reading public and to political power. Their position in this field correlated with their interests, roles and expectations. Subsequently, within the different groups of intellectuals, various forms of identification arose with the different social and ideological values existing in their societies. In the political and economic spheres the important changes happening between the 1930s and 1950s were reflected in the artistic and cultural fields. The position of intellectuals increasingly fluctuated and varied. Maintaining distance and autonomy, or declaring obedience and allegiance to a political party or identification with a political movement became a part of the intellectual mood. In this context the image of the so-called universal intellectual reached its climax (Foucault 1981). Taking advantage of their increasing political-expressive autonomy (between the 1960s and the 1970s) many intellectuals interfered actively in the field

17

of politics (e.g. N. Chomsky). Jean-Paul Sartre typifies this group of intellectuals, whom Bourdieu (1995) calls 'l'intellectuel total', identifiable by their engagement in various social and political debates and issues.

In terms of autonomy, it is the State and Academia (through their cultural and scientific institutions) which have become the main employers and, in a way, the 'new maecenas'. Naturally, intellectuals are not in the same dependency relationship as in classical times, because the academization of their activity has, to some extent, given them a relatively secure economic situation and provided them with better opportunities and means to carry out their intellectual and scientific endeavours. Nevertheless, as Jacoby (1987) has argued, the academization of intellectuals has alienated them from their traditional function, which is fundamentally to maintain an intellectual vigilance and a search for truth.

Thanks to the tremendous influence of the mass media, in the past decade, many intellectuals were harnessed and attracted to serve in such areas (Debray 1981, Garnham 1995: 359-361). This harnessing of their activity has been both very lucrative and a device for social visibility. The influence of the mass media is evidenced in its power to shape opinions and create images. The media have become a key element in constructing and imposing an intellectual self-image and in gaining success and fame. In this respect, Bourdieu (1994: pp. 3-9) contends that the mediatic intellectuals have unjustly gained prominence in cultural arbitration and commentary. Ambitiously striving for power, influence and visibility, they have been accused of having corrupted the integrity of the domain of the intellect and ideas. The prominence of mediatic intellectuals is double-edged. It provides them with opportunities to build reputations and gain publicity, but similarly it may embroil them in trivialization, vulgarization and 'intellectual prostitution'. And this new patronage by the mass media may result in the loss of their intellectual credibility and respectability, which are the essence of any intellectual autonomy.

Conclusion

Thanks to the universalization of education, the democratization of culture, the valorization of knowledge, and the spread of mass communications, intellectuals have attained the most influential and eminent position they have ever held in the modern society since their emergence as self-conscious groups. The tremendous increase in the numbers of the reading public has allowed intellectuals (e.g writers) to embark on freelance activity and to live autonomously on the sale of their cultural and symbolic production. But when compared proportionally with other groups of intellectuals, these represent a small minority beside the scholar-intellectuals, the journalist-intellectuals and the specific intellectuals who have emerged with the development of post-industrial society (Bon & Burnier 1966). The common denominator for all of these groups of intellectuals is that, compared with the past, they enjoy a relatively high degree of autonomy in various fields, especially at the intellectual, ontological and expressive levels (Sabour 1983, 1991). But economically and politically there is still much to be desired. As a matter of fact, most contemporary scholar-intellectuals are employed in academic institutions in addition to doing their literary and scholarly work. Their academic posts often constitute their main source of income, while the intellectual work remains a way of gaining respect and recognition and establishing an individual place in the intellectual community. In this regard, many would not have a decent life if their intellectual activity outside the academic field were to be assessed in terms of material gain. Boudin (1962: 37) states that 'when Napoleon founded the university the intellectuals looked at it with suspicion because it made them civil servants'. The intellectuals in modern society compete to be integrated as employees of the State or of academic institutions. These employee-intellectuals are often dependently autonomous and bureaucratically under 'implicit' supervision.

The mass-mediatization of culture and post-modern society have jointly and intercausally given rise to journalist-intellectuals (mediatic). By vocation and function these intellectuals are required to vulgarize and popularize knowledge and ideas to reach the common people or laity. However, since they are hired by official institutions (e.g. radio, TV) or private enterprises which are directed by a commercially minded policy of profit-making, consciously or unconsciously these intellectuals become domesticated and critically alienated (see Polan 1990: 343-362). In the process, they surrender their intellectual autonomy and bind themselves to a modern patronage as tenors and subjects of the 'mediacracy' (Beaud & Panese, 1995: 385-387).

In the light of the prevailing intellectual apathy, it appears that the species of the universal intellectuals is becoming rare or indeed extinct. This apathy or disinterest seems to confirm what Foucault (1981) predicted two decades ago, that the time of intellectuals with polyvalent sensitivities and concerned by local and global issues related to the common good is over.[6] The fragmentation of knowledge, expertise and the intellect has produced specific intellectuals whose domains of competency are limited and restrictively focused. Particularities and specific-orientedness have taken over the wholeness and globality. The field of knowledge has therefore become segmented and mosaic-like. In this situation an overlapping and interpenetration of specialities is inevitable. So, there is a conflict of competences where monopolies in certain fields are protected and the autonomy of intellectual-scientific exclusiveness is violated. In this conflict of intellectual and scientific positions and dispositions each group tries to win prominence for his know-how and knowledge (see Becher 1989). In propagating the domination of this knowledge and imposing its legitimacy on the other parts of the field or (other groups) the specific intellectuals aim at making it credible and indispensable. Any indispensable knowledge gives access to power in the social and political fields, and the brokers of this power are enabled to perpetuate the monopoly of their knowledge. This conflict of expertise can be seen, for instance, in issues related to ecological problems, especially between the so-called humanist intellectuals and the scientific intellectuals. It is also a conflict of autonomy.

Notes

1. Niccolo Machiavelli's (1965) dedication of his book 'the Prince' to Lorenzo de' Medici, ruler of Florence is worth mentioning here. Hoping for reward and protection he wrote:
   men who are anxious to win the favour of a Prince nearly always follow the custom of presenting themselves to him with the possession they value most, or with things they know especially please them...
   So, Your Magnificience, take this little gift [a book] in the spirit in which I send it, and if you read and consider it diligently, you will discover in it my urgent wish that you reach the eminence that fortune and your own accomplishments promise you. And if, from your lofty peak, Your Magnificience will sometimes glance down to these low-lying regions, you will realize the extent to which, undeservedly, I have to endure the great unremitting malice of fortune (pp. 29-30).
2. Among the best-known examples we can cite the Ptolemaic Dynasty with its famous Library-Museum in Alexandria (300 B.C.), the House of Wisdom (Dar Al-Hikma) in Baghdad (8th century), Catherine de Medicis, Catherine II of Russia.
3. Intellectuals and scholars (savants) migrated throughout history from one country to another looking for protectors and maecenas (Sabour 1994).
4. However, if we look at the composition of those active intellectuals who were involved in the Dreyfus affair it is noticeable that many of them were freelance intellectuals and men of letters, who were to some extent materially independent of the Establishment. They were not civil servants nor academically and economically self-reliant. Their freedom of movement and intervention in social affairs was, therefore, not inhibited by any significant dependency. This independence has reinforced their autonomy.
5. When we take into consideration the position of intellectuals in Latin America, Asia and Africa we are able to imagine what autonomous means. But there autonomy goes hand in hand with survival. Therefore, there arises the question of whether intellectuals should engage in open and self-destructive confrontation with their detractors (political power), which may be suicidal not only for their autonomy and existence, or whether they should proceed by imposing their own self-censorship and regulating their semantics and expression? Thus, they may continue to work in conditions of relative political-expressive and economic

autonomy. One intellectual in Syria has told me: 'It is better to be able to express two critical ideas out of ten than to be muzzled and voiceless' (Sabour, 1988). It is, sometimes, difficult for intellectuals who have never known censorship and restrictions on their freedom to imagine what it is like to be in a context where you have to produce a polysemic and double-loaded message in order to elude the rapacious eye of the censor.

6. The horror of the war in Bosnia and the rise of racism in Europe have not moved many intellectuals in the slighted way with the exception of a few groups of intellectuals in France and a few individuals here and there. There exists an almost total indifference to common and universal problems.

References

Andreski, Stanislav (1965), *The Uses of Comparative Sociology*, University of California Press, Los Angeles.

Beaud, Paul and Panese, Francesco (1995), 'From One Galaxy to Another: the Trajectories of French Intellectuals', in *Media, Culture and Society*, vol. 17, no. 3, pp. 359-384.

Becher, Tony (1988), *Academic Tribes and Territories, Intellectual Enquiry and the Cultures of Disciplines,* Open University Press, Milton Keynes.

Bon, Frédéric and Burbier, Michel-Antoine (1966), *Les Nouveaux Intellectuels*, Editions du Seuil, Paris.

Boschetti, Anna (1992), 'Jean-Paul Sartre: A Paradigm Case of the Modern Intellectual', in *Vanguards of Modernity: Society, Intellectuals, and the University*, University of Jyväskylä, Publications of the Research Unit for Contemporary Culture, no. 32, Jyväskylä, Finland.

Boudin, Louis (1962), *Les Intellectuels,* Presses Universitaires de France (Que sais-je?).

Bourdieu, Pierre (1992), *Les règles de l'art, Genèse et structure du champ littéraire,* Editions du Seuil, Paris.

Bourdieu, Pierre (1994), 'L'emprise du journalismey', *Actes de la recherche en sciences sociales*, no. 101, serie 2, pp. 3-9.

Bourdieu, Pierre (1996), 'The Intellectuals and the Internationalization of Ideas', (Interview with M'hammed Sabour) *Contemporary Sociology*, vol. 33, no. 1.

Coser, Lewis A. (1965), *Men of ideas*, The Free Press, New York.

Debray, Régis (1981), *Teachers, Writers, Celebrities: The Intellectuals of Modern France*, New Left Books, London.

Foucault, Michel (1981), 'Truth and Power', in Lemert, C. (ed), *French Sociology*, Columbia University Press, New York.

Garnham, Nicholas (1995), 'The Media and Narratives of the Intellectual', *Media, Culture and Society*, vol. 17, no. 3, pp. 359-384.

Gouldner, Alvin W. (1979), *The Future of Intellectuals and the Rise of the New Class,* The MacMillan Press, London.

Ibn, Khaldun Abdelrahman (1958), *The Muqaddimah*, Bollingen Foundation, New York, vol. II.

Jacoby, Russell (1987), *The Last Intellectuals: American Culture in the Age of Academe*, Basic Books, New York.

Janson, Sue C. (1991), *Censorship, The Knot that Binds Power and Knowledge*, Oxford University Press, Oxford.

Ibrahim, Saad Eddine (1985), 'Bringing the Gap Between the Decision Makers and the Intellectuals', in Tahar, Labib (ed), *The Arab Intelligentsia*, Dar Al-Arabiyya Lil-kitab, 1989.

Le Goff, Jacques (1985), *Les intellectuels au Moyen Age*, Editions du Seuil, Paris.

Lindley, Richard (1986), *Autonomy*, The MacMillan Press, London.

Nettl, J. P. (1969), 'Ideas, Intellectuals, and Structures of Dissent', in Rieff, P. (ed), *Intellectuals*, Doubleday & Company, New York.

Pels, Dick (1995), 'Knowledge Politics and Anti-politics: Toward a Critical Appraisal of Bourdieu's Concept of Intellectual Autonomy', *Theory and Society*, no. 24, pp. 79-104.

Polan, Dana (1990), 'The Spectacle of Intellect in a Media Age: Cultural Representations' in Robbins, B. (ed), *Intellectuals, Aesthetics, Politics and Academics*, University of Minnesota Press, Minnesota.

Popiel, Gerald and Mohan, Raj, P.(1987), *The Mythmakers: Intellectuals and the Intelligentsia in Perspective*, Greenwood Press, New York.

Roniger, Luis (1984), 'Civil Society, Patronage and Democracy', *International Journal of Comparative Sociology*, vol. XXXV, no. 3, pp. 208-220.

Sabour M'hammed (1983), 'The Creative Activity of Intellectuals and its Socio-Cultural Context', in Sarola, J. (ed) *Uria ja Ulottuvuuksia* , University of Joensuu.

Sabour, M'hammed (1988), 'Homo Academicus Arabicus', *Publications in Social Sciences*, no.11, Joensuu.

Sabour, M'hammed (1991), 'The Status and Ontology of Arab Intellectuals: The Academic Group', *International Journal of Contemporary Sociology*, vol. 28, nos. 3-4, pp. 221-232.

Sabour, M'hammed (1993), 'La lutte pour le pouvoir et la respectabilité dans le champ universitaire arabe', *International Social Science Journal*, Février, no. 135, pp. 107-118.

Sabour, M'hammed (1994), *La diaspora intellectuelle et scientifique Marocaine en Europe*, Dept. de Sociologie, Université de Joensuu, Joensuu.

Shlapentokh, Vladimir (1990), *Soviet Intellectuals and Political Power, The Post-Stalin Era*, Princeton University Press.

24

3. Intellectuals, Knowledge and Democracy

IDO WEIJERS

In Western Europe parliamentary democracy is at an impasse. The fall of the Berlin Wall and the euphoria about the worldwide victory of the market economy have not, up to now, led to a new democratic zest in this part of the world. On the contrary, in recent years political engagement has decreased. There is a good deal of complaint about a loss of political inspiration, moral leadership and legitimation. Many political parties are being confronted with an exodus and an increasing part of the electorate consists of protest voters. In this context many are looking for a new moral authority. The trade unions seem unable to act as a counterweight and strong moral single issue-movements also seem incapable of rising and flourishing at the moment. Some look for a counterbalance to this in the churches. Others turn to intellectuals. They think it is pre-eminently the task of the intellectual to guard our moral life. The intellectual should be above party-politics and daily conflicts and interests. He should intervene in the public debate to defend the crucial values of our culture and to break the political impasse.

In recent years the call for the social and political engagement of the intellectual clearly has been increasing and the phenomenon described above has to be seen in this context.[1] Some draw attention to the dramatic disappearance of the intellectual out of social life and even claim that we are witnessing the end of the intellectual in Western society. Authors like Alain Finkielkraut and Russell Jacoby have especially criticized the younger generation of intellectuals for not wanting any part in the defence of our culture, against what they see as the 'impoverishment of public culture',[2] or the 'triumph of stupidity over thinking'.[3] Jacoby laments that, 'The transmission belt of culture is threatened. The larger culture rests on a decreasing number of ageing intellectuals with no successors'.[4] In these pessimistic cultural indictments hope is not put in a *knowledge* elite as Mannheim had in mind, but in a *moral* elite: individuals such as Andrei

Sakharov, Edward Said, Salman Rushdie or György Konrád are held up as counter-examples for the intellectual in Western Europe and the States.

The Testifying Intellectual

Usually this call for social involvement or political responsibility entails a double mission for the intellectual, that is to act as political conscience or moral guard and as provocateur of the political professionals. As moral guard the intellectual claims to act as a consistent point of reference for the politician, whereas it is flexibility that he claims as a provocateur first and foremost. This double image of the intellectual, as garde and avant-garde, re-articulates an old dilemma with which generations of Western intellectuals have wrestled. It is the tradition of what may be called the 'testifying intellectual'. This tradition is marked, on the one hand, by Julien Benda, with his plea for universal, eternal values as the main concern of the intellectual, which is also a plea for the untouchable intellectual, superior to politics. At the other extreme it is represented by Sartre, with his plea for the intellectual 'engagé', committed to certain social and political values, who interferes in things that are 'none of his business', who takes sides and participates in politics as a provocateur of the political professionals.

Two difficulties need to be noted here. First, the ambiguous notion of the testifying intellectual presupposes a kind of social independence and individual autonomy, which intellectuals have hardly ever actually enjoyed. There are some favourite periods for this claim. In the United States this is the age roughly framed by World War One and Two. As critics of society thinkers like Lewis Mumford and John Reed on the one hand marked off their distance from a vulgar society, and on the other hand demanded their part in it as its enlightened voices. In Germany it is the Thomas Mann-age, in the Netherlands the age of Ter Braak. In France it is the post-war Sartrean age. But, as Bruce Robbins argues in the introduction to his collection on intellectuals, obituaries for the intellectual are so persistent a genre, because intellectuals have only incidentally lived the gloriously independent life so often ascribed to them.

The notion of the testifying intellectual must be seen as a piece of political rhetoric rather than an ideal historical past from which we have sadly fallen. In this genre the autonomy of the intellectual must always appear to be on the point of being lost. If, to be an intellectual involves first of all a rejection of all forms of social partisanship and all forms of 'business' in the sense of professionally devoting a great deal of time and energy to it, then the 'clerc' must always commit betrayal the moment his thought assumes any social embodiment or 'grounding'. It is at the moment of 'grounding' - that is of 'betrayal', when intellectual life is no longer a hobby, carried on in leisure time, touched only lightly in the course of a life centred elsewhere - that the subject comes into existence. Characteristic of this genre are the agitated exclamations that 'there are no more poètes maudits',[5] or that 'few American intellectuals live in exile'.[6]

Secondly, the moral notion of the testifying intellectual ignores a crucial element, which makes it meaningful to talk of intellectuals in modern democratic societies at all: that is their *knowledge*. We cannot relapse here behind the line articulated through the lineage Weber-Mannheim-Gouldner. The call for the social responsibility of the intellectual in Western democracy has to be related directly to his or her specific knowledge. An appeal to someone's personal testimony, aside from his specific knowledge, is more fitted to a closed society, not an open, dynamic information- or knowledge-society, which enjoys political legitimation, freedom of the press and freedom of organization.

The testifying intellectual, e.g. Emile Zola, is the intellectual who speaks in defence of 'the common good': Pramudya Ananta Toer, Breyten Breytenbach, Andrei Sakharov, the young Vàclav Havel. Characteristic of this intellectual is his/her confrontation with a closed public opinion, the invulnerable cynism of power and the political monopoly of knowledge. Whether he/she wants to or not, the fact that they state their opinion about certain social questions gives that statement the quality of a testimony against the political system. It is only in this political context that the two dimensions of the testifying intellectual; garde and avant-garde, fuse together organically. In the social 'übersichtlichkeit' of the closed society the intellectual can act as an alternative voice, a moral guide and general conscience of politics, he can articulate a clear alternative, respectable and provocative.

In Western democracy with its complex powersystem, its political 'unübersichtlichkeit', the figure of the testifying intellectual is overshadowed by the figure of the expert, whose public role is inextricably bound up with his specific knowledge or expertise. The expert does not claim a mission as Mannheim thought as the 'predestined advocate of the intellectual interests of the whole'.[7] He does not assert a claim to a 'complete theory of the totality of the social process', to a master science of political practice nor to a moral master view. The modern expert asserts a claim to a problem specific, professional 'Übersicht'.

Intellectuals who view their social responsibility here as one of personal testimony, are actually giving a comic replay of what was once really a tragic social role, as it still is in innumerable places in the world. To get up to speak is not an heroic deed in a democratic society. At least since the end of the sixties, that is since the re-introduction of republicanism in our political culture, to take the floor in public debate has become an essential aspect of Western citizenship. That is the 'price' the intellectual pays for our political civilization, for modern mass democracy, imperfect and open to improvement though it is.

The stratum of experts, counsellors and advisers is not only the fastest growing segment of the labour force in our societies. They are functionally indispensable in the political and economic administration of contemporary advanced societies. Some observers contend that the experts have infused these societies with a modern 'mandarin logic' and that they wield immeasurable power in public discourse.[8] Some, such as Brzezinski, have even predicted the dawn of a new age as the result of the construction of 'political knowledge' by a new professional elite.[9] Others, including Daniel Bell, caution against exaggerating the power of the experts.[10] The notion of power is only relevant within intellectual institutions, while in the larger world in which policy is made, the experts only exert influence. Nico Stehr has pointed to the fact that, at best, experts constitute rather loose associations of individuals. This is not so much the result of their humility or unwillingness to assume power, but the outcome of the substance of the forces they master, namely knowledge and expertise. The very employment of these forces diminishes the ability of any group to assume a 'master position' in society. Knowledge not only constantly de-mythologizes itself. The 'scientification' of social relations also generates a fragility of social structures which dissipates and operates against formations attempting to monopolize decisions.

In our society the number of experts is constantly growing, yet they do not monopolize and control society in any direct way. Nevertheless, in advanced societies expert knowledge is crucial as it affects the (self)-conceptions of the individuals, sets normative standards, and defines what counts as relevant knowledge and rational argument in public debates. The professional experts, counsellors and advisers with their claim to specialized knowledge surely have become crucial in the democratic knowledge-society. Simultaneously, the claim for the importance of 'general knowledge', the idea of one central intellectual forum; the cultural magazine, and of one favourite genre; the essay, and the notion of the primacy of the authority of the word over the authority of knowledge, all these key-elements in the vocabulary of the testifying intellectual have been relativized.

The Responsible Specialist

Among intellectuals two extreme and completely different reactions have developed in response to the fact that in Western democracy the intellectual can function only rarely as a general conscience for politics. On the one hand, some claiming to speak in defence of the tradition of Enlightment warn of a new 'betrayal of the intellectuals', as Alain Finkielkraut does very eloquently and passionately in *La défaite de la pensée*. He calls on the younger generation of intellectuals to involve themselves in politics and culture in a clearly self-conscious and coordinating way. They should stand up for classical, Western values and defend *culture* against the logic of consumerism and modern barbarism. This is the militant idealistic response, which refuses to accept that modern Western society has valued the intellectual primarily as a man of knowledge and a professional and hardly as a prophet of the good life.

On the other hand the radical criticism of modernity is concerned with just that hybridization of the prophetic and the professional social role of the intellectual. It is said that, since the république des lettres, intellectuals have made themselves spokesmen of the ideas of rational government and of the rational individual, whose thoughts and behaviour are depicted as flexible and malleable entities and understood as objects of purposeful redirection. The kind of authority in which such a vision of the world established men of knowledge is described by Zygmunt Bauman as 'legislative'. In *Legislators and Interpreters* Bauman presents a complete opposite of the social role of the intellectual to that of Finkielkraut. He sees their so-called 'legislative role' in functions such as surveillance, correction, welfare supervision, medicalization, which he summarizes as 'panoptic control'.

Bauman thinks that the intellectuals' self-identification with what they articulated as Western values remained unfaltering as long as the expectation that Western politics would be hospitable to knowledge-based political blueprints seemed plausible. It gradually came home to them however, that political technology developed by the modern state rendered their legitimizing services increasingly redundant. In a fully developed modern state, Bauman says, the effectiveness of state power can be maintained regardless of the scope and intensity of social commitment to the 'ruling values'. The only realistic intellectual role then would be that of the 'interpreter', for whom culture is not something to be made as an object for practice, but something in its own right and beyond control, an object for study, something to be mastered only cognitively as a meaning, and not practically as a task.

This approach implies, however, a view both of Western politics and of the social roles of knowledge and expertise, which is as narrow as that of Finkielkraut. It is a kind of superrealism which easily overlooks complexity. Firstly, democratic mass-politics cannot be reduced to political technology, as the present legitimation crises of many political parties make clear. These crises and other dramatic changes in our political systems are incompatible with the notion of a political technology. The fact that we face a legitimation crisis in West-European politics does not mean that politics in our societies do not need legitimation, rather the opposite.

Secondly, there is no reason at all to suppose that the social role of knowledge in our society has become less important than a century ago. In fact it is the other way round. Our lives and deaths have become more dependent than ever on medical and biochemical knowledge. Our social capabilities are conditional upon different networks of knowledge. Schooling, mass-higher education, in service training and lifelong-education are crucial for the distribution of social positions. Since the end of the sixties, that is since Daniel Bell and Radovan Richta drew attention to the crucial role of knowledge and expertise in our society, the importance of knowledge has been increasing. Knowledge, especially scientific knowledge, became a productive force in the industrial society, but in the latter part of our century it has become an immediately productive force. We can state indeed, that we live in a 'knowledge-society', where we are confronted with a permanent scientization of most spheres of social action.

Thirdly, the social roles of intellectuals cannot be reduced to social control as Bauman states. To speak of the social functions of judges and psychiatrists, doctors and educators in terms of techniques of 'panoptic control' gives a grotesque impression of their actual complex and often contradictory role in modern democracies. This image withers away as soon as one studies any kind of intellectual expertise at close quarters. The emergence of intellectuals has not made them a new class or power elite, as some social theorists expected.[11] Neither has it made them an elite of panoptic control, as Bauman says, precisely because of the character of the forces they master: expertise is constantly contested. Knowledge is not something stable and fixed in itself. Expert-knowledge can lend itself for control, but also for criticism of control. But the rise of knowledge-based occupations, be they experts, counsellors or advisers, forms one of the core attributes of advanced society.

Simple characterizations of the power-knowledge-relation in the West brush aside the question of the present role of the intellectual in society. The role of the 'interpreter', for whom culture is something in its own right and beyond control, purely an object for study, is clearly socially irrelevant.

Certainly, the democratization of Western society has implied a decentralization of the 'traditional' social role of the intellectual, that is of the social role they played from the end of the nineteenth century up to the 1960s. If they have not lost their social and political hubris, they have been knocked off their pedestal as the general conscience of politics and society. But it would be a serious mistake to overlook their vital social role as experts and advisers, that is as 'responsible specialists'. Our world has become 'interwoven' with the knowledge of specialists in an unprecedented way. Therefore the call for social responsibility on the part of the intellectuals in Western democracy has to be related directly to their specific knowledge or expertise.

This responsibility has to be marked in the first place by reflection upon the boundaries and uncertainties of one's own specialism. Not aloofness, but intellectual modesty, that is what we require of our responsible specialists. And here the notion of reflectivity seems crucial. I want to elaborate this point for its educational consequences, that is for its implications for academic training, because in my conception of the question of the social role of the intellectual we are not concerned with a few exceptional minds, but with the mass of our university graduates. So in my view this question is soon answered with another question: how does one educate the reflective expert?

Educating the Reflective Expert

Let me return to my starting point, the recent call for social involvement of the intellectual. The fact is, this demand has been accompanied by a criticism of the university. The university is held responsible by some for the supposed disappearance of the intellectual out of social life. We live in an 'age of academe', as Russell Jacoby puts it sharply. By the 1960s the universities virtually monopolized intellectual work, Jacoby says, and this monopoly involved a fundamental change in the character of higher education, from liberal generalistic intellectual education to narrow, vocational and professional training. This change has led to the disappearance of the classical intellectual habitus.

Usually these critics think and speak of the historical 'mission' of the university which is supposed to have been forgotten or threatened and which should be recovered. They refer to Humboldt's notion of *Bildung*, or to the resolute statement of Mill about what a university is not: 'It is not a place of professional education ... Their object is not to make skilful lawyers, or physicians, or engineers, but capable and cultivated human beings'.[12] Or they refer to Newman, who stated that, 'if a practical end must be assigned to a university course, I say it is that of training good members of society. Its art is the art of social life, and its end is fitness for the world'.[13] In the eyes of Newman useful knowledge was a deal of trash. He favoured a university training aiming at raising the 'intellectual tone' of society, at cultivating a public mind and 'purifying' the national taste.

The major difficulty with this criticism, to put it simply is its inappropriateness in time: we do not teach and study anymore in the age of Humboldt, Newman or Mill. A university is not outside, but inside the general social fabric of a given era, as Abraham Flexner noted in 1930. But in 1930 the universities had, for their part, already moved a long way from Flexner's 'Modern University', where the heart was a graduate school of art and sciences, solidly professional schools and research institutes. As Clark Kerr has observed, they were becoming less and less like a 'genuine university', by which Flexner meant, an organism, characterized by highness and definiteness of aim, unity of spirit and purpose. 'The "Modern University" was as nearly dead in 1930 when Flexner wrote about it, as the old Oxford was in 1852 when Newman idealized it. History moves faster than some observers' pens. Neither the ancient classics and theology nor the German philosophers and scientists could set the tone for the really modern university - the multiversity.'[14]

Flexner's idea of a 'Modern University' still has its supporters - the scientists, the specialists and most of the graduates. Newman's idea of a university still has its devotees too - the humanists, the generalists and some of the undergraduates. But the fact is that academic life and its social meaning have completely changed since the age of Newman and since the days of Flexner. We do our research in modern labs, with the most up-to-date techniques and complicated financing, and even more importantly, we teach in modern mass institutions with thousands of students who have no memory of the character-formation these founding fathers of the Western university of the nineteenth century had in mind. And more fundamentally, we teach in universities where philosophy has lost its central position. Philosophy was supposed to guarantee both the unity of the sciences and the unity of scientific training and research and cultural Bildung. Philosophy was crucial to educate men of science and to mould men of character.[15] The fate of the academic status of philosophy and the combined development of our universities requires two critical remarks relating to two different historical academic settings.

The first point is that we cannot and do not want to return to the elite-institutions of the last century, that is to the Bildungs-university of the beginning of the nineteenth century. Almost a century ago, Max Weber, who balanced between two scientific cultures, described this point as the struggle between the old Man of Culture (*das Kulturmenschentum*) and the new Expert (*der Fachmenschen-Typus*).[16] He decided in favour of the latter, that is against the old elite-institute of the university-mandarins. Those who want to step back and still opt for the Man of Culture have to be aware that they are choosing an elite institute. Given the widespread consensus and force of the meritocratic ideology in Western culture this would be a much harder choice than in the time of Weber.

The second point, however, is that we cannot and do not want to return to the pure research institutions of the beginning of this century either. Two factors are important here. First, a sociological consideration: from the beginning of this century our universities have changed slowly into 'multiversities', as Clark Kerr has called the American university, which definitively set the trend. Our universities have become complex mixtures of research and professional training. Again, the meritocratisation of our culture has been an important stimulus to this change. The rapidly increasing role of knowledge in our economy, in our politics and culture, has been another cause. The dynamics of our society require the mass production of academically trained professionals. In comparison with Weber this implies that the call for 'scientific passion' is no longer adequate for the university as a whole. Scientific passion presupposes a pure research university, while research is only relevant for a part of the institution nowadays.

There is also a philosophical consideration: Weber was concerned about the political disinterestedness of scientific knowledge. Science and scholarship had to be purified of ideology, that was the constant responsibility of the expert. This presupposes a degree of confidence in scientific and scholarly knowledge that we no longer possess. Our idea of responsible specialism is a reaction to this disenchantment with the world of pure knowledge. It is also a reaction to the hope of a *Grundwissenschaft*, Mannheim's dream of a complete theory of the totality of the social process.

For the idea of the responsible expert the notion of reflectivity becomes relevant. The responsible specialist reflects on their knowledge, they consider what their expertise does, both in cognitive and in social respects. They grasp the fact that modern science is pre-eminently, as Ulrich Beck puts it, a societal risk producer. This social and cognitive reflectivity should be part of the specialists' intellectual habitus. But to develop this broad-mindedness he/she has to be deliberately educated in that direction. That does not mean that their education has to be oriented to the past, to character-formation and to philosophical training. On the contrary, it has to be oriented to the future, to practical learning and to problem-solving strategies, it has to reflect continuously on learned strategies and to

33

reconsider our know-how. From the beginning he/she has to 'learn to learn', or to become a real 'reflective practitioner', as Donald Schön has interpreted this orientation.

So called 'integrated curricula', with an interplay of different perspectives, may be helpful here as long as they are part of 'problem-solving' educational strategies. Gerald Graff's idea of integrated and jointly taught courses to help, as he puts it, 'turning conflict into community', may be useful as long as we clearly see that we are trying to form a community of experts. We do not need a group of blinkered specialists but a community of reflective experts. We might say, that the first and crucial educational task for higher education becomes to teach students higher learning. However, as Ronald Barnett says, learning is a 'misnomer', or at least an inadequate way of construing higher education. The learning that goes on in higher education justifies the label 'higher' precisely because it refers to a state of mind over and above conventional recipe or factual learning. What counts for the sake of higher education and what is indicated here as higher learning, is the student's ability to understand what is learned or what is done, to conceptualize it, to grasp it under different aspects, and to take up critical stances in relation to it. In my view, the main question in higher education now is a practical one: the question is whether the student can go on in unfamiliar circumstances. The learning we want our students to acquire is learning how to respond to what they encounter. They have to learn how to form informed critical evaluations. And they have to learn to place their learning in a wider context. All these forms of learning are not learning that such and such is the case, but learning how to do such and such.

The educational aim of the reflective expert may, at the same time, offer the vital answer to the tendency to change university-study into purely functional, vocational training. To assign a central place to reflectivity in higher education, with its professional doubts, with its passion for reconsideration of learning, does not only stem the tide of academic functionalism. It also offers the best support to hold on to against the trend to attune the university directly to the labour market. We need to shift attention from the dominant human-capital approach to the so-called filter theory that is well known among sociologists. This means that the economic benefit of higher education is looked for not so exclusively in the increased productivity of people, that is in their specific professional training, but rather in the social sorting function of their education. This implies that the accent shifts from absolute skills and know-how, which students have to acquire, to relative suitability or 'trainability': higher education has to make students ready for a specific professional training. This approach seems to fit with the observation that employers looking for university graduates are

34

looking in most cases, in fact, for something that has got less to do with what one has precisely studied, than with a certain flexible availability for problems with a high degree of complexity, problems that ask for something in the form of a trained intelligence for 'this kind of issue'. The university is neither a 'producer' of graduates nor a 'service' institute for students. The concept of trainability seems to compel a shift from the training of 'ready-made' researchers and professionals to the training of relative and 'unfinished' suitability.

If we want to discuss the role of the intellectual in our society, then the question of the formation of the intellectual is crucial. Perhaps the notion of the reflective expert can be further developed here as a useful point of reference. The main educational goal then becomes the training of the capacity to analyse and formulate problems adequately, that is to indicate what solutions that one suggests do, in fact, bring about and where doubts and questions remain. Western democracy does not need a new moral elite of testifying intellectuals. But the formation of a mass of experts who feel themselves responsible for the consequences of their knowledge is crucial for the vitality of our democracy.

Notes and references

1. Maclean, I., Montefiore, A. and Winch P. (eds) (1990), *The Political Responsibility of Intellectuals*, Cambridge University Press, Cambridge.
2. Jacoby, Russell (1987), *The Last Intellectuals: American Culture in the Age of Academe*, Basic Books, New York, p. IX.
3. Finkielkraut, Alain (1987), *La Défaite de la Pensée*, Gallimard, Paris, p. 161.
4. Jacoby, *The Last Intellectuals*, p. 8.
5. Finkeilkraut, *La Defaite*, p. 145.
6. Jacoby, *The Last Intellectuals*, p. IX.
7. Mannheim, Karl (1968), *Ideology and Utopia*, Routledge and Kegan Paul, London, p. 140.
8. Derber, C., Schwartz, W. and Magrass, Y. (1990), *Power in the Highest Degree: Professionals and the Rise of a New Mandarin Order*, Oxford University Press, New York.
9. Brzezinski, Zbigniew (1970), *Between the Ages: America's Role in the Technotronic Age*, Viking Press, New York.
10. Bell, Daniel (1973), *The Coming of a Post-industrial Society: a Venture in Social Forecasting*, Basic Books, New York.
11. See Goulner, Alvin (1979), *The Future of Intellectuals and the Rise of the New Class*, Seabury Press, New York.
12. Mill, John Stuart (1984), Collected Works, vol. XXI, (ed) Robson, J. M., Routledge and Kegan Paul, London, p. 218.
13. Newman, John (1960), *The Idea of a University*, Holt, Rhinehart and Winston, New York, p. 134.
14. Kerr, Clerk (1963), *The Uses of a University*, Harper and Row, New York, p. 6.
15. Baggan, P. and Wiejers, I. (1995), *De Toekomst van der Universiteit*, Amsterdam University Press, Amsterdam.
16. Weber, Max (1972), *Wirtschaft und Gessellschaft*, Mohr, Tubingen, p. 578.

4. The Intellectual as a Social Engineer: Gunnar Myrdal and the Formation of the Good Society

LENNART OLLAUSON

Introduction

Within the last ten years or so there has been an intense debate on the welfare state, both on the question of whether we can afford previous levels of expenditure and on whether it is legitimate to use the welfare state as the means to redistribute surplus wealth among citizens. One could say that there has been a form of legitimation crises for the model of welfare state which was established in the decades after the Second World War. In Sweden the debate has been focused on the foundations of the so called Swedish or Scandinavian model, a model, which has been seen as a product of the long lasting political and ideological hegemony of the Swedish Social Democrats. But now many social scientists have declared that the old model is redundant; it must be replaced with something else, but they are unclear what the new model should be.

In the critique of the welfare state and in the descriptions of the crisis and its causes, one of the central questions has been the relationship between the social sciences and the political processs in the context of the welfare state, and in particular the role played by intellectuals. Or, in other words, the problematique of social engineering as a goal for the use of social scientific knowledge. This ideal or way of using knowledge has been criticized for being one of the causes of the present situation. At the same time a debate has ensued indicating that the Social Democratic party has a very problematic relation to intellectuals. It is suggested that the party has always been pragmatic and has thereby never been attractive to intellectuals in Sweden. Or, to put it another way; to be an intellectual means not to be pragmatic.

Gunnar and Alva Myrdal are two of the names most often mentioned in the Swedish context, as they played an important role as ideologists for an Enlightenment-movement in Sweden. And indeed the Myrdals did plead for a form of social engineering. They were also active intellectuals, taking part in the formation of the new Sweden from the thirties and onward.

In this chapter I shall discuss this problematique in relation to the formation of the welfare state in the decades around the Second World War.[1] If one addresses this issue I think that an analysis of the work of Gunnar Myrdal is an exemplar, both from the point of view of how to make use of social knowledge, but also because the decades from 1930 to the 1960s are interesting from the point of view of the changing position of intellectuals in modern society. Here I will assess Myrdal as a phenomenon in this process and at the same time I will also make use of his own consciousness of the problems inherent in this process.

I don't think it's necessary to describe Gunnar Myrdal in more detail; he was a famous economist and social philosopher, an MP in the Swedish Parliament, civil servant in the UN, and Nobel Prize winner in Economics. His most known works are an *American Dilemma: The Negro Problem and Modern Democracy*, (1944) and *Asian Drama: An inquiry into the Poverty of Nations*, (1968).[2]

Intellectuals and the Problem of Social Engineering

In the title of my chapter there are two problematical concepts, the intellectual and social engineering. By way of introduction I will give a hint of how I make use of these two concepts by means of a short historical framework, before I go on to discuss my case study on Gunnar Myrdal. To conclude I will return to the problems associated with these concepts and discuss them in relation to my historical example.

In the last few decades there has been an intense debate on the concept of the intellectual. Are intellectuals to be seen as a new class or are they just a stratum, floating between the main classes in capitalist society? This is the more sociological approach which is often opposed to a normative one. In the normative approach the intellectual is seen as a critic of tendencies in modern society, here the question of which values and norms should be dominant in society is crucial. In this latter picture there is a strong tendency towards defining the intellectual as an isolated individual. He - seldom a she - can never trust anybody and never be trusted. The intellectual is only loyal to his or her values.

If you take a more historical approach to the problem of intellectuals I think that it's obvious that you must take as your starting point the more sociological perspective, as this will make it possible for you to see the changes in the social position of intellectuals. And, with this approach you can assess the institutional conditions in which intellectuals function.

This is the approach that Carl Boggs takes in his book *Intellectuals and the Crisis of Modernity* (1993). Boggs claims that nowadays intellectuals can no longer function as rationalizing elites, social engineers, and state planners without compromising their oppositional identity. The simple alliance of intellectuals and powerful organizations was the hallmark of traditional, Jacobin and technocratic types, but these models have either broken down or were blocked by strong counter-trends.[3]

It is this kind of problem wihich interests me, i.e. whether it's possible to be a social engineer and an oppositional critic of modern society at the same time. And if so, what are the reasons for this? Boggs's starting point is an analysis of the traditional intelligentia, consisting of clerks, literati, artists and philosophers, which constituted a cultural elite. They usually saw themselves as above the classes in society. They seemed to have their social roots in the Church, the Monarchy and the Military. With the nascent modernization of Europe at the end of the 18th century a new layer of intellectuals emerged. The Jacobin intellectual was born.

In modern society these intellectuals had the key role in creating and sustaining ideological hegemony. They were the theoretical architects, striving to overcome the imperfections of society; they formulated plans in relation to universal values and goals. Here we could see a fusion between politics and intellectuals, as well as between knowledge and power.[4] A new elite was formed, which saw itself as central in the social development and the building of the good society. In the 20th century the modernization process gave rise to a new technological rationality, which assumed ideological hegemony. Technological and bureaucratic solutions to social problems was part of this ideology, with science or scientism playing an important part. If we follow this conception which Boggs has of the intellectual, we see a new vision of intellectuals, one where they have left their 'Promethean capacity to reshape society' behind. A key reason for this is that norms of professionalization have been imposed on the intellectual.[5]

It was in the decades between World War I and II, that the idea of social engineering took hold, even though it took another decade or two before it was established as an important political concept. There are of course different definitions of this concept, but a useful starting point is the definition of social engineering given by Karl Popper in *The Poverty of Historicism.*[6] For Popper the belief among social engineers that human beings are masters of their own destiny is central, as is the idea that we can regulate the world we are living in. These notions are clearly related to the model of social scientific knowledge, which is the tool to be used in the reforming of society. But what kind of knowledge is this? Is it possible for political scientists to find the same kind of basis for their work as it is for doctors in relation to medicine or technicians in relation to technology?

> ... the social engineer conceives the scientific basis of politics like a social technology, as opposed to the historicist who understands it as a science of immutable historical tendencies.[7]

The key concept here is social technology rather than social engineering, but they are both part of the same ideology, even though they can be seen as having been formed under different historical circumstances.

In recent times there has been much dicussion concerning social engineering, where catch phrases like 'scientifically based activity' and a 'better social world' are frequent. These echo problems in relation to the concepts I have discussed above. One of them is the tendency to ignore political antagonism and the opposing views about values and define ends as apolitical. Related to this view of social engineering is a notion of social knowledge, as neutral in relation to classes, sexes and races. This knowledge is the key means to be used in the formation of the good society.

There are clearly serious problems here, I don't believe that it's possible to ignore the political or ideological features of social knowledge, even if they are not always manifest. Another problem here concerns the ideal of social science to which you adhere, i.e. what is worth knowing and what is possible to know with those methods you are allowed to make use of? You can of course avoid problematizing the ideal of science, but I suggest that we have a key problem here. If this is true then the capacity to criticize society is relative to different forms of social knowledge. Here the intellectual, in one sense of the word, can be seen as opposite to the social scientist and professionals.

But if you define the concepts of intellectual and social engineering in a too strict way, you will only be able to reveal what is already said in the definitions. My analysis of the problematique concerning intellectuals and social engineering is closely related to my view that we can distinguish between two types of social engineering, one where the question of values within social knowledge is put to one side and the other where this is seen as the key question. The position one takes here will determine how you look at the whole relationship between intellectuals and social engineering. For now let us leave these conceptual problems and turn to my case study.

The Problem of Welfare and Economics

The so called Swedish or Scandinavian model of the welfare state was mainly developed during the 1950s and 60s, it can be seen - partly at least - as the result of the ideological debates and twists within the Social Democratic party, which had started during the late twenties and thirties. From 1932 Social Democratic ideology became more or less hegemonic in Sweden as the party became the dominant political force in Sweden. The ideology underpinning the model was based upon a belief in a universal form of welfare system in combination with a strong conviction that it was possible to form the good society by organizational means. There was no question of social or political revolutions, the reformistic ideology was firmly established. In this context the Keynesian revolution in economics fitted well into the frameworks of the Swedish Social democrats. It made possible a scientific legitimation of the politics the party wanted to practice.

The organization of the welfare state was part of a big modernization project for Swedish society. In the 1930s Sweden left the European backyard with respect to its standard of living and started its way towards becoming the number one. In this process a thorough going change in the position of intellectuals in Swedish society took place. A new group of intellectuals found their place in society at the beginning of the thirties: one of them was Gunnar Myrdal. In the early thirties Myrdal, together with a group of modernizers, conducted investigations on the housing question in Sweden. Urbanization had led to a situation where many people lived in overcrowded houses. So in this field there was a clear need for better and more functional houses and apartments. At the same time the building of houses was also a key part of the Keynesian programme. Enlightening the people could go hand in hand with an economic programme.

This was the main road in the modernization process of Sweden. Enlighten people so that they behave as modern people, i.e. in a rational manner. Education would be built upon scientific knowledge, and this knowledge should also provide the politicians with the facts they needed in order to organize the rational society. The social engineer could be the new hero in the formation of the welfare state.

But who should the knowledge producers be? And who were the intellectuals that could enlighten the people? Prior to this period engineering, as well as medicine or eugenics, was the dominating form of knowledge up until the 1930s, but then we can see a change towards the social sciences and especially economics. But it was a gradual process, as is shown in the middle of the 1930s, when the Myrdals wrote a book within the framework of social planning, entitled *Crises within the Population Question*, where they discussed the problem how to raise the living standard of the Swedish population. This was done within the frameworks set by the eugenic or biological form of knowledge, but it was simultaneously, an attempt to say that we can use modern social scientific knowledge in order to better the lot of the population. So this book can be seen as written in the transformation period where you still have to talk within the old dominant language, but a new grammar is emerging concerning social engineering.

We can say that in the thirties the first steps were taken towards a more organized and rational society. In this process economists became more and more important together with other social scientists. This process accelerated after World War Two when there was a broad debate in Europe on freedom or rather a free market versus an organized and planned economy. Some of the arguments in this debate were political, but we can also see how fundamental problems on the question of the role of intellectuals in this process were involved and also the issue of which form of social knowledge was needed in order to be able to modernize society.

Welfare economics

The relevance of this can be seen if we consider a meeting that took place in the late forties among young political economists from the Nordic countries in Uppsala, Sweden. Long discussions ensued on the problem of whether welfare economics fulfilled the criteria to be met in order to be a good social science. Afterwards a Danish economist, Bent Hansen, wrote a review article of a book by Warren Reder, *Studies in the Theory of Welfare Economics* (1947). In his review article Hansen commented on the debate at the meeting in Uppsala. He said that many of the economists that took part in the discussion rejected the theory of welfare economics of Gunnar Myrdal and were hostile to his views of science and politics developed in his *The Political Element in the Development of Economic Theory*.[8]

With reference to the Uppsala School of Philosophy, the young economists, according to Hansen, argued that welfare economics could not be a real social science since it did not stick to the distinction between fact and value. A key argument from the defenders of welfare economics was that political economy, just as medicine, must have a goal for its activity, an idea which is at least fairly well accepted among researchers within medicine. For medicine the goal was to make people healthier and for economics it was to make people wealthier. Thus, just as you can't doubt that medicine is a real science, you cannot doubt that political economy is a good science in the form of welfare economics.[9]

One of the economists Ulrich Herz, who was criticized by Hansen, wrote in response that Hansen apparently had not understood his arguments. On the one hand, Herz says, you can find some methodological problems related to the problem of doing calculuses on the level of welfare comparing different actions in the economic field. And on the other hand the problems of making use of the economical theories in the economical planning of society, which is on another level than the methodological problems. Here the references to the Uppsala School of Philosophy are relevant as its representatives have said that there is a logical rift between judgements of facts and judgements of values, a divide which cannot be bridged. And even if we don't accept this distinction, Herz says, welfare economics does not fulfil the criteria in order to be a fully fleshed social science.[10]

What interests me here is not the question if welfare economics is a science or not? I interpret the debate as a sign of a more general problematique which was discussed and which raised many of the questions posed in this chapter. One central problem was how to legitimate the use of social scientific knowledge in building the welfare state. Another more specific issue was whether you could build into the theory the political goal of more welfare for the people? As they seem to have done in welfare economics. And who should decide what these goals should be?

All these questions are related to what form of knowledge is needed in order to build the good society and what role the intellectuals should play in this process.

Myrdal As An Intellectual and Social Engineer

So far I have tried to give a general framework for a more precise discussion on the position that Gunnar Myrdal took within this field. Now I will shift perspective by making use of Myrdal's views in order to give another strand to my general argument.

In the decades I'm referring to here Myrdal worked as a professional economist; an expert for the Social Democratic government, and as a critic of modern society. He had the ambition to be both a social engineer and an intellectual. My starting point is how Myrdal understood his own position and specifically how he understood the relation between science and politics.

The intellectual

In the aftermath of the World War One the professional economists were outsiders in relation to politics, control over the economy was exercised by men from law, business and politics. Part of the explanation for this situation can be found in the dominant theory in political economy, which posited that all political intervention was harmful for a sound economy. But through the

43

thirties and during the Second World War and afterwards the positions changed. Myrdal describes the new situation in the 1950s, suggesting that in all countries they now,

> ... drew upon the services of a whole cadre of economists; they had already been trained in the depression years in collaborating with the politicians and the administrators on planning and even executing control schemes.[11]

Myrdal was one of these economists. It seems to have been obvious to him that political economy, as well as other social sciences, should take a responsibility in the formation of the new society.

Since the end of the 19th century there had been an intense debate on what constitutes social scientific knowledge, and more precisely on the role played by value-judgements within this field. Max Weber, for example, had written on the problem of objectivity in the study of society. Weber was influenced by Neo-Kantian philosophy in the Windelband-Rickert tradition. They understood the problem as related to the so called value question. In modern society it was important to find a solution to the problematical relation between politics and science, a solution which accepted this difference and tried to make a strength out of it.

Myrdal had formed the so called Stockholm School of Economics in the late twenties and early thirties together with a group of other economists.[12] Some of these economists were influenced by the Swedish philosopher Axel HŠgerstršm. HŠgerstršm, according to Myrdal had,

> ... clearly and strikingly expressed the importance of drawing a line between beliefs about reality and valuations of it. The two are not on the same logical level, for beliefs cannot be judged by the criteria of true and false.[13]

This meant that Myrdal and his colleagues thought that there were no objective values, which could be known scientifically. The significance for Myrdal of this thought can be seen in the book he worked on in the late twenties, *The Political Element in the Development of Economic Theory* (1930). The dominant message in this book was that all theories in economics were laden with values. Myrdal demonstrated this in an effective manner by going through all the dominant political theories from the late 18th century until his own period.

But already Myrdal had begun to doubt if it was enough just to cut off the metaphysical elements in theory in order to have a theory free of subjective values. The conclusion was that ...

> it should then be possible to reach solutions of practical and political problems simply by adding to the theoretical knowledge of facts and relations a set of premises from the sphere of valuations and by drawing the conclusions. But was this thought not just naive empiricism, at heart not dissimilar to the crude belief in 'facts' established without theory, of which I saw so distressingly much in America where I then spent a year?[14]

As a development of these thoughts he wrote an article for *Archiv fŸr Sozialwissenschaft und Sozialpolitik*, but the article was not accepted by Joseph Schumpeter and Emil Lederer because its conclusion was that it was impossible to insert value premises into economic analysis.[15]

What was the message in Myrdal's article? He discussed - based on the distinction between ends and means - the problem of values within social science. Usually, he said, the problem of value is related to the discussion of ends, while the means are seen as neutral. But for Myrdal it was obvious that means are not neutral and this entailed that the distinction between value laden ends and value neutral means collapses. If we accept this we will find that there are many places within scientific work where values come in. In scientific work elimination of alternatives and simplification is essential. But if:

> ... the elimination is not guided by objective principles the remaining choice between alternatives is arbitrary, and the practical results of the analysis of these alternatives have no claim to scientific objectivity.[16]

This, in reality, was quite a harsh critique of utilitarianism, the core philosophy of neo-classical economics. Although Myrdal criticizes the solution given to the means-ends discussion he says that we cannot dispense with it. It is necessary for a practically oriented political economy. But, Myrdal asks himself, can we not shut our eyes to these problems as the general normative theorems within political economy fulfil an important function? In this way we get a directing principle for how to treat practical questions. We find what Myrdal calls, '...an illusion of coherence and consistency, and this is always pleasing to a scholar'.[17]

But Myrdal rejected this answer, because it would mean that the social scientist preserved 'pseudo-scientific political doctrines'. Myrdal didn't believe in the attempts made to rationalize or theorize basic political ideologies. His solution is to let the value premises stand as value premises and nothing else. If economists want to bring in these premises, they must use methods used by sociologists and psychologists. Systematic studies of political attitudes must precede the theories of a practical political economy. This leads to the view that elements of social psychology will be woven into the problems of practical economics.This foundation of economic theory in social psychology must be done through empirical studies of the behaviour of individuals and groups of people. I think that we can see here the result of the Myrdals' visit to the US the year before he wrote this article. Indeed, Alva Myrdal did much research on social psychology in these years.

The social engineer

After doing scientific work as well as political work in the thirties and forties, Myrdal had changed his position somewhat. He had been an MP for some years and member of the Social Democratic government in the middle of the forties. From the thirties he had worked very close together with the Minister of Finances, Ernst Wigforss. In this decade he and his wife were working on some problems concerning the planning of society as well as of people's everyday life. In the thirties the eugenics or 'Rassenhygiene' was the dominant model from which social questions were posed. Alva and Gunnar Myrdal wrote a lively much discussed book on the crises concerning the population question in Sweden in 1934. The problem discussed was how to raise the standard of living of the Swedish population. One of the answers to this question was related to the other big problem they worked on, viz. the housing question. On the one hand enough houses and apartments must be built, and on the other hand people must be taught to use their houses or apartments in a rational way. This could be done by means of architectural solutions, at least partly. So the introduction of social engineering in Sweden in the thirtes was related to these two fields, the quality and quantity of the population and the building of proper places to live in. The housing question was also a very important step on the way towards a more planned economy, within the framework advanced by Keynes in the thirties. And it has since been one of the cornerstones of the policy of Social Democractic governments in Sweden, when they have been trying to find the right balance in the economy, between savings and consumption.

In 1940 Myrdal had had a call from the US and was asked to do a larger social study on the so called Negro problem. He accepted and carried out this project during the War. This was one of the first 'big science' projects within the social sciences in the world. So Myrdal learned to think big just

46

as he also learned to work with social problems in other countries than Sweden. In his research on the lack of citizenship for blacks in the US it was important for Myrdal to show that this was not in accordance with the constitution of the US. There everybody was an equal, but in practice some were more equal than others. So one problem for Myrdal was how to actualize the correct values in modern American society. This research project deeply influenced Myrdal. In the late fifties Myrdal could summarize his changed position as :

> ... certain that valuations are necessary in all scientific work, from the beginning to the end. The final solution of the value problem in economics and in the social sciences generally must therefore be to set up a method by which human valuations are rationally and openly introduced into theoretical and practical research to give it direction and purpose, to make it both unbiased and relevant of life. These valuations must themselves be ascertained as social facts: and the value premises by which they are represented in our scientific work must be tested as to relevance and significance in our society.[18]

Myrdal in the Fifties

I will now try to show how Myrdal conceived the problem of how the social sciences could contribute to raising social welfare and how Myrdal looked upon the relations between science and politics during the 1950s.

An American dilemma

Sweden had a very privileged position in the early post-war years, as it had been able to stand outside the war. The time was referred to by Gunnar Myrdal as the 'harvest-time'. Now the Social Democrats were to make use of the political influence that they had achieved, the period of compromise with the bourgeois parties was over. The late forties was also, as Leif Lewin, wrote '... the classic period of the debate on the planned economy in Sweden'.[19] Developments in Western societies went towards more and more planning of the economy. Demands for social security for different groups of people in need, together with public intervention in the fields of housing and construction, were part of this development towards planning in the modern sense. Pension reforms, school reforms and the commitment to full employment were other parts on the road towards the welfare society. In a short time, the modern welfare states were born.

47

This new situation placed new demands on the use of social science and also created a market for new professions, which had their educational background in the social sciences. One of the questions was what kind of knowledge was needed in order to be able to form the new, good society? And it was in this context that political economists discussed the problem of welfare economics.

In 1951 Myrdal wrote two articles on the theme 'the development towards a planned economy'. His message was that it was not a conscious development towards planning. It was more the product of economic development, an adaptation to an economic reality, which had been hastened by the crisis within the economy in the previous decades. There had been a development away from the more or less perfect competition of the market towards a more regulated economy. These institutional changes also affected the attitudes of people towards the economic processes of which they were a part. The old society had been questioned and people were more reflective and rational in their actions. They emerged free from taboos and prejudices, and they were becoming more economically rational.

Paradoxically, Myrdal says, when people started to behave as they were supposed to by the liberal idea of economic man, the foundation of the liberal economic society was crushed. Neo-classical economics had utilitarianism as one of its basic principles, where the general welfare would be raised automatically if individuals followed their own interests. The explanation Myrdal gives to this paradox is that the liberal theory, in reality, was built upon the idea that human beings acted contrary to the ideas of 'economic man'. So now liberal society was not working because people behaved as its core theory prescribed. Some years later Myrdal described the development in his book *Beyond the Welfare State*:

> When the mesh of diversified state intervention and all other public policies of various sorts, including those of the big enterprises and the organizations within the institutional infra-structure of the democratic Welfare State, have had to be coordinated in one field after another, under central state control, into unified structures of laws, rules, regulations and agreements, and also fitted into a forecast and a plan for the development of the entire national economy.[20]

This development leads to a regulated society, which is not merely formed from a new perspective on economic problems, but also by the so called social question. Different social reforms have been proposed and carried out. Justice and equality are the primary values protected by means of regulations from the state and these values are steering the development towards a more planned economy.

Following from these remarks Myrdal sees that the discussion on the question of whether we should have a planned economy is meaningless, as there is no alternative. 'The planned economy is our fate.'[21] The planned economy is not a threat to our democracy. Thus it seems as if the debates on how to organize the good society back in the thirties were also meaningless, as the development could not be affected anyway. But it also seems as if Myrdal believes that it was a form of society regulated by certain values. Perhaps we could say that there was a parallel development in these two fields.

The development of state control was questioned by many liberals, but Myrdal was, as we have seen, of another opinion. This was clear in his book on what will come after the welfare state. There he was more of a utopian. But even so Myrdal wrote about the more or less perfect welfare state and depicts it as a utopia, where the citizens are taking more and more responsibility for organizing their work and life. He argues that this utopia is,

> ... a real goal. It is inherent in those ideals of liberty, equality and brotherhood that are the ultimate driving forces behind the development of the modern democratic Welfare State. If we made the ideology of the Welfare State more explicit, i.e. if we clarified our direction and aims, this utopia would stand out as our goal.[22]

But many aspects of this citation should be discussed. A first simple question is who the 'we' are? Does this word refer to the whole of humanity? Is this the position of Myrdal in the late fifties trying to fulfil what he wrote in the last paragraphs of *An American Dilemma* in 1944:

> To find practical formulas for this never-ending reconstruction of society is the supreme task of social scientists. The world catastrophe places tremendous difficulties on our way and may shake our confidence to the depths. Yet we have today in social science a greater trust in the improvability of man and society than we ever had since the Enlightenment.[23]

Or we can ponder what he wrote a couple of years later, discussing the international integration of national economies.

> There is no way of studying social reality other than from the viewpoint of human ideals. A 'disinterested social science' has never

49

existed and, for logical reasons, cannot exist. The value connotations of our main concepts represents our interest in a matter, gives direction to our thoughts and significance to our inferences. It poses the questions without which there are no answers.[24]

This remark brings us back to the core problem for this chapter concerning social engineering and intellectuals and the more general problem of science and politics.

Social Theory and Social Policy

We have so far discussed in general terms the views of Myrdal on values in the social sciences. It seems as if, during the decades discussed here, he is changing his position from being a more or less ideal type of social engineer to a position as an intellectual. But in order to get a more precise picture of this I will now turn to what he thought about the division of work between the different social groups in society, the social strata which are important in the use of social scientific knowledge in changing or reforming society. We can see Myrdal's views as implicit comments on Max Weber's views on science and politics.

I think that the best starting point for this is the opening address Myrdal gave at the Conference of the British Sociological Association in 1953, *The Relation Between Social Theory and Social Policy*. The central theme in his address was that the social sciences during the 20th century had influenced social policy a great deal:

> My thesis is that, while there was little participation on the part of social scientists in the actual technical preparation of legislation and still less in administering induced social changes, their influence was nevertheless very considerable, and that this influence was due in the main to their exposition and propagation of certain general thoughts and theories.[25]

As examples of influential social scientists Myrdal mentioned Malthus, Ricardo, Marx, Darwin and Keynes. Myrdal also argues that the influence of these theoreticians was essentially ideological. By this statement he did not mean that social scientists were blurring or confusing the minds of ordinary people. On the contrary, the social scientists were fighting against superstitions and prejudices and were constantly trying to enlighten people. This, according to Myrdal, is the ideological use of the social sciences.

But what was the relation between politics and the social sciences and what should it be? Myrdal first explains what most scientists think, using a formulation which presupposes a sharp distinction between what is and what ought to be:

> ... though it is not possible for science to pronounce on the ends of social policy, it is a scientific problem which can be scientifically solved to establish what means are most appropriate for reaching an end which is postulated.[26]

But Myrdal does not accept this formulation, though he accepts the distinction between is and ought. He says that we can separate out the problem of ought from the means-end discussion. Most social scientists believe that the question of means are value-free. But Myrdal says that it is simply not true that means are only instrumental to ends. Many means have an independent value as well. So when the value premises are stated, premises which are extra-scientific, they must be concerned with the means as well as the ends. Furthermore, Myrdal adds, all means used for reaching an end have accessory effects, which also must be taken into consideration.

But who should decide on the values to be chosen? Myrdal points out some factors which condition the politician's ways of working in a democracy. There are three groups of public servants - the politicians, the civil servants and the journalists - all who must make intellectual sacrifices. Their freedom is limited and they can't freely pursue ideas. The politicians, for example, can't work for longsighted goals, as they must take into consideration daily changes in the opinion of people. Moreover, they must take collective responsibility, which means that they can be criticized for actions that they don't support themselves, but still have to defend. The primary aim of politics is power and all that goes with that is contra-rational:

> ... the steady pedagogical urge to rationality in political questions must be provided largely by people who have their status independently of the general public and for this reason can afford not to sacrifice long-range influence for immediate power.[27]

One group of people who should be able to bring this rationality into politics are the civil servants. They can have a great influence on politics now and in the future. But this only applies as long as they don't say anything on the broader issues of the time. This is so, Myrdal continues, because:

51

... they often disclose an astonishing lack of perspective and sometimes a general ideological confusion. Their field is the details and the routine, not the larger motives for policies, the general relations between social acts or the broad trends of social development which raise basic issues.[28]

The journalists are also trapped in their institutional conditions. So how can we then guarantee some kind of rationality in a political democracy? And the value of rationality is one that Myrdal can't sacrifice. Myrdal gives the social scientists the decisive role. This is the group in society which can give it a long-range intellectual leadership and which makes it possible for society to move in a direction of '...rationality and progress'.

This sounds like the idea of social engineering that Myrdal had pleaded for since the early thirties. Now, in the beginning of the fifties, he still sticks to these ideas. In the years after the Great Depression a kind of economic engineering was started. Large numbers of economists found their way into the government offices. But not only this group of social scientists, but also psychologists, political scientists, historians and geographers, to mention but a few.

The social sciences should and could contribute to the rationality of politics. In the late forties and early fifties there was an ongoing discussion on the problems of planning modern society. In his address Myrdal comments on the message from von Hayek that state economic planning leads to serfdom. He doesn't care much for von Hayek's arguments, but he can see that there is a kernel of truth in the notion that too much planning can lead to a crises for democracy. But this isn't a big problem, according to Myrdal. The knowledge produced by social scientists can and should be used in planning for the good society, which for Myrdal seems to be the welfare state.

One of the dangers that Myrdal points out for democracy is that the social scientists in modern society become more and more specialized. They don't involve themselves in broader issues anymore. This means that certain critical problems are bypassed. I think that we can interpret this as meaning that there are such institutional conditions for the sciences, which point towards this situation. The only cure that Myrdal can think of to ward off this problem is to strengthen the universities. This is the only institutional place within society where you can give yourself time and also have the opportunity to deal with long term social problems.

This belief in scientific knowledge was quite typical in the fifties, even though not too many social scientists shared either Myrdal's view on the welfare state or his ideology of science. In order to find a contrast to the views of Myrdal I will refer to a book by the American sociologist, *George A Lundberg*. In *Can Science Save Us?*, which was translated and published in Swedish in 1952, he asks where shall we seek help in order to be able to solve our social problems? Lundberg's answer is of course that social science, and more specifically sociology, can give us this help. Perhaps not right now, but later on. Here his view-points are close to the ones of Myrdal. Lundberg also deals with the so called value-problem. He thinks there are no specific reasons why we cannot study values just as objectively as any other phenomenon. He argues that we can deduce the values people have from their actions and that this is what can be studied in a scientific way. Of course social scientists also have values, but when they act as professional social scientists they are objective, according to Lundberg. The only value-judgement a social scientist should make explicit in his scientific work concerns the importance of certain facts in relation to his research. In order to get the most effective help for people to reach their goals they must rely more on scientific knowledge. 'Give science what belongs to science and to metaphysics what belongs to metaphysics.'[29]

To Be An Intellectual or A Social Engineer: That Is The Question

Let me finish this chapter with a short discussion on the problem of the relation of intellectuals to social engineering. Also I will make some remarks concerning democracy and the role of the critique of social development in relation to the problems of value within the social sciences. My central focus will concern whether it is possible to be an intellectual at the same time as a social engineer.

If we follow the usual way of defining the two concepts, it is clear to me that it is not possible to be an intellectual and social engineer at the same time. To be an intellectual is to be a critic of social development; to be a social engineer is to take an active part in the formation society. To be an intellectual in this meaning is not first and foremost to be a member of a profession, this is more the position of the isolated individual. It is the social engineer who is the professional. For both categories there is a close relation between politics and science, but for the social engineer knowledge is ideologically neutral, while it is ideologically laden for the intellectual.

From my point of view the problem of values within social sciences is crucial to this whole discussion. If you accept the views of Myrdal on this problem, questions such as how the values are to be chosen and who is going to make the choices are important. Hence in relation to this we have the problem of elitism versus democracy. I contend that in order to shed light on this we must separate at least two different models of social engineering from each other. One of them is based upon an ideal of neutrality, both concerning the position of social scientists, and the idea that values are not part of a truth-seeking social scientific knowledge. The ideal of scientific knowledge here is very close to the positivistic or scientistic tradition. Otto Neurath, the propagandist of the Vienna Circle, was an excellent spokesman for this model. There is a tendency towards elitism within this tradition.

The other model is based upon an ideal of knowledge where values are seen as permeating scientific work. Frequently advocates of this model are of a rationalistic orientation, but they can also be of a relativistic nature. Within the second model we can also distinguish between those who are democratic and those who have more elitist leanings, when questions such as who is going to decide what values will be the best and how active the people should be in the transforming process of society are discussed. Is this seen as a mere technical problem or does the reforming process of society presuppose that people take an active part in political work? The last model in its more democratic versions is then possibly not part of a social engineering model, but I would say that it could be.

Myrdal is part of the second model and belongs to the more elitist tendency here. I will say a few words on this. We can summarize Myrdal's point of view concerning the question of the role of values within social scientific knowledge as follows. It is not enough that you accept the value premises to be extra-scientific, they must be deliberately chosen and made explicit. The value-premise must not be arbitrarily chosen. It must be:

> ... relevant, even significant, and it must be practicable. This means that it must correspond to the real valuations of existing groups in society, large enough or for other reasons having power enough to make it realistic.[30]

We can see in this citation that there are two different kinds of problems; one is internal in the ideal of social social science and the other one is more political, i.e. how values are chosen. Within the part integral to social science we can identify two levels, on the one hand we have the value-premises needed for the practical application of social analysis and on the other hand we have the values, which are involved directly in the scientific work. The scientific problems we work with, Myrdal says, are chosen and these choices in their turn are products of our valuations. And Myrdal formulates this as the principal paradox of science;

54

the value premise ... cannot even be formulated except in relation to all elements in the alternatively possible development processes laid bare by factual analysis: the factual analysis cannot be carried out except when guided by the value premise.[31]

Let's continue our analysis of this so called paradox of social sciences and see how Myrdal pursued it in the 1950s. In 1958 he published *Value in Social Theory*, which consisted of a selection of essays written earlier. This text gives a good picture of Myrdal's views on the problem of value and the intricate interrelations between facts and values. In his philosophy of science Myrdal is clear about the need for theory. He says that scientific knowledge does not emerge by itself, which means, according to Myrdal, that you can never do raw empirical studies. Problems must be raised and the empirical studies selected must have a theoretical basis in order to be meaningful. At the same time, just as theory is a priori to facts, science has as its first principle, that 'the facts are sovereign'. Myrdal goes on to argue theory is only a hypothesis, which means that:

> ...the criterion of its truth can never be anything other than the pragmatic one of its usefulness in bringing our observation of facts into a meaningful and non-contradictory system of knowledge. And so scientific progress can be expected to result from a process of trial and error.[32]

Within the moral sphere we can find a corresponding process, where the logical basis is consistency between the values within the value system. Myrdal goes on:

> As the valuations refer to social reality, and as therefore their interrelation logically involve people's beliefs concerning this reality, the process of correcting their theories to fit the facts plays at the same time an important role in the attempts to give clarity, honesty and consistency to their moral ideas: to purify and strengthen the public conscience. For people want to be rational. Scientific truth-seeking, by rectifying their beliefs also inflences their valuatons.[33]

Myrdal's comments here are interesting, especially on the way people's values are corrected by means of research. But still we haven't discussed the question of how you select the values from which you start your research. If we look at what Myrdal did in his study *An American Dilemma*; there he chose to start with the values expressed in the Declaration of Independence.

55

In other places Myrdal asserts that you should make use of values which important groups in society are attached to. The core concept here is of course 'important', which can be interpreted as either the powerful groups in society or as the largest groups in society. The consequences of which of these you pick are very important. It's not possible within the framework of this chapter to go more deeply into this problem, but an interesting follow up would be to compare Myrdal with Max Weber and how he and the Neo-Kantians saw this part of the value-problem. In their views the academics or the so called 'mandarins' should play a more active role in this process than they would in the world of Myrdal.

One could describe Myrdal as a 'Philosoph', which means that he is a child of the Enlightenment, who wants to teach mankind 'the real values', such as rationality, solidarity and freedom. If you follow these values they are not chosen because important groups in society like them, but because Myrdal thinks that they are worth following. If we interpret Myrdal as a man of the Enlightenment, I think that we find as much elitism in his thinking as in the Neo-Kantian tradition.

The picture I have given of Myrdal here is more an image of an intellectual, discussing especially the foundations of social scientific knowledge. I have done this in order to show that there is also another Myrdal than Myrdal the social engineer, working closely with the Swedish Social Democratic government. In this respect he was eager to show that social knowledge was an important part in reforming society and the reform process must be built on scientific knowledge. So in a way it is perhaps correct to say that Myrdal was more of an intellectual in relation to the social sciences than to the political field.

I contend that his way of posing the question of values within social scientific knowledge made it possible for him to be a social engineer, taking part in the transformation of society, at the same time as he was a critical intellectual, criticizing the values chosen as well as criticizing the general direction of the political work. It is also possible to make use of the analysis made by Myrdal on the institutional changes affecting the possibilities of a critique of social development. This critique points out the necessity of having institutions within society, preferably universities, where people of different kinds have enough time and autonomy, in order to be able to discuss more longsighted solutions to the social, economic and environmental problems of modern society. Late in his life Myrdal was critical of the tendency of the universities to become more and more of an educational apparatus for modern professions, forgetting its other purpose of being a focus for the critique of society. The multiversity seems to point in another direction, but it has always been the task of universities to educate civil servants of different kinds. But this task now seems to dominate over its other aim of being the institutional foundation for the development of more longsighted views on the development of the social and natural world.

Notes and references

1. Halsey, A. H. and Karabel, J. (1977), *Power and Ideology in Education*, Oxford University Press, Oxford.
2. Myrdal, Gunnar (1944), *The Negro Problem and Modern Democracy*, Harper, New York.
3. Boggs, C. (1993), *Intellectuals and the Crisis of Modernity*, University of New York Press, New York, p. 10.
4. Ibid. p. 16.
5. Ibid. p. 97.
6. Popper, Karl (1957), *The Poverty of Historicism*, Routledge, London, p. 66.
7. Popper, Karl (1962), *The Open Society and Its Enemies*, Routledge, London, p. 22.
8. Myrdal, G. (1953), *The Political Element in the Development of Economic Theory*.
9. Hansen, Bent (1948), 'The New Welfare Economy', *Ekonomisk Tidskrift*, pp. 248-252.
10. Herz, Ulrich (1949), 'Science and Politics in Political Economy', Ekonomisk Tidskrift, pp. 27-39.
11. Myrdal, G. (1958), *Value in Social Theory*, p. 248.
12. Hansson, B. (1991), 'The Stockholm School and the Development of Dynamic Method', in Sandelin, Bo (ed), *The History of Swedish Economic Thought*, Routledge, London.
13. Myrdal, *Value in Social Theory*, p. 250.
14. Ibid, p. 254.
15. Myrdal, G. (1933), 'Ends and Means in Political Economy', *Zeitschrift fYr Nationalokonomie*, vol. IV.
16. Ibid. p. 213.
17. Ibid. p. 221.
18. Ibid. p. 221.
19. Lewin, Leif (1967), *Planhushållningsdebatten*, Diss, Stockholm, p. 529.
20. Myrdal, G. (1958), *Beyond the Welfare State*, Yale Law School Publications, New Haven, p. 70.
21. Myrdal, G. (1951), *Ultvecklingen mot Plahushållning*, Tiden, Stockholm, p. 148.
22. Myrdal, G. *Beyond the Welfare State*, p. 70.
23. Myrdal, G. *An American Dilemma*, p. 1024.
24. Myrdal, G. 'International integration' (*Appendix to Value in Social Theory*), p. 1.

25. Myrdal, G. (1954), 'The Relation Between Social Theory and Social Policy', *British Journal of Sociology*, p. 215.
26. Ibid. p. 238.
27. Ibid. p. 219.
28. Ibid. p. 219.
29. Lundberg, G. A. (1952), *Can Science Save Us*, Tidens Förlag, Stockholm, p. 32.
30. Ibid. p. 240.
31. Ibid. p. 240.
32. Myrdal. G. (1958), 'The Logical Crux of all Science', in *Value in Social Theory*, p. 233.
33. Ibid. p. 234.

5. The Taylorization of Intellectual Labour

LENA DOMINELLI AND ANKIE HOOGVELT

Introduction

There is a distinct climate of anti-intellectualism in Britain today. It is important therefore, that intellectuals once more become a subject of serious sociological analysis. This paper makes a start in the re-examination of the role of intellectuals which must be sustained by further systematic research. In it we examine critically the fate of intellectuals in post-war Britain to make sense of various apparently disparate yet confluent developments. We use our own experience as intellectuals situated in British academia, augmented where possible with the limited available statistical data. There is a small literature that is critical of the transformation of the university system in the UK and indeed elsewhere[1] which we have barely tapped. We have desisted from dwelling on it because, to our knowledge, no one has addressed the present transformation from the point of view of (a) the context of globalization and Contract Government, (b) the privatization of the welfare state of which education is a part, and (c) the functional management of intellectual labour.

We cover each of these three areas. However, we focus primarily on the issue of how Contract Government has changed the working environment of intellectuals through economic instruments and, in the process, has altered the make-up of the intellectual class. Moreover, within the broad category of intellectual class, our chief preoccupation is the relation between intellectuals in universities and the state.

We conclude the chapter by considering the different types of intellectuals that have developed in the last two decades as Britain moved from the reconstruction of a war torn economy and the creation of a welfare state to a deepening integration into the world economy combined with a restructuring of the public domain.

The Welfare State: Expansion of Academic Intellectuals

The immediate post-war period resulted in an expansion in the number of intellectuals and the social roles and locations in which they became involved. Much of this was attributed to the expansion both of the welfare state with its demand for highly qualified professionals and of universities following the Robbins Report.[2] Between 1963 and 1973 the total numbers of full-time students in the 'old'[3] universities almost doubled from 130,562 to 251,226. This was parallelled by an equally robust growth in full-time tenured academic staff from 16,881 to 26,429.[4] This expansion provided a home for intellectuals critical of society and looking for alternative visions as well as for those supportive of the status quo. Both were funded by the state. The growth of mass higher education increased the number of bureaucratic professionals within the welfare state undertaking intellectual work alongside the elite responsible for the intellectual's role, i.e. professional academics. Borrowing from Gramsci's[5] useful concept of the 'organic' intellectuals, we argue that during this period there emerged two types of 'organic' intellectuals: the professional bureaucratic/technocratic intellectuals or 'hegemonic' organic intellectuals who serviced the welfare state and endorsed the Establishment in its activities, and the critical thinkers or 'counter-hegemonic' organic intellectuals who organized around welfare issues and demanded changes in welfare state structures including the delivery of personal social services, as well as more radical changes in the allocation of power and distribution of resources in society.[6]

In the late sixties, as a result of changes in the economy, the expansion of state funded intellectual activity came to a halt as the state began to reshape itself to deal with the demands of international competition and assert control over its organic intellectuals and the activism of the labour and community movements.[7]

At this time we see the state change from being a promoter of intellectual activity to a controller of it. Whilst this shift in direction explains in part the decline of the intellectuals' critical function that followed, the intellectuals contributed to their demise as generators of ideas. For, rarely did they analyse the implications of their dependency on the state. They did not stop to think that the state had after all provided them with the wherewithal to act as change-agents, and engage in politically motivated intellectual work which fed into grassroot organization and mobilization in the community and the workplace. They were therefore especially vulnerable when the state changed its agenda and re-aligned social relations in monetarist directions.

Globalization, Economic Restructuring and the Changing Nature of the State

By globalization we understand a dual process of both widening and deepening of capitalist relations on a world scale. While many have tried to trace the intensification of those linkages in terms of trade, investments, communications, and speed of informational interaction,[8] we believe that the currency of the concept since the 1980s owes to the growing visibility of three principal interactive features:

(1) The establishment of a global market principle, that is, the imposition of a new categorical imperative, namely global market quality and price, upon the domestic supply of goods and services, and upon domestic factors of production. For various reasons that we cannot go into here, namely the growth of multinational companies and the organization of international production, global competition has become the most powerful structural force shaping domestic economic behaviour.

(2) The deregulation and liberalization of financial markets, which, coupled with timely technological innovations, has rendered the capitalist world system increasingly one global system in which money as bank capital and money as productive capital merge in cross-frontier activities and in which - as a consequence - return on capital can be earned regardless of restrictions of either space or time.

(3) Flexible accumulation. By this we refer to the circumstance that the global market principle now affects production capacity itself. Owing to technological developments, production capacity at least in some leading branches of industry, has become sufficiently flexible to be viewed as a commodity.[9] Global manufacturing industry is developing networks of small independent businesses who are providers of flexible capacity and who compete with one another within the network. The articulation problems associated with today's economic networking has led international business to develop certain patterns of regulation and governance, such as Quality Management and advance process certification. The need to ensure that such controlling mechanisms are spread throughout the entire national economy has drawn the state in as a regulating force. For example, the British Government has institutionalized certification through the imposition of British Standard 5750 (BS5750) which has recently harmonized with EU standard ISO9000. This standard certification now applies equally to businesses in the private sector and services in the public sector.[10]Thus, even parts of the welfare sector which had always regarded themselves as outside of the commodity relationship, have been drawn into this same regulatory

framework. For example, Cheshire Social Services has registered under BS5750, service provisions for people who are long term mentally ill.[11]

The internationalization of the state

From this, it can be seen, that globalization, as Cox[12] has pointed out, is accompanied by the 'internationalization of the state' in which the state becomes a vehicle for the adjustment of the domestic economy to the imperatives of the global market. This adjustment, we would argue, involves a whole range of tasks and functions which the state undertakes on behalf of international capital. These cover: monetary and fiscal policies; industrial legislation; social policies; the restructuring of the welfare state; and the reconstitution of social obligations, for example, an ideological attack on alternative lifestyles, and prioritization of traditional family values through social policy initiatives.[13] In this list we also include the transformation of 'higher education' from a critical activity to short-term training for the labour market and from basic research to research that is 'relevant' to the needs of industry. Consequently, training for certain professional work previously requiring university education is now being reduced to technical training to be undertaken solely in the workplace. This degradation of professional work is part and parcel of the Taylorization of intellectual labour which we address below.

In the 1980s many of these policies went under the name of deregulation. But this term is correct only in so far as it relates to the lifting of restrictions within the financial markets. The further application of 'deregulation' in fact involved a considerable amount of centralization and interference by central government in local government, in the public domain, in education and in the every day private life of citizens. Indeed, today there is emerging what the Regulation School identifies as a whole new mode of Regulation, necessary for the materialization of a new, global, regime of accumulation.[14]

The difficulty for any theorist of Regulation is that the forms of regulation of the new epoch are - compared with the past - quintessentially a form of deregulation. That is the paradox. Deregulation in one sense implies a dismantling of state-sponsored forms of regulation of the market, a shrinking of the public sector, indeed even a diminution of the public domain. However, this is not happening for the government is financing 'quangos' (quasi-nongovernmental organizations) and freelance consultants to conduct many of the activities formally undertaken in the public sector, but without public accountability.[15] In the higher education domain too we witness the growth of a private sector feeding off the public sector.

How can a deregulated society be regulated? That, of course, is the sociological question of how the various subunits of society from family to educational establishments and economic enterprises can still hang together, and be coordinated, in some sensible way. The only way to understand this process is to describe it in terms of the emergence of new 'regulatory codes'. These regulatory codes pervasively penetrate every sphere of organized human activity, be it schools, universities, hospitals, prisons, business enterprises, or family life. They include quality control, performance indicators, flexible work organization and so on.

Contract Government

What is confusing about the current role of the 'internationalized state' is the government's 'regulation through deregulation'. That is, the government imposes new regulatory codes, which whilst clearly having been invented and developed within business enterprise, particularly globalized business, are now deliberately foisted upon those organizations in the public sector over which the government still has some financial leverage whilst promoting a reduction of its own direct involvement in these organizations. In those countries where the central state has been strong, the government can exercise greater direction over the 'regulation through deregulation' process and initiate changes in social and economic relations more swiftly.

These changes were implemented in Britain during the 1980s with relative ease because here, not only was the government ideologically committed to monetarist doctrines, but the state was also one of the country's key economic players through its control of the assets which were locked in the welfare state and the large workforce it employed. Also, the state could feed off the public's hostility to a bureaucratic interventionist and unaccountable 'socialist' state. Thus, fairly quickly around £50 billion worth of state assets were sold to the private sector, often at knockdown prices.[16] In transferring assets from the public sector to the private sector, an infrastructure was created whereby the private sector could trade with, and carry out, services for the public sector whilst being paid for by the state through contracting out. This, however, required a different managerial approach.

In Britain, as in other countries, the public sector has seen far reaching management changes in the last decade under the broad heading 'deregulation'. These public sector management changes have been put into place in two successive, planned, stages: the Financial Management Initiative (FMI) of 1982 and the Next Steps Initiative launched in 1988. Characteristically, these two management initiatives involved the imposition of a new logic of seeing the (public) resource provider as a 'purchaser' of services from 'provider' units (commercial or voluntary organizations and individual entrepreneurs) whose actions are contractually defined and held accountable. In the FMI stage these provider units were still largely public sector departments themselves. The Next Steps Initiative, by contrast, created semi-independent executive agencies from the operational arms of Government with the further aim of having these agencies in their turn contract specific tasks to other, private sector, agencies and enterprises. To this end, compulsory competitive tendering legislation was also introduced in 1988, to accompany the Next Steps Inititative. Thus, the objective of Next Steps was to create a series of clearly specified client/contractor relationships, that is, arm's length government or Contract Government.[17]

Consequently, staff were transferred from public to private sector. This transferral was accomplished in the main through four processes of privatization which occurred alongside the well known sell-offs in which the public sector owned companies were sold on the stock exchange. These were: management buy outs, facilities management, independent trading agencies and quasi-independent service agencies, and, joint ventures.[18] As a result, the complement of 732,000 civil servants which were in post when the Conservatives took office in 1979 was reduced by 440,000 who had gone to work for these arm's length agencies by the middle of 1995. A further 185,000 jobs were lost altogether under successive cost cutting drives, leaving a core of just 55,000 civil servants and a further 50,000 working in areas too small or too sensitive to be turned into agencies.[19]

In the section on the Circulation of Intellectual Elites, we consider the changing structural relationships between private and public sector more precisely and pinpoint the re-location of professional academics in the interstices created in the new privatized welfare state. But first we look at the cultural framework of Contract Government because we believe that it sheds light on the changing parameters of what constitutes 'knowledge' and 'intellectual practice'.

The Cultural Framework of Contract Government

Greer,[20] in her description of the philosophy and ideology of the Next Steps Initiative, makes the point that Contract Government was developed on the back of 'agency theory' which is a micro-economics theory arising from the experience of contemporary enterprise organization in achieving contract compliance. It is a point that has also been made elsewhere.[21]

Agency theory is a framework for the analysis of 'agency-problems'. 'An agency relationship is defined through an explicit or implict contract in which one or more persons (the principal(s) engage another person (the agent) to take actions on behalf of the principal(s).'[22] The contract involves the delegation of some decision-making authority to the agent. Problems arise in agency relationships fundamentally because it is assumed that individuals will always pursue their self-interests possibly at the expense of others. The key problems for the 'principal' therefore are:[23]

1. To motivate the agent in such a way that the agent's self interests coincide with the principals' objectives (referred to as the problem of 'bonding');

2. To monitor the activities of the agent in meeting required ends; and

3. To reduce the 'asymmetry of information' in which either the agent or the principal has more information about what or how they do or decide things than it is willing to share with the other.

The solutions to these problems are largely what is now driving the conceptual or cultural paradigm of Contract Government. This includes: the definition of overall strategic goals and the identification of sequential performance objectives within these; the operationalization of performance targets; the clear and detailed specification of input and output measures and the costing of these, including a critical scrutiny of 'value for money'; concrete specification of the relevant contributions and responsibilities of all the actors involved; and amongst other things, the formulation of reporting and monitoring tools.

The Taylorization of Intellectual Labour

How does this cultural paradigm affect our concept of 'knowledge' and 'intellectual activity'? Our answer to this question is through the 'Taylorization of Intellectual Labour'. Admittedly Taylorism is a concept, and a managerial practice, that dates from a very different time and a very different place. And just now when it is disappearing as a tool for controlling manual workers, it is being introduced as an instrument for reorganizing mental labour! Yet the crucial similarity between the two is the scientific management of work and the consequent managerial control of the workforce. In the early part of this century, Taylor[24] had put forward three principles of work reorganization whereby managerial control was achieved: (1) An extension of the division of labour by the breaking down of every activity into ever more simple component parts, thus allowing cheaper unskilled labour to be hired; (2) Full managerial control of the workplace, separating mental from manual labour; and (3) Systematic costing of each step of the work process in order to provide managers with the information necessary for exercising control over the labour process and the workforce. How does this apply to intellectual work today as it is being reorganized under Contract Government? We believe it applies in two ways:

Commodification of service delivery

Much of the public sector involves the delivery of services which have essentially a complex processual character. Education, health care, provision for the elderly or the disabled, are not finite, tangible, commodities in the way that roadworks, houses, vehicle licenses or passports are. Nevertheless, the agenda of Contract Government requires that such processes are fragmented into component parts or activities, each part being able to be translated or 'operationalized' into empirically identifiable and quantifiable 'indicators' or 'measures', i.e., discrete 'technical competencies', which may then be subject to cost-efficiency scrutiny and put up for tender to enable private sector providers to compete with public sector providers in an internal market. Even policy advice and indeed basic academic research in this way becomes 'commodified' and tendered in open competition between public sector service units, private consultants and academic departments. The creation of a single 'internal' market for research was recently formalized in the Government's White Paper which set the agenda for publicly funded research.[25]

The elimination of professional autonomy

The contractor or purchaser has to control and limit the provider's ability to use discretion and set their own agenda, as identified in agency problem number 3 above. This is achieved, again, by breaking down the task into discrete, identifiable activities (called 'elements')[26] and, next, enforcing by contract the delivery of each discrete, separate step. This has been done by using functional analysis to define 'competences', for example, in social work education,[27] mechanical engineering, management, nursing education[28] and teacher training. 'Competencies' have become the vehicle through which the Taylorization of intellectual labour and hence the privatization of service provisions is managed. To this end, the Government has set up yet another quango, the National Council for Occupational Standards which has produced the paradigm for national vocational qualifications (NVQs) that are to define the competencies required for any professional occupation. Consequently, a complex critical activity has been reduced to de-skilled fragmented work which no longer merits an academic award, thus fulfilling Braverman's critique of Taylorization as the degradation of labour.[29]

The competency approach is the incarnation of Taylorization in the service sector. What it does, in the formulation of the Government's own official publications on the subject,[30] is the following:

1. Identify a key purpose for an area of work, occupation or role, which clearly summarizes 'what the occupation sets out to achieve (rather than how or why)';

2. Agree this key purpose with the potential providers;

3. Identify the 'key roles' or statements which describe the main functions required for achieving the key purpose;

4. Breakdown each key role to a further level of detail, which describes 'what needs to happen to achieve the key role';

5. Identify those statements which provide the units of competence which can stand as the national occupational standards;

6. Breakdown these statements further into elements of competence. These are then qualified by performance criteria and range statements; 'Taken together, these form the national occupational standards - the assessable outcomes of performance'.[31] Note the 'assessable outcomes of performance'. This strikes at the heart of the commodification process. For it is these, and not the expended labour time that is now being put out to competitive tender in the quasi-market. It is no longer 'hands' that are being hired, but the final product which is being contracted for. What this means for institutions of higher education is that they become relatively uncompetitive in this market because they lack the flexibility of response necessary to be included in this competitive process. This then leaves the quasi-market open to people who have exited from these institutions, either through redundancy or early retirement, to tender on the basis of self-employment. This whole process becomes the linchpin for the 'circulation of intellectual elites' which we discuss below.

What is interesting about this management of intellectual labour through fragmentation, sequencing and commodification (i.e., the Taylorization of intellectual labour) is that it is being brought about not during a period of fordist accumulation but precisely in the period of post-fordist or flexible accumulation! We have seen before how flexible accumulation is one of the principal features of globalization. Taylorization of intellectual and professional labour, echoes, or mimics, the manner in which in global manufacturing industry, industrial processes and production capacity are 'flexibly' accessed, relieving the buyer of the costs of accessing capacity by committing to its continued use, thereby allowing companies to externalize employment and hence become more profitable.[32] In this way, globalization, we believe, culturally impacts on the manner in which, through contract government, commodification is stretched to the public sector, including the academic sector.

The Circulation of Intellectual Elites

In this section we examine the implications of Contract Government for the social positioning of the intellectual classes. Deregulation brought to intellectuals a realization that they were not, after all, a 'free floating intelligentsia',[33] but dependent on the state for their continued existence. This realization necessitated a re-alignment of their relationship with the state and made them scrabble for resources which would allow them to carry out intellectual activities whether in support of the state or not.

The re-structuring of the state (through privatization, Contract Government etc.) re-located bureaucratic professionals to the private sphere. This process we call the 'circulation of intellectual elites'. We are aware that the use of the phrase 'circulation of elites' has a tradition in political sociology going back to Pareto, Mosca and Michels,[34] which does not strictly apply here. Nevertheless we use the phrase because of its heuristic value: it gives us an image of revolving doors through which elites pass from one sector to the other depending on which offers the best opportunities for employment. Figures released by ministers in a series of Parliamentary answers show that in 1989, one-in-eight civil servants leaving Whitehall went into consultancy work; by 1993, this figure had risen to one-in-two.[35] This transfer encourages a deepening of the organic linkages between the bureaucratic professionals and the globalized capitalist class. And, in this interactive process, it enables the state to implant the regulatory codes from the business world upon the public domain. This is so because these elites are now working for a private sector carrying out activities which were formerly done in the public sector but which are now only financed by public monies. Examples of these regulatory codes are: customer driven supply; performance-related pay; flexible work organization and contracts; total quality management.[36]

The contractual nature of their employment compels a focus on economic targets to be achieved and on pay being related to their achievement. This creates the conditions under which only a certain type of intellectuals can flourish, namely the organic hegemonic type. This occurs because the only legitimated form of intellectual thinking that can develop is one which concentrates on technocratic 'competencies' and economic indicators. This produces a mechanistic understanding of social processes and human behaviour which draws upon a separation and compartmentalization of intellectual activity and the abstraction of everyday experience. The separation of intellectual activities from their social base disguises important political processes and forms of social control. Non-intellectual activity parades as 'professional' intellectual activity through notions of 'competency' and 'open management'. This, for example, enables freelance consultants with limited qualifications and teaching skills to set themselves up as trainers who compete with qualified and experienced academics. Thus it is not qualifications and ability to do the job which determines their employment, but whether they are asking the right price and are willing to subordinate their critical capacities to do what is being asked in a contract which has been defined neither by the consumer (student) nor the qualified professional (the academic).

These cultural shifts exclude, from the contractual bargaining process, counter-hegemonic intellectuals whose skills become irrelevant. For what they do is focus on the holistic process whereby links are made precisely between the social, economic and political aspects of any one activity under review.

The Intellectuals in the Academic Sector

We have argued in the section on the circulation of intellectual elites, that one segment of the intellectual class, namely the professional bureaucrats, have found a 'part state-funded' niche in the private sector. By contrast, those remaining in academia, have experienced an increase in workload (student numbers), a contraction in unit of resource, a dramatic decline in their social status and a truncation of their functions. The empirical evidence for this has been published and is readily accessible.[37]

When Thatcher took office in 1979, the restructuring of academia began in earnest: total spending per student (capital and recurrent) has declined by some 50%.[38] This was accompanied by changes in how academic work was done and in the composition of the workforce, moving it away from tenured, permanent, staff to a more casualized, insecure, workforce whether in research or teaching. A marginal rise in number of 'core' staff of 1.2% accompanied the near doubling of student numbers in the 1980s.[39] This was supplemented by a 23% rise in staff employed on temporary and short term contracts, between 1988-1993.[40] Timely legislation, in the form of the Education Reform Act 1988, enabled this casualization of the academic work force through the abolition of tenure. Casualization gives intellectuals a precarious hold in their profession and is more conducive to the development of the hegemonic organic intellectual than the counter-hegemonic one, for challenging the status quo can only be done at the expense of one's own livelihood.

The squeeze on the university sector also manifests itself in a lowering of the socio-economic status of academics. The average pay of academics in universities has declined in relation to comparable white collar workers in the public sector, though more so in relation to the private sector. Ironically, newly qualified Ph.D holders employed in the private sector, will earn upon commencement of their careers a salary easily equivalent to or exceeding that of their professors who have supervised them and who are at the end of theirs. Comparing the growth of real pay of teachers in higher education between 1980-1990 with other OECD countries, the UK stands out as the only country with a negative growth of 3.8%.[41]

What is unusual and interesting about the way the Government re-structured the university sector is that it did so not by confronting academics with a direct ideological attack on academic freedom, but rather ingeniously used that very 'freedom' to harness peer pressure and scrutiny so as to create an 'internal' market and competition, for both research and teaching. In some ways the system which emerged has disconcerting similarities with flexible production in industry. For, there too, changes in work organization are driven by the utilization of peer pressure and benchmarking to set the standards for continuous improvement.[42] This industrial workplace phenomenon has been described for example as worker's self-subordination.[43] It is a concept that helps us understand how professional academics too have been co-opted into creating the conditions for their own disempowerment.

The British Government has succeeded in subverting the critical scholarship and the 'value-free' and 'non-commercial' ethos of the academic community through the following four economic steps, although within the space of this article we focus largely on the first two, which we regard as the most critical in terms of the fragmentation of the professional academics:

(1) Decentralized budget management;
(2) Peer-judgement of quality in cost-effective teaching and research;
(3) Flexible production principles of organization;
(4) Increasing involvement of employers in setting academic agendas including curriculum matters.

Each step of the way illustrates the profound relevance of Foucault's concept of 'discourse and practice'. Through discourse and practice, the individual and the group become gradually drawn into a new world of lived experience that gradually detaches them from their own critical consciousness, ideology or value commitments including, in the case of

71

academia, the value commitment to 'value-free' scholarship and basic research.

Decentralized budget management

Given that the internal market had to be introduced in what had always been a budget financed operation, in the past driven by criteria defined by autonomous professionals, the way the Government proceeded was to turn academics into managers of cash limited budgets.

Successive, annual reductions in the Government's overall budget for Higher Education (otherwise known as 'efficiency gains') set the framework for a method of accounting, known in industry as 'market price minus' as opposed to a 'cost-plus' system of accounting.[44] That is to say, starting from a given budget, universities and departments, in a cascading structure of decentralization, had to calculate 'back' the price of any activity. At first, promises were made that the cheapest provision of a certain output, say a taught degree programme, would be rewarded by the allocation, in the next cycle of funding, of increased numbers of funded student places. This is the essence of the 'internal market' principle. The Government purchases degree programmes for the nation's students from competing provider units. In this way, academics at all levels became implicated in a process of dreaming up 'cost-effective' production of their teaching. They invented ingenious if spurious measures of productivity whereby each individual academic would eventually be held accountable for the use of their time.

Notional relations were established between teaching and research (50-50% of time), thus separating in the individual's own daily practice that which previously had always been regarded as indivisible, while at the same time usefully pre-figuring the eventual formal separation of the two in the government's funding structure. Next, notional relations were established between preparation time and delivery of lectures, and between time devoted to teaching and administration. Average costs of teaching output were calculated by dividing total income from student funding and fees by staff costs, consumables and capital expenditure. This required ever further decentralization of budgets between departments and even between degree programmes within departments and disciplines. Average costs could be 'reduced' by admitting 'non-funded' or 'fees only' students (self-financed and overseas students) and not counting these as contributing to the Funding Council's unit of resource.

72

In an inspired move the Government abolished, in 1992, the binary divide between universities and polytechnics (where staff had never had a contractual commitment to do research, and consequently average teaching costs were a lot lower) thereby creating a single internal market for all 'universities'. Thus, in one fell swoop, the 'average' teaching unit of resource was reduced to the lower demoninator, while the mechanism was put in place whereby the unit of resource for the whole sector could be further driven down. For their part, research successful staff in the old universities responded by hiring their own casual teaching staff, thus further de facto separating teaching from research and scholarship.

Peer review

Competition within a declining total pool of funding was next regulated by peer review and judgment. Consistent with its ideological view of self-regulation by market participants in any sector of industry, the Government decided that the academic community should continue to be its own judge, this time not of academic value, but of value for money. In creating the internal market for universities, the Government had mimicked the emerging practice within global business of organizing internal markets between providers of flexible capacity (see above p. 61) and thus it had to adopt parallel procedures for assuring quality of output. In global business flexible, just-in-time, production implies that products cannot be assessed for quality at the point of delivery, hence the need for advance process certification. Likewise, the quality assessment procedures adopted for teaching output concentrated on 'assuring' quality of degree programmes by demanding the adoption within each university of certain nationally specified quality control and internal audit procedures. Periodic inspection visits by panels of experts drawn in the main from universities with a sprinkling of other interested parties certified the comparability of procedures and classed degree programmes in terms of 'excellent', 'satisfactory' or 'fail'.

Thus far, the award of 'excellent' has not resulted in more funded student places. The conclusion therefore is justified that this quality assessment was also designed to change the cultural climate under which academics work. Surreptitiously, the nature of undergraduate degree programmes has begun to shift away from subject specific content, to meeting quality assurance procedures. It is not 'what' one teaches that matters but 'how' it is taught. That is to say, the preoccupation is with the congruence between stated aims and objectives, the consistency between these and methods of delivery, and between these and modes of examination and assessment, not with the rights or wrongs of subject content (which is never directly scrutinized). Quality

73

assurance procedures have driven the breaking down of complex intellectual processes into discrete, measurable 'competences' and 'skills' and these by their very nature are only measurable and comparable at the broadest level of generality. Thus a new reality has emerged in which the purpose of undergraduate programmes is no longer to train students in subject specific disciplines, but rather provide a general educational experience measurable in terms of comparable outcomes such as: critical ability, transferable skills, inter personal skills, problem solving, oral and written communication skills. A corollary of this is that the boundaries between disciplines have become blurred, and the discipline specific content of courses has become less and less important, thus preparing the ground for modularization and broadening the reach of the internal market by a widening of the 'credit transfer' market between disciplines and institutions.

Meanwhile, academic administration and management have become a growth area of awesome proportion and absorbing increasing amounts of academic staff time. One report estimates that six tons of paper per year, £250,000 worth of photocopying, and the equivalent of a third of an average sized university in labour hours is devoted to frantic paper pushing! The timely arrival of new technology has given the budget managing academic community the illusion that they can save their own jobs by jettisoning those of clerical and other support staff. This is further evidence of the way 'market principles' have penetrated every day working practices.

Separate peer review cycles have been established for research assessment. In these assessment exercises there has been a clearer connection between manifest and latent functions: the desire to concentrate research funding into 'centres of excellence' means that this exercise has less to do with quality 'assurance' than with assessment of output. The perceived need to find operational measures for quality of research output has led to the adoption of a range of spurious but quantifiable outcomes: number of published papers in refereed journals, total money value of research contracts received, numbers of research students attracted, and so on. This process has resulted in the chaotic development of a transfer market in which cash rich universities have managed to buy the CVs of successful persons, not necessarily academics, although many moved between institutions, but also of those from private industry who came with industrial research contracts. The assumption that intellectuals can be bought, therefore, has become firmly established within academia.

Flexible production

The changes wrought through the 'discourse and practice' of managed budgets and quality assurance in teaching which we described above, paved the way for modularization and semesterization. Modularization not only widens the competitive scope of the internal market and echoes the principle of flexibility by now well ingrained throughout the post-fordist economy, it also usefully permits the educational sector to respond to the needs of a growing contingent of part-time workers and those whose careers are interrupted by spells of unemployment. The latter of course is also part and parcel of globalization and the post-fordist world. Semesterization potentially enhances this flexibility because it effectively permits the throughput of twice as many students on a degree programme by halving the content and offering it twice in one academic year.

Employment led agendas

The restructuring of the intellectual workforce and the growing prominence of market-led principles in teaching and research activities gave employers increasing influence in setting the agendas for what was taught and how. Their role has been evident in the universities' rush to include employment relevance in their 'mission' statements - itself a practice directly imported from the world of business management - and to demonstrate that this requirement was being adhered to by including it as one of the criteria which the quality assurance process examined. Thus, employers were brought into teaching assessment exercises, to give their verdict on the suitability of graduates from particular courses for employment in their firms or sector. Degree programmes had to trace their graduates' destination in the labour market. Moreover, some disciplines, for example, engineering and social work, already have the requirement that they include employers in consortia. These have been specifically set up to design the curriculum, its delivery and assessment, monitor standards and ensure that quality assurance procedures are observed. For their part, government funded research councils have been instructed to set monies aside for schemes such as the Foresight Challenge and Ropas (Realising our Potential Awards) the guidelines of which stipulate that the research councils must match any money that academics are able to obtain from industry.

The latest development in employer led teaching, and in the separation of teaching from research, has come in the form of a merger between the Department of Employment and the Department of Education accompanied by the transfer of the Office of Science and Technology out of Education and into the Department of Trade and Industry.

The Responses of Intellectuals in the University Sector

The introduction of the market discipline into the public sector including academia has changed the relationship between intellectuals and the state. The new conditions which Contract Government has imposed on their working life has fragmented their ranks and re-aligned their numbers in new ways. What we have referred to previously as hegemonic organic intellectuals (i.e. those supporting of the status quo) have re-grouped into two social categories which we call 'privatized professional' intellectuals and 'petty bourgeois' intellectuals. The former include those previously employed within the state sector as well as those academics who have gone into the private sector. The second is a social category which is made up of academic managers and academic entrepreneurs, i.e. those academics within universities who are good at grasping the opportunities that the market presents.

The counter hegemonic intellectuals whom we have defined as those wishing to oppose the status quo, have fragmented into two kinds: activist intellectuals and postmodern intellectuals.

We believe that this social fragmentation has accompanied the changing working conditions of intellectuals. Instead of being comfortably ensconced within the public sector as had hitherto been the case, they have become overwhelmed by the demands that threaten their security, the fundamental reordering of their priorities, a diminution in their numbers, a loss of professional autonomy and bleak prospects for the future. The lack of a stable predictable order has fostered movement and interaction between these different groupings of intellectuals as well as within them, thereby lending a novel dynamism to the concept of the 'circulation of elites'. The constant movement of academics, and of resourcing opportunities, in and out of the private and public domains have created conditions under which three broad strategies of response, adaptive, fugitive and resistant,[45] have emerged through which people have sought to carve out a niche for their continued survival. These responses straddle the social categories which we have identified above.

The adaptive response

The groups of intellectuals whom we have identified as making an adaptive response are the privatized professional intellectuals and the petty bourgeois intellectuals who have become academic managers and academic 'entrepreneurs'. The privatized professional intellectuals consisted of those elements of the new hegemonic organic intellectuals which had set up small independent consultancies and businesses to take advantage of the potential for publicly funded research and training commissioned by the state. Funding released under the impetus of contract government, particularly through compulsory competitive tendering has unleashed an explosion of short-term projects which has attracted privatized professional intellectuals seeking employment possibilities.

The thesis of the circulation of elites is relevant here. Many of the privatized professional intellectuals had been made redundant as a result of privatization measures which redrew the map of the welfare state. Thus, instead of being state employees, they now work from within the private sector of their own homes. Moreover, these consultants are able to utilize the networks of contacts from their previous jobs in the civil service, academia or local authorities to unearth opportunities for them (or their firms). They either exploit these directly or subcontract certain aspects out to the academic entrepreneurs who have the knowledge and expertise necessary for completing the original contract. Thus, a revolving door has been created for professional academics and professional bureaucrats from the welfare state to constantly enter and exit as they interact with each other, thereby giving their status a fluidity which exacerbates their insecurity at the same time as it increases the likelihood of their learning about further potential employment prospects.

The contracts which authorize their work are controlled by government departments whose agendas impose the global market discipline on the public sector and reduce the power of the autonomous professional. Their commissions, therefore, revolve around contingent funding aimed at achieving certain objectives which are compatible with the government's agenda. Seeking 'truth' or undertaking research for 'the sake of research' is deemed impractical and irrelevant. This is amply demonstrated by the government's selective publication of the research findings which conflict with its ideological stance. Thus, the Home Office's failure to release findings which conflict with its ideological agenda have exposed the political purposes to which intellectual labour is being subordinated. By publishing only those results which justify unpalatable ideological realities,[46] the state has played one set of intellectuals off against the other, lending legitimacy to those whose research outcomes give it the upper hand in the struggle for ideological hegemony.

Similar objectives seem to be emerging in conjunction with teaching, where the government's agenda is aimed at taking as many disciplines as practicable out of universities and into the workplace where a reduced unit of resource, or so it is assumed, will yield better returns. Professional vocational based disciplines such as teaching, health and social work are amongst the first to experience an erosion of their status as university based subjects by having their training transferred to the workplace. In some vocational courses, this process has gone further than in others. For example, probation training looks like it will be the first of these to be completely based 'in-house'.[47]

This strategy of contracting out teaching on vocational programmes will give the employer the right to define what constitutes appropriate training for any given occupational category at the expense of consumers whether service users or workers. Competency based training has underpinned the move to work-based education by denuding professional tasks of their intellectual content, that is, theoretical and analytical basis. Our analysis of modularization leads us to anticipate that the practice of outcontracting will eventually go beyond vocational training and embrace all 'credit transferable' modules of teaching.

'Flexible specialization' and the opportunity to draw on a wide range of expertise has provided the state with an ideological cover under which to popularize the 'circulation of elites'. Being funding driven, flexible specialization has also facilitated the mystification of broader economic forces which have curtailed the power of professionals. Accustomed as they are to autonomy in defining their research agendas, flexibility in choosing which set of funds to pursue gives professionals the illusion that they have retained intact their freedom to work according to their own plans.

It is the social role of academic managers and academic entrepreneurs to remain within the university sector and mediate between it and the privatized professional intellectuals described above. As managers of the time and expertise of other intellectuals, they are implicated in transforming the scholarship culture to a business culture by pushing through reforms which: redefine teaching and research more in keeping with funders' demands; bring in quality assurance measures of control to assist in this redefinitional process; and quantify work processes to enable the performance output of individuals to be identified, measured, and evaluated in a pseudo-exact way.

The academic managers and entrepreneurs have also drawn on their personal expertise, professional skills and knowledge of networks to facilitate the entry of privatized professional intellectuals into the university sector. Additionally, they have been able to identify those activist intellectuals whose critical capacities have had to be defused and harnessed in favour of anchoring market-led change in the academic community. Thus, whatever their personal predilictions, by facilitating interaction and making connections between two opposing sides in the name of progress, this group of intellectuals have become trapped in promoting a neo-liberal economic agenda.

Both the privatized professional intellectuals and the petty bourgeois intellectuals in academia, through their adaptive response, play midwife to the new social and political formation which is being brought into being. Their role as organic intellectuals in the change process has become one of mobilizing people for rather than against the new social order and lending legitimacy to the process of globalization.

The fugitive response

The 'opting out' intellectual attempts to retain intellectual integrity through an individualized refusal to act as mediator in the transition between the destruction of the culture of scholarship and its replacement with the business one. The individualized negation of social change characterizes the fugitive response which features in the strategies favoured by the 'opting out' intellectuals and postmodern intellectuals alike, as they adjust to their new working environment. We have classified the reaction of the 'opting out' intellectuals as a fugitive response for it represents an attempt to escape from the market discipline which is being resisted for its debilitating impact on their customary holistic ways of working and for precluding the option of relating to colleagues and students as people rather than as factors to be used in meeting production targets.

The ranks of the 'opting out' intellectuals are swollen by the large numbers of early retirees who withdrew from the labour process in academia by taking advantage of generous retirement schemes which the government funded during the latter part of the 1980s.[48] These initiatives have accelerated the processes whereby the casualization of the workforce has been progressed because the full-time permanent posts previously held by the early retirees have been converted to short-term, often part-time, contracts. This group of intellectuals also competes with the privatized professional intellectuals and academic entrepreneurs for small-scale research and training projects which they undertake from their homes feeling that self-exploitation is a lesser evil than that which is imposed upon them by their former employers. Ironically, those early retirees who feel that they still have a great deal of useful life left in them have often accepted new employment opportunities with their former employers at lower rates of pay. The tenuous nature of their employment signals the way in which employees are

79

being required to shoulder the costs of their own longer-term reproduction. Moreover, since returning employees cost employers less to hire, they add a further downward twist to the ever declining unit of resource.

The casualization of academic intellectuals has also enabled the imposition of a labour discipline on reluctant subjects by playing on fears of the individual's unemployability. It has also opened up more employment opportunities, many of which have been taken up by women, whilst simultaneously locking them further into lower paid, casualized, part-time work.[49]

Postmodern intellectuals are committed to challenging the status quo - an aim they share with activist intellectuals. However, they seek to realize this commitment by using the individual rather than collective organizations as their reference point. Their philosophy rejects grand theory and mass actions predicated on universalistic aspirations with their attendant promise of human progress and liberation in favour of individualized ones rooted in the politics of identity.[50] In grounding their intellectual processes on this foundation, they have contributed to the depoliticization of intellectual work and have devalued an historically important avenue for promoting change, namely, collective organizing.

Thus, the postmodernist intellectuals like the 'opting out' intellectuals start from a resistance position only to end up with a fugitive one which merely serves to reinforce market discipline and Contract Government. Moreover, in rejecting collectivist solutions to the social process which we have called the 'Taylorization of intellectual labour', postmodernist intellectuals have become incapable of studying the overall structure within which their own individual lives are articulated. They have therefore lost the possibility of utilizing understanding it as a basis for changing society. Since they eschew theories which posit collective mass action and the historical traditions on which these have been based, they seek like-minded individuals with whom they share ephemeral bonds. Together, but acting singly, they focus on the postmodernist lifeline which offers them a rope out of disillusion and despair, namely, changing themselves. Insofar as postmodern intellectuals think that they can initiate change by changing themselves, they share a commonality with the privatized professional academic: the grasping of individualized solutions to provide an avenue out of a compromised situation and a self-delusion in thinking that by choosing which 'part' of reality or contract (in the case of privatized professionals) to bid for, they are exercising choices which enable them to keep their hands clean of the dirty politics that guide market-led organizational change. The ultimate destination of the fugitive response, therefore, is adapting to social conditions set by more powerful others. In other words, their efforts inadvertently maintain the status quo.

The resistance response

Like the postmodern intellectual, the activist intellectual pursues resistance strategies to begin with. But unlike the postmodernist, the activist intellectual keeps trying to mobilize others and persists in the belief that the monumental changes which are disempowering intellectuals and the general populace can be halted. However, the resistance responses hold limited chances of succeeding. To begin with, their scope for organizing the grassroots is limited. Populist ideology over the past fifteen years has ensured that the flow of change follows monetarist directions rather than those advocated by allegedly idealist or 'utopian' academics who stand accused of being out of touch with reality. Their lack of access to the media means that there is little interest amongst opinion-formers - now usually located amongst the political elite - in spreading their message. Indeed, the sidelining of the critical intellectuals in academia is a marked feature of the British neo-liberal regime. Ideologically oriented 'think tanks' and privatized professional intellectuals are more suited to working in a climate which applauds the advantages of market-led welfare provisions.

Whilst the postmodern intellectual dismisses forms of resistance rooted in collective action for ideological reasons, the activist intellectual on the other hand finds that it is structural limitations which restrict their room for manoeuvre. The state's refusal to fund 'political' activity either amongst its own employees as it had previously under the Community Development Projects,[51] or within the voluntary sector by withdrawing charitable status from those organizations deemed to have been ignoring this injunction has exacerbated the difficulties activist intellectuals have encountered. In addition, the central state has promulgated legislative initiatives designed to curb the organizational power of the trade union movement, the key to mass action amongst the British working class.

Thus, the 1980s unleashed a deluge of legislation which successfully disempowered trade unions. Its impediments to collective action included denying workers the right to: strike on their own behalf; support others through sympathy strikes; amass in large numbers in one location; conduct 'political' strikes; and spontaneously call 'wildcat' strikes. The intellectual elite, never a strongly unionized segment of the workforce, found that fragmentation intensified the tensions between those who wished to oppose the prevailing trends and those who were in favour or at least did not object to them. Hence, most of the industrial action which took place during the

81

1980s,. for example, working to contract, not marking examinations, not registering students, were limited to points which did not breach their contracts of employment and aimed at securing pay rises rather than resist the 'Taylorization of the intellectual labour' or protest about the decimation of a conducive learning environment for students. Thus, fragmentation and differentiation amongst the intellectual elite ended up dissipating militant action.

What motivates activist intellectuals to keep chipping away in such adverse circumstances? Their reasons include: a grave concern that the space for practitioners to exercise critical thought is disappearing; a value system that values others; the knowledge that their own awful conditions are but a minor reflection of the dreadful life situations confronting others; a determination to resist alienating change because they have an alternative vision of society which they believe is achievable; and the knowledge that their own moral integrity is sustained through struggle.

Moreover, their work remains relevant through their commitment to facilitate and empower grassroots movements by exchanging information and skills. However, their opportunity to translate what they write into practice is thwarted by their lack of independent finances and access to mass systems of communication. Hence, they become involved in a small, local, precariously funded, projects which challenge the status quo to a limited extent, for example, community development projects; projects run by feminists, environmentalists, disabled people and black activists. These they nurture and participate in as much to keep up their own morale and sense of injustice as it is to protest the abuses of power which aim to impoverish other people and keep them in their place.

Concluding Remarks

We have analysed the changing role of the intellectuals in the current transformation of society and argued that globalization has had a profound impact on the nature of intellectual work, the relationship between intellectuals and the state, and their strategic role in class formation and legitimation. Moreover, we have concluded that whilst their overall responses at the present time indicate that in so far as intellectuals are exercising agency in circumstances which are largely beyond their control, the results reflect their inability to fundamentally alter the direction which developments in academia are taking.

Notes and references

* This chapter was previously published in *Studies in Political Economy.* See Dominelli, L. and Hoogvelt, A. (1996), 'The Taylorization of Intellectual Labour', *Studies in Political Economy*, vol. 49, no. 1.

1. See Wilmott, Hugh, 'Managing the Academics, Commodification and Control in the Development of University Education in the UK', Paper presented at the Third Workshop on Changing Notions of Accountability in the UK Public Sector, University of Manchester, October 1992. See also Buchbinder, H. and Newson, J. (1988), 'Managerial Consequences of recent changes in university funding policies, a preliminary view of the British case', *The European Journal of Education*, vol. 23 (1/2), pp. 151-166.

2. Baron Robbins, Lionel (1968), 'Higher Education Report of the Committee on Higher Education, 1961-63, HMSO, London, Cmnd 2154.

3. The binary divide in higher education between the universities and the polytechnics was abolished in 1992. Since then the former polytechnics have been referred to as the 'new' universities, and the former universities as the 'old' universities.

4. These figures are taken from HMSO (1974), Statistics in Education, vol. 6.

5. Gramsci, Antonio (1971), *Selections from Prison Notebooks*, Lawrence and Wishart, London, p. 10.

6. We refer here to the work particularly of the Community Development Movement which flourished in the 1970s. See for example, Loney, M. (1983), *Community against the Government: The British Community Development Project 1968-1978*, Heinemann, London. See also Bennington, J.(1976), *Local Government Becomes Big Business*, CDP, London and J. Bennington et. al. CDP Final Report, London: CDP 1975.

7. Loney, *Community Against the Government.*

8. McGrew, A. (1992), 'A Global Society?' in Hall, Stuart, Held, David and McGrew, Anthony, *Modernity and its Futures*, Polity Press, London.

9. For an excellent description of the commodification of production capacity, see Ramchandran, Jaikumar and Upton, David, M. (1993), 'The Co-ordination of Global Manufacturing', in Bradley, S. P., Hausman, J.A. and Nolan, R.L. (eds) *Globalization, Technology, Competition:*

The Fusion of Computers and Telecommunications in the 1990s, Harvard Business School Press, Cambridge, MA, pp. 169-184.

10. Bannock, G. (1992), *Small Business Perspective*, Graham Bannock and Partners, London.

11. Dobson, R. 'Quality Street', (1993), *Community Care*, 24, p. 24.

12 Cox, R. W.(1981), 'Social Forces, States and World Orders: Beyond International Relations Theory', *Millennium*, 1981, vol. 10, no. 2, p. 146.

13. For examples of this development, see Showstack-Sassoon, A. (ed) (1987), *Women and the State, London: Hutchinson*, 1987 or Walby, S. (1990), *Theorising Patriarchy*, Blackwell, Oxford.

14. The Regulation School is a loosely knit group of scholars who address the present period of crisis and transformation from a perspective of change that transcends the structural limitations of both Marxism and equilibrium oriented neo-classical economics. For a concise summary of the Regulation School's main conceptual apparatus see, Boyer, R. 'Technical Change and the Theory of "Regulation"', in Dosi, Giovanni, Freeman, Christopher et.al. (eds), (1988), *Technical Change and Economic Theory*, Pinter, London. For a comprehensive review of the diverse approaches loosely federated under the label Regulation School, see, Jessop, R. (1990), 'Regulation Theories in Retrospect and Prospect', *Economy and Society*, vol. 19, pp. 153-216.

15. The public sector is directly state controlled and publicly accounted for. While this sector has indeed been reduced in size, this does not mean that the Government has reduced the public sector defined as all those areas of activity for which it is responsible, financially or administratively. Much of the conventional public sector (i.e. the sector for which Government is not only financially and administratively reponsible but also accountable to Parliament) has been transferred to 'quangos' appointed by government ministers, but no longer accountable to Parliament, or indeed Local Authorities.

16. During the 1980s more than one third of state owned enterprises were privatized, raising about £27 billion for the Exchequer, but at a market capitalization value of between £50 and £60 billion. See Vickers, J. and Yarrow, G. (1988), *Privatization, An Economic Analysis,* MIT Press, Cambridge, MA, p. 169. See also Hyman, H. (1989), 'Privatization: The Facts', in Veljanovski, C. (ed), *Privatization & Competition, A Market Prospectus*, Hobart Paperbacks, London.

17. Greer, P. (1994), *Transforming Central Government: The Next Steps Initiative*, Open University Press, London.

18. See, *Labour Research* (1990), see also *The Economist*, 19 March 1994.

19. Hugill, Barry, 'A Civil Service on its Last Legs', *The Observer*, 29 May 1994, p. 22.
20. Greer, *Transforming Central Government*.
21. Broadbent, J., Dietrich, M. and Laughlin, R. (1993),'The Development of Principal-Agent, Contracting and Accountability Relationships in the Public Sector: Conceptual and Cultural Problems', Sheffield University Management School Paper.
22. This definition of agency problems is based on Smith, C. W. (1987),'Agency Costs', in *The New Palgrave: A Dictionary of Economics*, vol. 1, Macmillan, London.
23. This list of key problems to be addressed through Contract Government is derived from the Mainframe Consultancy Services document which was commissioned by a Government quango to develop the 'competences' for Social Work Education in 1994 (see endnote 26). It is also consistent with the definition of 'agency problems' identified in the The New Palgrave dictionary definition.
24. For this summary of F.W. Taylor's Scientific Management, see Abercombie, N. et.al. (1984), *Dictionary of Sociology*, Penguin Books, Harmondsworth.
25. 'Realising our Potential: A Strategy for Science, Engineering and Technology', presented by the Chancellor of the Duchy of Lancaster, HMSO: May 1993, Cmnd 2250, London.
26. In contractual framework documents, the word 'element' is used to designate 'identifiable activities'. See for example, Mainframe Consultancy Services Document, Consultation on the DipSW Review of Competences for Professionally Qualified Social Workers, London:NISW, July-August, 1994; The Central Council for Education and Training in Social Work, Revisions to Paper 30, London: CCETSW, (1995), Butters, S. *Competences; Project Report for the Department of Trade and Industry*, Milton Keynes: Quality Services Centre, Open University.
27. *Mainframe*, (1994).
28. Butters, S., *Competences*.
29. Braverman, H. A. (1974), *Labor and Monopoly Capital*, Monthly Review Press, New York.
30. *Mainframe* (1994), p. 4. See also, Probation Training Unit, (1994), 'Introducing Competences', Home Office, London.
31. *Mainframe* (1994), emphases in original, p. 4.
32. On the broader implications of organizational change in industry, see, Kanter, R.M. (1991),'The Future of Bureaucracy and Hierarchy in Organizational Theory: A Report from the Field', in Bourdieu, Pierre

85

and Coleman J. S. (eds) (1991), *Social Theory for a Changing Society*, Westview Press, Boulder, pp. 63-87.

33. Mannheim, Karl (1940), *Man and Society in an Age of Reconstruction*, Routledge and Kegan Paul, London.

34. These classic writers had focused on the historical inevitability of elite formation, even in democratic society. Our own interest, on the other hand, is focused on the manner in which, during a period of profoundly changing class relations, members of one elite manage to join the rising ranks of another. See Pareto, V. (1935), *Mind and Society*, Mosca, G. (1939), *The Ruling Class*, and Michels, R. (1915), *Political Parties*.

35. *The Guardian*, 13 February 1995.

36. SSI (Social Services Inspectorate) Purchase of Service: Practice Guidance and Practice Material for Social Services Departments and Other Agencies, London: HMSO (1991).

37. Between 1987 and 1993 alone, student numbers in universities (including the former polytechnics) rose by 50% to more than 1 million full time equivalents, while academic staff numbers increased by only 10% to 72,000. The unit of resource decreased by more than 20% in that period. Higher Education was being obtained on the cheap. See Association of University Teachers, 'Bursting at the seams', London: Summer (1993), p. 6. These figures may also be worked out from Universities' Statistical Record, *University Statistics*, vol.1.

38. The AUT has calculated that between 1979 and 1994 student numbers (full time equivalents) increased from 547,000 to 1,220,000 while recurrent spending per student declined (in real terms), from £6,090 to £4,537, and total capital spending for each student declined from £487 to £356. See AUT, *Higher Education, Preparing for the 21st Century*, London: Spring 1995, p. 16.

39. See Universities' Statistical Record, University Statistics, vol. I (Students and Staff), Cheltenham: USR 1993.

40. Universities' Statistical Record.

41. Association of University Teachers, *Bursting at the Seams*, p. 6.

42. For an excellent collection of empirically based research reports on changing shopfloor industrial relations consequent upon the introduction of flexible production, see Elger, Tony and Smith, Chris, (eds), (1994), *Global Japanization? The Transnational Transformation of the Labour Process*, Routledge, London.

43. Garrahan, P. and Stewart, P. (1992), *The Nissan Enigma: Flexibility at Work in a Local Economy*, London, Mansell.

44. Cf. Womack, J. P. et. al. (1990), *The Machine that Changed the World*, Harper, New York. Womack et.al. describe the changing system of

accounting that accompanies the transition from fordist to flexible production methods.

45. We are grateful to Roger Murray, who gave comments on an earlier draft of this chapter, for summarizing and labelling this three headed distinction.
46. For example, the Home Office commissioned research on 'Law and Order' issues which were intended to demonstrate that family breakdown, the rise in women headed single parent households and the lack of male role models in their households were responsible for the increase in the number of young offenders. When counterindications were evident in the findings, it refused to publish the results.
47. Stone, K. 'Get Tough', *Community Care*, 16-22 March 1995, pp. 16-18.
48. Between 1980 and 1993, 2394 non-clinical full time academic staff took early retirement. This figure is based on table 32 of Universities' Statistical Record, University Statistics, London: various years. We have, from this table, taken the total number of retired staff and deducting the 65 + category, to obtain the total 'early' retirees.
49. Coyle, A. (1984), *Redundant Women London*: Women's Press, London. Walby, S. (1990), *Theorising Patriarchy*, Basil Blackwell, Oxford.
50. Cf. Nicholson, L. (1990), *Feminism/Postmodernism*, Routledge, London.
51. Armstrong, J. (1977) 'Analysis of the Inner Area Partnership Scheme Applications'. Leicester: Community Work Training Unit. See also Loney, M.(1987), *The State or the Market: Politics and Welfare in Contemporary Britain*, Sage, London.

6. Democrats against Democracy: the Charter Movement in Hungary

ANDRÁS BOZÓKI

This chapter outlines the history of a political movement of intellectuals, the Democratic Charter. The movement, which had its peak from 1991 to 1994, served as an umbrella organization to meet the demands of several, quite different groups. Such demands included a re-awakening of a formerly politically active civil society, which seemed to have been drained of energy as a result of party pluralism, which came into being in 1989. Also an articulation of a democratic consensus that could surpass partial interests, an opposition to authoritarian tendencies, an emphasis on the idea of participatory democracy, as opposed to the practice of an élitist democracy, based on the idea of representation and, finally, setting out an experimental field for a possible socialist-liberal political alliance within a political movement. Social, cultural and political goals were mixed in the movement, of which not only participants but also organizers were often unaware. In my chapter I describe and assess the above, varied characteristics through an empirical analysis of the Democratic Charter. The chapter is prefigured in an earlier study, which focused on the part played by Hungarian intellectuals in the political re-structuring of the country.[1]

Why Was the Democratic Charter Set out?

Problems of the Liberal Party and liberal intellectuals

The Alliance of Free Democrats (SZDSZ), the representative party of Hungarian liberal intellectuals, which had initiated the political changes of 1989 and was considered their originator by many, lost the first free elections in 1990 and became an opposition party in Parliament. A coalition government took office in Hungary. Coalition parties on the one hand included groups that actively opposed the Kádár regime from 1956 to 1989.

On the other hand, they also covered groups, whose main strategy was that of survival at all costs and whose set of values were closer to pre-communist Hungary, to a paternalistic policy led by the descendants of the landed gentry who wished to maintain state intervention in all walks of life. The leaders of the SZDSZ, many of whom had come from the democratic opposition of the totalitarian state, realized rather early that their party would have to change from an opposition of the *government* into an opposition of the *system*. There were signs to suggest that the centralizing efforts of the government, dominated by the Hungarian Democratic Forum (MDF), which took over in 1990, as well as an anti-parliamentarian, populist rhetoric used by MDF extremists might be leading to the build-up of a new orientation; one that would acquire economic power and stabilize a system that seemed to be democratic, but was, in effect, semi-totalitarian. The fact that the idea of opposition to the system could re-surface, indicated that a group of intellectuals who had been extremely successful in 1989-90 were facing difficulties when in opposition.[2] Their problem was not only finding their place in the new system, but in a quickly forming political élite as well. The members of the SZDSZ and part of the public could not understand why the party, having achieved considerable success with its anti-communism in 1989-90, concentrated on institutional rather than personal changes, why it turned against not only the new government but also the new regime. In 1991 intellectuals, who earlier had been sympathizers, turned their back on the party; the popularity of the SZDSZ was quickly decreasing.

The political heirs of the former democratic opposition, who shared the principles of a liberal economic policy, suffered additional setbacks because the majority of their adversaries in 1989, representatives of a 'new technocracy' consisting of members of the then communist party (MSZMP), found their place in the new hierarchy and built up links with the first representatives of a slowly forming 'new bourgeoisie' rather easily. These people would form the 'new clientele'. The SZDSZ's main political adversary, the MDF, sought in its programme a 'country of owners' and the creation of a national middle class and national bourgeoisie. But following heavy internal fights and realizing that the programme could not be implemented in the short run, they reconciled with some groups of the 'new technocrats' who had attained considerable influence during the last decade of the Kádár regime. The radical populist wing of the party, on the other hand, exerted strong pressure to carry out the original programme in a militant fashion. Government policy fluctuated between permissive methods of embourgeoisement and aggressive interference, sometimes replacing one with the other at random. The breadth of vision of the opposition part of the 'politocracy' of 1989 gradually narrowed down in official politics.

In the 1980s dissident intellectuals led a kind of undergound existence. Their independence ensured that they had been the most outspoken critics of the Kádár regime. They served as an example for Hungarian journalists in the transitional period. As a group they efficiently mobilized the public. In the autumn of 1989 they were able to terminate communist party privileges and, by enforcing a referendum, which was an absolute success for the opposition, they blocked the way to a premature presidential election planned by those in power. It was the same group that openly supported several days of unrest following price rises, during which taxi-drivers blocked the main roads and bridges of the capital bringing traffic to a standstill in Budapest. By supporting the taxi-drivers, the group helped prevent the use of force by the government against those taking part in the blockade. The democratic opposition in the 1980s was able to set up a political public domain, though rather isolated, and create, within its scope, the missing link of a political society, in de Tocqueville's sense, between state and society. When political changes started in 1988, the opposition did not establish a party but a movement. The Network of Free Initiatives (SZKH) was created in order to co-ordinate the activity of politically active civil groups that had been working informally. The Network later gave birth to the SZDSZ, although its leaders maintained a kind of undergound attitude for a long time to come. The popularity of the new party grew as long as it was able to give an undergound interpretation to its politics. But the taxi-drivers' blockade was the last chance for that. Being an 'opposition to the regime' and the demand to take over the government did not prove to be popular. Indeed, these moves left many sections of society unimpressed. A professional political élite and bureaucracy slowly came into being, which limited the scope for the appearance of a critical intellectual attitude. It was a painful experience for the party leadership to realize that the situation had changed and that a considerable number of party sympathizers had grown disillusioned with their politics. As Garton-Ash has pointed out, circumstances in a parliamentary democracy demand, so to speak, a replacement of an anti-political diction with an openly political one.[3] But both the party leadership and liberal intellectuals were dissatisfied with the changed state of affairs, since they felt that the principles they so successfully followed in 1989 were disintegrating, falling victim to the struggle for power.

Liberal intellectuals and the media

Following the elections in 1990, the media having regained its freedom only two years before, provided a major playing field for former dissidents. A proliferation of papers began. Never before had so many interesting studies been published in Hungarian magazines and journals than following the fall of the former system built on censorship and self-censorship. The majority of intellectuals, however, read daily papers and watched political programmes on television rather than reading magazines and journals. A state of mind of feverish political interest prevailed in the *intelligentsia.*

The liberation of 1988-89 created an ethical revolution in the majority of the media. Young journalists came into the foreground and older ones tried to change their attitude; to forget about the submissive practices of the past. A strong market competition started in order to keep or turn over readers. This meant that, contrary to the earlier propaganda function of the press, newspapers focused on news, interesting items and sensations. The majority of the papers were strongly critical of the new government, which the ruling coalition rather resented. Government politicians failed to realize that criticism would attract readers much more than the apologies which journalists had become fed up of writing anyway during the years of the dictatorship. Thus, a considerable part of the media had become an 'opposition' naturally, due to the very nature of democracy.

On the other hand, cracks appeared and grew within liberal intellectual culture; one that had never really been completely homogeneous. When those groups were organized as a government coalition on the one hand, and political opposition on the other hand, a difference between their norms and models became apparent. The constituents who had formed the coalition as 'natural allies' could also be divided into two groups from this point of view. One group comprised the followers of Prime Minister József Antall. They represented a model of a western social market economy and multi-party democracy, but their rhetoric was that of pre-war politics and symbols of the good old times. This group used a language of 'restoration-modernization' expressing the conservative values of a return to democracy. Their orientation, however, was utterly alien to the approach, and especially the language, of the media following political re-structuring. No conservatism linked to modernity could come into being in Hungary. Instead, conservatism appeared in a traditional form as opposed to modernity. In Hungary, the part of the press called 'liberal' was suspicious of the conservatism of the Antall government, not because it could not accept a conservatism using a modern language, but because it could not believe, due to the traditional language used, that it *was* a modern conservatism. On the other hand, due to historical reasons, its democratic grounds were felt to be rather unstable. The other group was formed of critical intellectuals, now turned into government politicians who preserved their critical attitude, but their criticism had been based on a romantic, anti-modernist gemeinschaft idea already formed in the years of the Kádár regime.[4] In their case there were fundamental - not merely

91

linguistic and stylistic - differences between the media and some politician-intellectuals turning towards populism.

Both the above factors and a campaign against journalists by the MDF increased the propensity of the majority of the media to sympathize with the opposition parties. They embraced modernity as a model, refusing to use archaic symbols and language. It was a question of two different approaches to history. One argued that the four decades of communism interrupted Hungarian history and involved a complete break with its continuity (i.e. for them history had to be continued from where it had been broken). The other represented the view that communism had been a distorted kind of modernization, which - in spite of its catastrophic effects - resulted in modifications in the structure and values of the society and that after its fall, the existing, post-communist status-quo had to be taken as a starting point following western norms. Both the media and the opposition parties interpreted the 1989 political changes in the latter way. Although political re-structuring actually finished by re-structuring the country's institutions, a 'fight of cultures' between norms and models continued.

The situation described above resulted in the short run in a state of affairs described as an 'interpenetration' of liberal intellectuals, politicians and the media. This created a rather chaotic form of political life which ran counter to a clearly functional differentiation of political activity. Maintaining this state of affairs served the interests of non-party member critical intellectuals who were trying to maintain their influence in the power structure. In many cases, politicians also encouraged or accepted it since they thought their support to be too weak not to need the *intelligentsia* in shaping public opinion. A complete break, a real differentiation between politicians and intellectuals, obviously needs a strong pluralism in the long term to give time for the media and political institutions to crystallize their functional roles. Breaking down the alliance was not in the interest of either player in the period under consideration; though some political minded intellectuals had become dissatisfied even with the opposition parties of the time. A withdrawal from parties to a 'political society' had begun.

In addition to the closed orientations of entering politics or making a professional commitment, critical intellectuals had to set out new forms of action, a new strategy to enforce their political interests. They needed a strategy that would not restrict intellectuals with a political interest to different professional areas of politics or trade but left an open path for them to play both parts.[5] A specific intellectual movement, the Democratic Charter, was meant to serve that goal.

The History of the Democratic Charter

From the appeal to the alliance: The first months

Some editors of former 'samizdat' Eastern-European journals, who had since been publishing their magazines in continuation of the democratic movements of the past, met in Budapest at the beginning of August, 1991. At the conference, the author György Konrád, then the president of International Pen Club and a member of the SZDSZ National Council, proposed that a Central and Eastern European Democratic Charter be proclaimed to lay down in a joint statement a minimum level of democracy for the post-communist countries of the region.[6] Konrád wished to model the Charter on previous solidarity initiatives of the opposition in order to ease newly arising ethnic tensions that were to bring about armed conflict in several places. Participants at the conference, however, rejected the proposal saying 'it's no use enforcing a romantic role of intellectuals that used to be topical in the past but is not so any more'. They argued that 'key issues are now in the hands of professional politicians and the whole idea would come to some aborted drive of the highbrow'.[7]

What did not seem feasible internationally, became topical in Hungarian domestic policy a few weeks later. A few days after the failed Soviet coup, Imre Kónya, the head of the parliamentary faction of the largest government party, the MDF, published a paper urging 'a stricter' policy by MDF regarding privatization, the mass media and punishing the guilty of the past regime. The paper caused a shock because Kónya had not been known as somebody to agree with the views of MDF extremists such as István Csurka or those of other radicals. In his paper Kónya emphasized the steps he had proposed had to be done even if the majority of Hungarian society were against them, further, western responses should not be feared as Europe had already recognized Hungary as a democratic state.

The Kónya paper was interpreted by SZDSZ leaders as a threat. Proposed by János Kis, President of the party, the executive body of the party decided, in order to prevent a shift to the right by the government coalition and authoritarian tendencies in its wake, to appeal to democratic citizens by issuing an open Charter stating that democratic re-structuring had not been completed. To support their proposal, two leaders of the party analysed authoritarian tendencies in the MDF in a lengthy article.[8] Although some intellectuals, especially those close to the government parties but also some others, doubted the correctness of their findings, the authors refused to change their views. On analysing the situation, leading politicians of the former communist party, the Hungarian Socialist Party (MSZP), joined

SZDSZ leaders. The arguments by SZDSZ representatives, however, included an important statement addressed directly to the critical intellectuals of 1989:

> The group of liberal intellectuals, who have done so much in the press, in clubs and other public forums to prepare the ground for restructuring during the late Kádár period, split as soon as political changes took place and have been unable to recover from the split to this very day. Some of them have been absorbed by the opposition parties. Some stayed out and turned their back on party politics. Those who are in, often fail to see what is outside Parliament, those who are out are increasingly antagonistic to Parliament and the whole new political structure.[9]

In order to bridge the gap between insiders and outsiders, Bauer and Kis proposed a division of labour for them.

> Intellectuals working within the parties should realise that, lacking support by independent intellectuals shaping the public view, their voice is crying in the wilderness. Non-party member intellectuals should realise that their fate is also at stake in political struggles and it is no use maintaining their independence by saying six of one and half a dozen of the other.[10]

The proposal still used the old language of dissidents by speaking about insiders and outsiders and not making a distinction between intellectuals and politicians. If one accepts a definition of professional intellectuals as individuals who legitimize their given social position by their knowledge and objectivity, then politicians cannot be considered professionals. A politician's social-political position is legitimized by the votes of his electors rather than by his professional knowledge, which is the case even if 90 per cent of the Hungarian MPs elected in 1990 had a professional university degree, and often behaved as political minded intellectuals rather than politicians.[11] The cited paper, however, was not a sociological analysis but a political article with the aim of mobilizing people. 'All who are for freedom and against totalitarian rule by communists or anybody else shall join forces to defend democracy.'[12] Feeling a growing political apathy and disillusionment in the country, the authors wanted professionals, who were increasingly distancing themselves from politics, to return to the ranks of supporters of democratic, especially opposition, politics by taking part in the proposed public demonstration. Party executives emphasized that their initiative was not anti-parliamentarian, stress was laid on the collaboration of individuals committed to the same cause, rather than on party politics. Iván Petõ of the SZDSZ said: '...although the idea of establishing a Democratic Charter was born in the SZDSZ, it is not intended to be apparently linked to the party. AFD members would sign the Charter as individuals but the AFD would not be signatory as a party, a political organisation'.[13] At the same time the Publicity Club organized by journalists also published a statement condemning the principles of the Kónya paper but their call did not have a major effect.

The document was completed two weeks later compiled mostly by well-known members of the former democratic opposition with collaboration from authors like György Konrád and Mihály Kornis. The title of the document was a reference to the Czech Charter 77, one of the outstanding initiatives of the struggle for freedom in Eastern and Central Europe. The document was then debated on two occasions in a hall of the Merlin theatre in Budapest with the participation of a wide range of intellectuals. During the debate a difference of opinion arose between liberal and socialist minded participants on whether social rights could be regarded as an inherent part of democracy. In the end a demand for a social minimum was included in the text on a proposal by journalist Katalin Bossányi, former socialist MP, while some anti-government phrases in the introduction were omitted. The participants wanted to publish a generally acceptable document that could be signed by everybody, including members of the ruling parties.

The document was issued on the 26th of September 1991, signed by 162 mostly left-wing and liberal intellectuals. The full text was published next day in four national dailies: socialist *Népszabadság* and *Népszava*, liberal *Magyar Hirlap* and *Pesti Hirlap*. The latter used to stand close to the government, but was basically independent at that time. The document listed the criteria of democracy in different areas of society in 17 points. The first lines explaining the need for a Charter ran like this:

> We, signatories to the Charter, Hungarian Democrats, independent of our party politics, believe that the democratic process is held back in our country. Many have turned away from politics not only as a result of our declining living standards but because they do not believe this to be a democracy. We know that, as in all historical transformations, this is a decisive period in our history which brings not only hardship but benefits as well. We would like to safeguard them, and thus we deem it necessary to make public the sort of Hungarian Republic we want.[14]

The declaration was signed by four thousand people by early December. Although its text was not openly anti-government, Prime Minister József

Antall thought it was. He called it, 'a collection of elementary constitutional theses' that could be signed by practically anybody. Therefore on the one hand he saw it as meaningless, but on the other hand he considered it an action by the opposition directed against the government that coalition sympathizers could not stand for. He took the stance that *there is* democracy and not that *there will be* when the conditions in its 17 points have been met, as it has been worded in the Charter. And if *there is* democracy, whoever doubts its existence questions indirectly the democratic legality of the government and existing institutions, i.e. is anti-democratic. There was an obvious difference in the language of interpretation of democracy. Democracy was a political concept for the Prime Minister and his supporters, based on institutions and representation, while from the point of view of the signatories of the Charter it meant a wider, social concept based on civil participation. The existence of political democracy in Hungary was not questioned by the signatories, they themselves fought for its birth in the 1980s. These people, however, felt a need to identify with the role of the *critical intelligentsia* and to maintain that identity by turning from claimants of political democracy into claimants of social democracy.

Both political and critical intellectual motivations were inseparably mixed in the Charter from the moment it was born. Politicians supporting the Charter were probably endeavouring to widen the political base of opposition politics and regarded the Charter as a *means* to that end, while critical intellectuals in it were unwilling to interpret it in the dimensions of party politics (or if they were, they did not reveal it), but regarded the Charter as a new 'public social' form of a critical intellectual identity. It was regarded as an opportunity for the *intelligentsia* to break away from partial party truth and continue to be a representative of some 'universal truth'. In this sense the Charter gained an independent life; it turned from being a means to an end. In addition to shared ideals and a critical attitude, the Charter had another, less explicit, but important generational relevance. One of the signatories, Tivadar Farkasházy, said in an interview: 'I feel some anger inside, as it is my generation that should be governing the country now. The group of people termed "the Big Generation" should shoulder the burden and the responsibility. Instead, what happened was that an even older group of people said it was their turn in the dodgem'.[15]

Following Prime Minister Antall's response, signing or not signing the document turned directly into an issue of political loyalty. Therefore the representatives of the government coalition and their sympathizers did not sign. The action seemed to remain on the level of a quickly rising and quickly falling 'highbrow' intellectual initiative. When some of the Charter signatories held a press conference on the 29th of October, 1991, only a

96

dozen people were interested. A month later, however, when the Prime Minister sacked the President of the independent National Bank of Hungary, György Surányi, an extremely well qualified economist, because Surányi had signed the Democratic Charter, the slumbering initiative was given a new impetus. Antall thought Surányi to be disloyal for signing. He said, 'if somebody is crying for freedom at a place where there is freedom, that person has become the victim of a misconception or is lying. Nor the President of an independent National Bank, nor any member of the government can give their name to such a document'.[16] István Csurka, the leader of MDF radicals used harsher wording: 'it should be realized that the Hungarian people authorised the MDF at free elections to govern the country. Overemphasizing a need for professionalism is a dirty trick by the Bolshevik'.[17] The signatories to the Charter, however, thought their earlier fears had come true and that the government wanted to implement anti-democratic goals. Both parties thought they were true democrats and wanted to protect democracy against each other. The sacking of the President of NBH caused a scandal in domestic policy. In response the leading bodies of the opposition parties joined the signatories of the Democratic Charter, which enhanced its political weight. Signatories protested against the government assessing their economic officers by their political loyalty rather than by their performance. Daily papers published the 17 points of the Charter again. A group of economists addressed MPs in an open letter, some of the signatories to the Charter met in the Pilvax café in Budapest on the 2nd of December to discuss strategic issues. At an impromptu press conference following the meeting György Konrád made three proposals: 1) the Democratic Charter should be established as an organization with spokespersons to take a stance on topical issues from time to time; 2) neighbouring Central and Eastern-European countries should start their own Charters; 3) collaboration between such movements should be launched.[18]

A group of signatories to the Charter including a number of journalists issued a protest statement on the following day condemning the way the President of the Bank had been relieved, calling Charter sympathizers to join and announcing a rally to clarify the appropriate way of further actions to be taken. At the same time a full page political advertisement was published. On it, the words 'It can be your turn tomorrow' reminded people of the symbolic case of the relieved President.

A rally of the Democratic Charter took place at the Budapest Town Hall on the 7th of December, 1991. The Mayor, Gábor Demszky of the AFD, a member of a prior democratic opposition, let Charter organizers use the Town Hall free of charge; an offer that was repeated many times. More than a thousand people (not only intellectuals) took part. Participants agreed that the

Charter, which started as a single move of protest, needed to be changed into a movement-like initiative. In his opening address György Konrád identified the Charter, not as a party or political movement, but as 'a spiritual alliance of democrats', which, he said, was a kind of 'shield of the mind', a 'genre for self-arrangement of the civilian society'. Several speakers reiterated that the Charter did not wish to be a move by the opposition but a common denominator of the principles of democracy. The audience was reminded of the intellectual movements of the 1980s. It was declared that former dissidents and their sympathizers did not wish to be subjected to authoritarian power again, on the other hand, former reformers might achieve their goal: an opportunity of uniting the parties that had lost the elections. Two politicians, MPs, remarked on the relationship between the Charter and the political institutions. Miklós Tamás Gáspár of the SZDSZ said: 'the Charter is gaining importance as the crisis of parliamentarian democracy is growing in Hungary', while Gábor Fodor of the Federation of Young Democrats (FIDESZ) remarked, 'the Charter cannot replace either parliamentary opposition or any element of the political institutions'.[19]

Spokespersons of the Charter were elected in an open ballot for a year and participants adopted a proposal by György Konrád to the effect that the Charter should have signatories and spokespersons rather than members and leaders. All signatories should symbolically become spokespersons as well. Elected spokespersons included four journalists, two sociologists, a psychologist, a chemist, a film director, a high school teacher and a professional politician of the MSZP. It was important to include as many journalists among the spokespersons as possible to ensure publicity for the Charter. It was also important to delegate people close to the (mostly) opposition parties. The majority of the spokespersons were intellectuals who had stepped into the limelight at the time of political re-structuring, but later quickly withdrew from politics, as well as sympathizers, but not members, of the opposition parties. No one from the first line of former dissidents took up a position as a spokesperson of the Charter. Thus a newly organized group of intellectuals achieved their goal in the enthusiastic atmosphere of the rally at the Town Hall. Intellectuals hesitating between political and professional roles found an arena, as well as a chance of withdrawal, in the Charter to shape a spiritual and political alliance. Professionals who had quickly withdrawn from politics could again get closer to decision-making without being forced to join the rank and file of politics.

Following the rally, the influence of the Charter grew among intellectuals. The number of signatories rose to 7000 in the following week.[20] Spokespersons received dozens of supporting letters and declarations of joining every day. HUF 80,000 (app. USD $1,000 at that time) was collected at the rally or transferred to the Charter's account. The mood was somewhat like that of the revolutionary times of 1988-89, though the government press were, naturally, unenthusiastic. It was pointed out that the Charter was an opposition movement and the question was posed: 'whose freedom has been endangered by a democratically elected government, who would like the public to share their own fears and why do they openly wish a change of the system without personnel changes?'.[21] The FIDESZ was the opposition party that openly criticized the Charter for becoming something different from that which they had originally joined. The Parliamentary faction of the AYD underlined in a statement that 'by signing the Charter, they did not wish to approve of the establishment of a political movement and do not wish to participate in it'.[22] The other two opposition parties, the MSZP and the SZDSZ did not mind. In response to the FIDESZ separation, spokesman Tivadar Farkasházy remarked that the Charter, 'does not wish to become a branch office of any party', the Charter does not wish to become a party, it is merely a citizen's appeal independent of any parties.

Elected Charter spokespersons initially wanted to arrange a Christmas peace demonstration or collection of signatures, but the idea was given up due to lack of time. Instead, an open letter of self-identification was addressed to the signatories. Avoiding the term 'political movement', it identified the Charter as a citizens' initiative. It was emphasized that, 'the Charter is not directed against any party' and 'the Charter is not backed by parties'. At the same time thousands of signatories were sent sheets to collect further signatures. The number of signatories increased at a record speed in the history of the Charter, from 7,000 in December, 1991 to 200,000 in mid-February 1992. The Democratic Charter Foundation was set up during the winter and the Charter's own database was separated from that of the SZDSZ. However, a separate PO Box could not be rented due to lack of money, so new signatures were still addressed to the SZDSZ.

The then spokespersons decided to issue reports from time to time on the current state of democracy in Hungary. The first (and last, as it turned out later) occasion for that arose at a press conference on 13 February, 1992 held in the Kossuth Club. At the conference Charter signatories talked or circulated reports on certain phenomena in the press, the economy or the political scene that seemed to be endangering democracy. The press conference went largely unnoticed, and the reports were not published. But a conservative signatory, Pomogáts, caused some sensation with his report on a meeting of the World Association of Hungarians held in December 1991 where he was publicly accused of high treason for signing the Charter. The spokespersons viewed the press conference as a failure. It was indeed rather weightless: too few people attended and those who did had known the reports

99

in advance. The spokespersons learnt an important lesson and turned to arranging open political actions.

The first major demonstration of the Charter took place on the national holiday, of the 15th of March, 1992. It was the first time that supporter parties were faced with a fait accompli when the spokespersons announced a separate Charter rally and demonstration in downtown Budapest along a traditional route of former dissidents. The event, to be held on the day of Free Press, had become quite topical because the government was trying to exert increasing pressure on the presidents of independent Radio and Television. Also, using their pre-emptive right, they wanted to purchase the only liberal daily, *Magyar Hirlap*. The arrangements for the demonstration gave rise to the first confrontation between Charter spokespersons and the AFD administration of the capital. Budapest Mayor, Gábor Demszky, (a member of former underground opposition) did not think the action was justified because it competed with his festive address. At a reception held at the Town Hall on the eve of the National Day the Mayor reprimanded Charter spokespersons, 'How dare you make a revolution against us; organize a movement against me who have fought for your freedom!'.[23] The parties reconciled at that time, but the weekly *Beszélő,* edited by AFD sympathizers, attacked the Charter later on with the objection, 'why did not they co-ordinate their plans with their friends in advance'.[24] The demonstration, the first occasion when the Charter took masses to the streets, took place with about fifteen thousand participants. In addition to Charter spokespersons and sympathizers, two symbolic figures of the movement, György Konrád and Iván Vitányi (MSZP) addressed the crowd. It was emphasized that it was not an opposition demonstration. An umbrella, 'para-party' identity of the Charter was underlined, saying 'We are not supposed to defend one party, one way of thinking or one kind of taste alone but every taste, every party and every thought even ones we dislike'.[25] Their political opponents, however, were of a different view. A few members of a rightist group demonstrating close by insulted nearby Charter sympathizers, including György Konrád, and a journalist. To wind up the demonstration, the Charter published a statement in protest against government threats to the political neutrality of the public media.

Following the demonstration Charter spokespersons arranged two meetings in Budapest in an endeavour to set up a permanent, informal nationwide network. Spokespersons at the meetings met the most active supporters, most of whom urged the Charter to be organized into a formal movement. Participants included representatives of the Democratic Trade Union of Researchers (TDDSZ), the League of Citizens' Rights and the Young Socialists. Clubs of the Democratic Charter were formed in the country and spokespersons often visited country towns and cities on the invitation of such clubs or to mark their opening. But in spite of this, the Charter did not become a viable social movement and there were just a few occasions when its influence was felt beyond groups of the *intelligentsia*. It was proposed by a few socialist spokespersons to organize an anti-fascist demonstration on the 8th of May to mark the end of World War II in Europe. The proposal, however, was rejected saying that May the 8th had a different meaning in the countries of the former Soviet bloc than in Western Europe.

An action by the Charter arranged for May Day, however, was a success. Spokespersons had got hold of a government draft on the Social Act. It was believed to be unsuitable to ensure adequate social support, thus a call was issued, written in collaboration with social politicians, in defence of social minima. It was issued in a period when 15% of the population were living under the poverty line and the number of the unemployed exceeded five hundred thousand.[26] It contained a reference to point 5 of the 17 points of the Charter, which said, 'there will be democracy if the state guarantees all its citizens basic social welfare'. Although point 5 was opposed by liberals right from the start - arguing that welfare/social demands should not be confused with a demand for democracy - it had found its way into the Charter. The Social Charter based on it and published for May Day was embraced by all trade union associations. Together with the Pensioners' Association and youth organizations it meant the representation of five million people. Overall support by the trade unions was sensational at the time, as it was the first occasion in the post-communist history of the trade unionist movement that all trade unions agreed on an issue. Collaboration was agreed between the Charter and major trade unions. The former Communist trade union association (MSZOSZ), and an independent trade unionist organization set up following political re-structuring (FSZDL), printed Charter leaflets in their own printing houses and distributed them jointly. Charter spokespersons took part in May Day arrangements in Városliget and Népliget (two parks in Budapest, traditional scenes of May Day celebrations) collecting hundreds of signatures for the Democratic Charter. The Social Charter, however, created the first conflict between liberal and socialist members. Liberals warned that the Charter was going to shift too far to the left and fall prey to MSZP ideologues.

Increasing attacks by the government coalition against the presidents of public radio and television gave rise to another Charter event. In the cultural committee of the Parliament, government coalition MPs voted for a proposal to relieve from their position the radio and television presidents who had been appointed by a consensus of coalition and opposition parties. In an open letter on the 18th of May Charter spokespersons protested against 'government policy violating the consensus'. Following this, Head of State Árpád Göncz refused to sign a move by the Prime Minister to relieve the presidents of the media. In response the government coalition proposed to discuss a statement by Parliament condemning the Head of State for his alleged anti-constitutional action. President Göncz was in the crossfire of political attacks by the ruling coalition parties. As the stakes had risen, the Charter issued a solidarity statement on the 26th of May to support Mr Göncz. 'The coalition parties consider the Head of State, Árpád Göncz's move made in defence of democracy and the freedom of the media anti-constitutional. We protest against the unjustified series of attacks against the Head of State. A threat to constitutional order is posed by forces trying to evoke hysteria, to disturb the order of society and to divert attention from an economic and social crisis',[27] said the statement also calling for another rally. At the same time, 25 sympathizers (mostly authors and artists and one of the leaders of the taxi-drivers' blockade in 1990) published a full-page paid advertisement to support Árpád Göncz. It started another wave of collecting signatures which was promoted by the Publicity Club.

By the time Charter signatories and supporters gathered on the 3rd of June, 1992 in the crowded Budapest Town Hall, 12,000 people had already signed a statement to support the President of the Republic. György Konrád was the leading speaker of the rally, where Iván Vitányi and others also addressed the participants. All of them spoke about a disintegration of the consensus that had tacitly joined the government parties and the opposition despite their differences of opinion. Contrary to previous occasions, open criticism of the government coalition was dominant.

> The President of the Hungarian Democratic Forum, the Prime Minister, has found the time ripe to set out rules for the mass media, an attack has been launched against the Presidents of the Radio and Television, who are trying to maintain their relative independence. The President of the Republic has also been attacked as he was unwilling to take part in such an attack and remained true to his oath to defend the freedom of the press, of speech, of thought and of belief refusing to play a subordinate role to the Prime Minister's censorial will.[28]

Later on in June the constitutional crisis seemingly abated, the draft statement condemning Árpád Göncz was not submitted to Parliament by representatives of the government coalition. 32,000 signatures had been collected by the end of June to support the President of the Republic, with active participation from MSZP and the MSZOSZ, the number later increased to 35,000 and that was the end of the campaign.

As it turned out, however, from letters continuously received by Charter spokespersons and from a debate on the Charter's future held in the second part of the Town Hall rally, sympathizers were far from satisfied with their achievements and urged the Charter to become a wider movement or an active network. Debates on the Charter's future increased as well. Members who emphasized the Charter's (party) political function viewed it as a framework for political alliance between liberals and socialists. Others believed that the Charter should maintain its independence from party politics and be socially oriented instead.

The most important event in the history of the Democratic Charter took place on the 24th of September 1992. It was triggered by a provocative political analysis by István Csurka, a vice-president of the ruling MDF, and published in the weekly *Magyar Fórum* in August, 1992. Analysing the failure of coalition parties at by-elections and the stalemate of the 'media war' between government and opposition, Csurka had drawn the conclusion that the extreme right of the MDF should either force the government to step down or demand that political conflicts are settled by force rather than by compromise. In its language the paper openly used some terms of German Fascism, such as the notion of *Lebensraum* or a 'genetic degradation' of the population on ethnic grounds.[29]

The Csurka paper caused an outrage among intellectuals. The public was also shocked when the issue was debated in Parliament and Csurka reiterated his views on television. Prime Minister Antall was hesitant and uncertain about whether to distance himself from the paper stating merely that he 'did not identify with it'. Fear was growing that the largest government party would fall into the hands of extremists. Pressure was increasing on Charter spokespersons to do something. They met on the 30th of August to discuss the issue. It was stated that Csurka's extremist views could not be tolerated by the democratic forces. One group urged the immediate arrangement of a rally, while others thought a few weeks' preparation was needed to organize a real mass demonstration. Co-operation was started with the opposition parties, trade unionist organizations and other social groups turning up in growing numbers to prepare a demonstration. An appeal was published by the Charter on the 10th of September urging the government to condemn anti-constitutional views and announcing at the same time a 'grand demonstration' in defence of democracy at an appropriate time. It was already known at the time that István Csurka was going to speak at a rally of his followers in front of the television building and Charter spokespersons wanted to hold their demonstration after that. On the other hand, they could not foresee what

103

effect the Csurka rally would have, so two versions of the demonstration were prepared, a rally, if Csurka did not have a major effect, and a spectacular mass demonstration in case of a major threat.

In the end, the latter version was used. The rally of the right-wing radical, Csurka, not only attracted marginal groups but also many middle class people and the number of participants reached 15,000. It became vital then to organize a much larger demonstration of the Charter. Initially it was thought, with the agreement of the opposition parties, that speakers at the Charter demonstration should be independent of parties. The Young Democrats also announced that their support of the demonstration depended on that. In the end, however, it turned out differently. Following the Csurka rally, SZDSZ leaders believed that the Charter demonstration should be given major political support and convinced spokespersons, with support from György Konrád, about the need for party speakers. Spokespersons' opinions on the change varied, some were pleased to enter big politics, while others felt they had been faced with a fait accompli on the part of the SZDSZ, ignoring their independence.

Social expectations increased day by day. More and more organizations joined the demonstration, some of them providing financial support as well. In the end the FIDESZ also supported it, though no speakers were appointed. The MSZP did not object to party speakers. All three parties as well as major trade unions helped print leaflets. The Democratic Charter made another public appeal on the 21st of September announcing the place and time of the demonstration and stating:

> In Hungary the extreme right have been pushing forward over the past few weeks. Racist, anti-minorities, inciting views supporting fascism were publicised at different forums. The vice-president of the MDF announced a nationalistic program called *Magyar Út* (Hungarian Road), different from the coalition program, and antagonistic to national endeavours to join a civilised Europe. (....) The Democratic Charter is warning. This is not what we voted for in 1990! Let us defend the achievements of a peaceful political re-structuring, let us protect jointly the freedom and democracy we have attained in heavy struggle![30]

A long list of organizations joining the appeal showed all the colours of the rainbow. It ranged from anarchists to an evangelical youth organization, from former communists to liberal democrats, from greens to Christian sports clubs. The list of speakers was announced at a press conference arranged by the Charter on the 22nd of September, where different organizations could

104

also express their views. With collaboration from sympathizer journalists, opposition politicians and critical intellectuals, major dailies reported daily on the event to come. A political 'action-unity' of critical intellectuals and leftist-liberal journalists was apparent again, which used to be an important element of the Charter at the beginning.

Over 80,000 people, by reliable estimates, took to the streets on the 24th of September, 1992 in response to the Charter's appeal. It was the largest mass demonstration in Hungary since June the 16th 1989 when Imre Nagy (executed former Prime Minister and hero of the 1956 revolution) and fellow-martyrs were ceremonially re-buried. Demonstrators marched along their traditional route in the City. Speakers addressed the crowd in front of the House of Parliament, while the crowd listened with flowers and candles in hand, calling for a joint move against an anti-democratic right wing and emphasizing the importance of a quiet but firm response to aggression. Iván Vitányi again suggested that it was not an opposition demonstration but a meeting of the 'friends of society'. György Konrád reiterated, 'if there is democracy, being Hungarian is not forbidden. If there is no democracy, it is difficult to be a Hungarian minority in neighbouring countries. Hungarians, then, have a vested interest to see democracy prevail all over the Carpathian basin'.[31] The demonstration had a definite anti-fascist character. Participants included old age pensioners who, in their own words, last demonstrated against Fascism fifty years ago, in 1942. As part of the event, Charter sympathizer actors also performed. Major funding was provided by a religious community called the Community of Belief. At the same time, Charter demonstrations took place in Miskolc and Debrecen with a few thousand participants. Pál Forgách, a former President of the League (FSZDL) addressed the Miskolc rally. Although the government press were trying to discredit the Charter demonstration because of the participation of an alleged extremist group, but it was peaceful and dignified, free of extremists. A large banner with the words 'Fearless for Democracy' was carried by spokespersons, there were few other banners.

The success of the demonstration pushed the Charter onto the level of big politics. The initiative, which started as a loose association of intellectuals, was able to mobilize crowds that had been passive for a long time. It is true, the number of signatories was increasing slowly but their composition had changed. Following the Social Charter in May, the proportion of the unemployed and pensioners increased. The Charter did not change into a permanent social movement, but it functioned as a symbol or catch word for democracy that could mobilize a large number of people if the need arose. The demonstration also meant another step towards closer co-operation between the Charter and the opposition parties.

A month later a conference with the title 'Revolutions and Restorations' was held at the Town Hall organized by the editors of the international journal *Lettre Internationale* and other European intellectuals. György Konrád reiterated there his former idea of setting up an international democratic charter, which was supported by an overwhelming majority. Following the conference the Budapest Appeal was compiled by Konrád, Mészöly and Vitányi. The authors announced a proposal to set out an international democratic charter in order that democratic ideals could continuously be matched with 'the state of affairs in the world'. After identifying their joint values, the authors suggested an international dialogue on the issue.

In the meantime radical rightist groups including uniformed skinheads disturbed celebrations on October 23rd (Republic Day, and the day of the outbreak of the revolution of 1956), preventing by whistling and shouting, President Árpád Göncz from delivering his ceremonial address. Since there were off-duty border guards on the scene, who had been taken there on trucks, and the police did nothing to prevent the disturbance, a well founded suspicion arose of organized forces being in the background. Suspicion grew with Prime Minister Antall simply saying in his first statement that he 'is not pleased with' the disturbance but failed to condemn it. By the time Charter spokespersons gathered to express their protest, participants at the Lettre conference had already compiled a statement in protest. Charter spokespersons published a full-page political advertisement in protest against the appearance of neo-Nazi ideals. There were two photos in the advertisement: one recalled the take-over of the Arrowed Party (Hungarian fascists) in 1944, on the other one there was a neo-Nazi youth photographed on Kossuth Square on October the 23rd. The caption ran: 'Again? No!'

President Göncz was to inaugurate a restored Hungarian national symbol at Tatabánya on the 29th of November. But leaders of the movement feared a repetition of the disturbances which had characterized earlier events. Charter spokespersons asked supporters in a letter to attend and, if the need arose, to physically protect the President of the Republic. About 100 people responded. Police, however, were careful this time and skinhead groups gathering on the scene had no chance to disturb the inaugurating ceremony. Many people felt by that time that the Charter had remained the last force to safeguard democracy in the country. The events it organized made the Charter well-known in the country, many people joined by signing. The Charter awakened a new enthusiasm for democracy and reactivated civil society in Hungary. The following Table illustrates how rapidly support for the movement expanded. It shows the rate at which the number of signatories increased, and the events associated with accelerated membership.

106

Table 1. Rate of increase of Charter signatories

Date	Event	Number of signatories
1991		
26 September	17 points published	162
30 October	press conference	1,500
8 December	Town Hall rally	4,000
15 December	.. .. ..	7,000
1992		
31 January	Town Hall Rally	18,613
13 February	press conference	20,200
18 March	demonstration	22,082
6 May	social appeal	24,191
3 June	campaign for media presidents	25,713
29 June	campaign for the President	27,040
14 September	campaign against the far right	27,346
5 December	.. .. ..	27,600

Source, Horányi, *The Documentation of the Charter.*

The number of signatories increased steeply in the first months, (8/11/91-13/2/92). As well as initial enthusiasm, this was because the HSP actively participated in collecting signatures. Based on Horányi's data, nearly 12,000 of the 27,000 signatures were collected with the participation of the MSZP.

Comparing social distribution data of the first 10,000 signatories to a list of 2,000 collected exclusively by the MSZP (Table 2), there is a significant shift on the MSZP list to blue-collar workers, the unemployed and pensioners. The Charter list collected in a spontaneous action by sympathizers contains many more intellectuals. (The 2,000 sample of the MSZP has been based on data of signatories from 12,000 to 14,000, therefore it does not belong to the first 10,000.)

Table 2. Social distribution of signatories to the Charter

Occupation	Mixed Collection	HSP Collection
Blue-collar workers	12.7%	19.65%
Teachers, instructors	12.1%	10.4%
Engineers	8.1%	4.2%
University students	4.3%	2.4%
Pensioners	14.7%	33.7%
Office workers	8.3%	7.9%
Press	3.7%	0.7%
Doctors and health workers	3.6%	1.1%
Lawyers and economists	8.6%	3.7%
Researchers	4.3%	2.2%
Artists/actors	3.7%	0.5%
Businessmen	5.0%	3.5%
Housewives	0.4%	1.2%
Unemployed	0.9%	3.6%
Other	6.1%	1.3%
Occupation not indicated	3.4%	4.0%
	100% = 10,000 people	100%= 2,000 people

Source: Horányi, *The Documentation of the Charter*

Over 27,000 people joined the Charter in one year. It should be noted that the proportion of the unemployed and blue-collar workers was growing after May 1992, following the Social Charter, though the rate of increase at that time was considerably lower than at the beginning. The Charter mobilized about 15,000 people on March 15, 1992 and over 80,000 at its mass demonstration on September 24. Two rallies at the Town Hall were attended by 1,000 people each and 35,000 signed an appeal supporting President Árpád Göncz.

Party attractions - Changes in the function of the charter

A one-year mandate of Charter spokespersons expired in December 1992. The future of the Charter was discussed at several meetings. Some proposed that the Charter should suspend its activity for a year, because - with elections nearing - it might be used by some parties for their own campaigns endangering its very existence. Konrád, on the other hand, proposed with some support from others, that spokespersons should stay on for another year. At a meeting in December, following a lengthy debate, spokespersons decided to postpone their elections but meet again. At the meeting a political statement was also adopted in defence of the president of the television network who had been suspended from his position by the Prime Minister; a disciplinary procedure based on an (anti-constitutional) regulation that had accidentally survived political re-structuring.

The spokespersons and their friends met again on January 10, 1993. By that time the radio and television presidents had resigned due to government pressure. Due to tensions in domestic politics the Charter meeting opened in a rather depressed atmosphere. It looked as if the Charter was in a critical situation. Some participants expressed fears that the ruling MDF might postpone the general elections due in 1994. A lengthy debate followed on the relationship between the Charter and political parties, in which two approaches were outlined: 1. the Charter should be an independent organization of citizens with its funds separated from party funding, 2. the Charter should not be independent of parties and should not refuse party funding. At the end, 'independents' remained a minority so the dilemma ended in an open victory for political parties. A new, 16-member body of spokespersons was elected. In it there were four former spokespersons, altogether ten of the founders of the Charter were elected. The body of spokespersons was distributed by occupation as follows: four party politicians (including Konrád and Vitányi), three journalists, seven well-known scholars and one high school teacher. Spokespersons were elected on their merit rather than democratically, based on intellectual performance and former activity in the opposition. It was also important that potential spokespersons should belong to sympathizers of one or other of the opposition parties and should have access to the mass media. It was no accident that intellectuals of the humanities were dominant, those who were masters of word and picture, description and illustration.

Differences in the expectations regarding the future role of the Charter dominated a Budapest rally on February the 7th, where about 1,000 sympathizers confirmed the elected new spokespersons. Budapest Mayor, Gábor Demszky delivered the first address. He criticized the government for its overemphasis on party interests and said of the Democratic Charter, 'the Charter is wonderful, partly because its goal is to respect overall human rights and partly because it is a balancing, coherent power between different political ideas. It expresses a public feeling, a complete refusal of rightist views and the demand to create the scope of true democracy'.[32] The question how 'a complete refusal of rightist views' can be co-ordinated with the demand to create the scope of true democracy points up the internal contradictions of Charter policies. Mihály Kornis, for instance, urged 'an all-society union' of the opposition in his latest paper and envisaged the Charter in this framework. György Konrád, on the other hand, although he agreed with the necessity of action against a 'fascist-smelling democtatorship', emphasized that 'social control over government' embodied in the Charter 'will be needed even if a future government is made up of the parties whose members and leaders have signed the Democratic Charter'.[33] Charter events had lost their drive by spring 1993. The extreme right led by Csurka had been driven out of the MDF, domestic politics had normalized in Hungary. A dictatorship seemed less and less threatening. At March 15th celebrations the top speaker was Elemér Hankiss, the resigned president of the television network, while György Konrád dealt with foreign political issues in his address. A statement published by the Charter for May Day did not go beyond banalities asking political forces 'to stop useless fights with each other and rise above second rate political issues'. At about that time another movement started named 'Act against Hate!', which was different from the Charter because there were fewer intellectuals among its followers and it did not join any political group.

The Democratic Charter arranged a collection of signatures in late August 1993 in protest against broadcasting on television the re-burial of Miklós Horthy, the governor of pre-war Hungary. The majority of signatories then were socialists rather than liberals, many of whom had been prominent personalities during the dictatorship and had lost credibility. On the eve of the funeral ceremony Charter spokespersons said goodbye to the Horthy regime with a cultural programme in front of about 1,000 people, emphasizing that contemporary democracy could not be regarded an heir of the Horthy regime.

The last two mass events organized by the Charter took place in defence of the freedom of the press. The new management of Hungarian Television

110

wound up the last independent news programme with references to an allegedly biased presentation of an earlier political event - the disturbances on October 23, 1992, which prevented President Árpád Göncz from delivering his ceremonial address. On an initiative of the Chamber of Radio Employees, 15,000 people held a silent demonstration in front of the television building on October 30, followed by a mass rally at Budapest Town Hall organized by the Charter. Some of the speakers spoke of the threat of a political coup - following the coup in the media - while some proposed that, 'in the shadow of a coup that might become dangerous' the Charter should turn to international forums. Because of the events President Árpád Göncz emphasized in a letter addressed to Prime Minister József Antall that 'Hungarian Radio and Television have grown unable to meet their basic tasks and that voters will 'be deprived of the opportunity to freely express their views'. In his reply Prime Minister Antall expressed disagreement: 'a defence of the freedom of the press also means that an internal terror cannot be exercised by certain political forces and groups of journalists who sharply criticise everybody whose ideas are different'.[34] Both parties adopted the posture of guarding the freedom of the press, though Antall considered it an internal affair of the media. Charter speakers, on the other hand, emphasized, in agreement with President Göncz, that the issue had outgrown an internal debate of intellectuals as an oppression of the freedom of the press could lead to a red-brown dictatorship.

The last phase of the 'media war' began in autumn 1993. It was marked by a severe shift to the right of news programmes (compared to the government centre) and political purges, both in the radio and television. In protest many outstanding authors, poets and musicians forbade their works to be broadcast on Hungarian Radio and Television. At the same time, 83 intellectuals announced in an open letter the establishment of the Association of Independent Thinkers (FÜGE) aimed at reviewing news programmes every week and publishing their findings. 162 actors signed an open letter addressed to the Prime Minister protesting against a 'civil war of ideals' in radio and television, which had rendered 'creative work impossible'.[35] Some people were dismissed from the radio because they had played an active part in the Democratic Charter. The Executive Committee of Hungarian Pen Club expressed their solidarity with protesting authors. Although the Hungarian Writers' Association also agreed that the freedom of the press had been violated, they did not support a boycott. Instead, they urged the government to ease the tension in radio and television. Although a political motivation of the dismissals was officially denied, in fact it was obvious, and the majority of the public found it appalling. The procedure was legally unjustified, while it recalled the spirit of the Kónya paper and the Csurka pamphlet. Radio staff

111

held a protest demonstration on March the 3rd, which was joined by the Publicity Club, and 54 intellectuals demanded in an open letter that the dismissed should be re-instated immediately. The spokespersons of the Democratic Charter also published a protest letter condemning the government much more harshly than ever before. Similar sentiments were expressed at a press conference held a few days later and then at a mass demonstration organized on the eve of the National Day on March the 15th, where 20,000 people took part. The demonstration was addressed by some of those dismissed from national radio and then the 17 Points of the Charter were read, followed by a statement by spokespersons on the freedom of the press. The statement demanded that the government should withdraw from the media and that the next Parliament should adopt a suitable Media Act immediately after the elections. Opinion polls at that time already forecast that the government coalition were going to lose the elections because they had shifted too far to the right and had lost popular support, which was a promising item of news for many Charter sympathizers. Some were actually looking forward to the elections in May to end a period of misery.

Results of the second free elections held in post-Communist Hungary justified expectations of a change of government. The MDF-led coalition lost. In the first round of the elections the parties actively supporting the Charter received the highest number of votes (MSZP, 32.98%, SZDSZ, 19,76%). The second round of the elections ended in absolute majority for the MSZP with 54%, while SZDSZ received 18% of the votes. The MSZP could have formed a government on its own, but it was made clear immediately that they wished to form a coalition, and the only serious coalition partner was the SZDSZ. György Konrád supported the coalition in an article published after the first round of the elections arguing for a Prime Minister to be appointed from his party, the SZDSZ. Although many people failed to support the latter idea, there was a growing pressure on both parties to form a coalition. Articles were published in the papers arguing for an MSZP-SZDSZ coalition. The Democratic Charter went beyond its earlier scope and sought to shape party policy. On May the 31st, two days after the second round of the elections, Charter spokespersons organized a public debate on what kind of government should take over in the country. Though there were some opinions to the contrary, the majority of the speakers supported a coalition. Based on this, György Konrád on behalf of the Democratic Charter publicly asked the leaders of both parties to start coalition negotiations. Not only the parties wanted, then, to influence the movement, movement intellectuals also wanted to influence their parties.

A civil movement had turned into the 'king maker', or at least behaved in that manner. Supporters of the Democratic Charter contributed to the

112

overcoming of hatred between communists and anti-Communists that had been decisive in 1990. Also they helped achieve the collaboration of three social élite groups, political reformers of the Kádár regime, technocrats and leftist-liberal intellectuals. The common denominator of those groups, however, was not a social-liberal-democratic minimum represented by the Charter, but a promise of modernization. The Democratic Charter, often with true pathos, protested against the spread of a politics of ideologies though its supporters used value centred politics. The social-liberal coalition that took over in 1994, however, not only gave up ideologizing, but also refrained from a value centred discourse. In its language the coalition returned to a peculiar mixture of neutral technocratic terminology of the late Kádár regime and 'task-oriented' bureaucratic language.

Conclusions

For many the establishment of the Charter and the events organized by it meant saying 'yes' to democracy and 'no' to anti-democratic phenomena. When people were unwilling or unable to find their way in the labyrinth of party politics, the Charter simplified topical political issues to one single alternative. In this way, the Charter had become a benchmark, a point of reference - here is 'our' Hungary and there is 'theirs'. The Charter had been organized in order to restore a destabilized political consensus and in defence of a democratic minimum, but - partly in response to a pressure from the government coalition - it drove politics onto a moral field. It was not Parliamentary speeches, but peaceful demonstrations organized by the Charter that halted an advance by the extreme right. In many respects the Democratic Charter was one of the most successful political movements of Hungarian intellectuals, since it organized the largest anti-Fascist demonstration in Hungarian history. On the other hand, the existence of the Charter increased rather than decreased a polarization of political life, a deepening of society's differences. 'Popular-front politics' were the price paid for the defence of a democratic minimum and this probably contributed to a quick return to power of the former Communist party.

The extreme right suffered a severe loss at the elections in 1994. István Csurka's radical right-wing party received only 1.59% of the party-list votes. Still, it is not easy to tell, even in retrospect, whether the threat to democracy had indeed been as large as suggested by Charter spokespersons. Election results suggest that the threat had been exaggerated and 'a threat of Fascism' had actually been smaller than the anti-Fascist response it triggered. However, it could only come to light following the protest action organized by the

Charter. Using the tools of social science it is impossible to verify either that election results would have been the same had the Charter not been set up or that they would have been essentially different. Anyway, by keeping the issue of a threat from the extreme right on the agenda, the Charter ensured a natural framework for social co-operation against such trends.

From a sociological perspective a main characteristic of the Charter was its duality. On the one hand, it had become a club-like, network-style framework for talking politics by intellectuals. On the other hand, due to its openness, it had served as a channel for elementary mass demands that erupt rarely. It was a real 'umbrella movement' in more than one sense. Partly, it was able, at a given time, to act as an umbrella to cover different social groups that would not have communicated with each other otherwise. On the other hand, it was an umbrella in another sense suggested by György Konrád: its members did not wish to operate it permanently, at all costs. When it was needed, the Charter opened as an umbrella and closed for a time when there was no need for it. Because of this, it was not considered a real movement by some. This, however, is not true. It was a movement consisting of distinct actions, which seemingly ceased to exist from one action to the next.

The movement needed well-known, charismatic leaders in order to maintain its umbrella-like character, people who were able to catch and hold the attention of large numbers of people. Such was the role played, firstly, by György Konrád, an author known all over the world, the father and magician of the Charter, its symbol, a member of the former democratic opposition, who was at that time the Chairman of International Pen Club and member of the SZDSZ National Council. Similar figures were the novelist Miklós Mészöly, the aesthetist Péter Balassa, sociologist Elemér Hankiss, director Imre Kerényi and film director Miklós Jancsó. Charter spokespersons often spoke up in defence of President Árpád Göncz (a former dramatist), and they had been in contact with him and enjoyed his support. Iván Vitányi was another important figure who had a dual role in the inner circles of the Charter, as an intellectual and as a politician holding an important position in the MSZP, bridging a gap between younger socialist intellectuals and the Socialist Party. In addition to similarities, there were also differences between the parts played by Konrád and Vitányi. Konrád was in the Democratic Charter, because he was the 'magician' of democracy. He also sat on the National Council of the AFD because of his fame and past merits - he was firstly an intellectual and secondly a politician. Following 1989, Konrád had changed from an 'anti-politician' into a 'metapolitician', from a member of the opposition into a prominent figure of the Democratic Charter. The relationship between him and SZDSZ leaders is somewhat similar to that between the German author, Günter Grass and the German Social Democratic

Party of the 1970s led by Willy Brandt and then by Helmut Schmidt. Konrád's links with SZDSZ leaders were close because of the long years spent together in the democratic opposition. Iván Vitányi's credibility and legitimacy had different roots. It was partly due to the fact that he, who had been appointed the director of a research institute under the dictatorship (and was not far from the 'cultural policy' of the Kádár regime), offered 'shelter', i.e. job opportunities, to members of the opposition who had been removed from their positions. In 1989 he was an active participant in changing the former state-party into a socialist reform-party. He had been Chairman of the MSZP Board and an MP since 1990. Compared to such positions, the Charter was a kind of political hinterland for him. Unlike Konrád, Vitányi was a politician in the first place. He was hailed as an active member of the movement both by MSZP, preparing to break out from its isolation, and the Charter, in need of organizational support.

The Democratic Charter was represented by established intellectuals who had four key characteristics 1. They had a past history in the opposition (or at least could not be considered supporters of the old regime), 2. They were acknowledged professionals, 3. They were close to the opposition parties of the period (measured by influence rather than by membership), 4. They had the opportunity and ability to be effective in the media. The Democratic Charter was a movement of the age of mass communication, where the image of a message is almost as important as the message itself. Major Charter events were designed by professional theatre and film directors, professional communicators made the announcements and speeches. The image and communicational skills of a speaker were more important than what he/she represented politically.

In addition to established intellectuals, however, another group of 'movement intellectuals' also appeared. It consisted mostly of younger journalists or other intellectuals close to the party who had been selected (sometimes without being asked) by established intellectuals. Those people did not belong to the democratic opposition of the 1980s, on the contrary, most of them believed for a long time that a dictatorship might be reformed. Due to their reformist behaviour, they were a step behind events when political transition started. Because of their growing critical activity as journalists, they found it unfair that the politicians of the MDF-led coalition government simply treated them the same as the beneficiaries of the dictatorship. Most of them learnt the role of a critical intellectual in 1990-91 and became a Charter spokesperson. They were media people turned into movement intellectuals by the Charter. The role of movement intellectuals was a belated compensation for what they had 'missed' in the 1980s. The value of their opposition behaviour was enhanced because it was modelled on

115

the members of the former democratic opposition and 'endorsed' by their approval. In a period when people seemed to lose their faith in party politics the position of a Charter spokesperson enjoyed strong moral legitimacy in society. The democratic opposition of the 1980s symbolically 'accepted' media intellectuals of the 1990s with that alliance (or, putting it in another way, acknowledged their need for them) and continued to approach former party member intellectuals.

Movement intellectuals were identified by Eyerman and Jamison as people who had been 'trained' to become intellectuals by a movement. They regarded the movement as cognitive praxis, in which intellectual activity is conceived as a process rather than a product.[36] Established intellectuals can operate in the context of a social movement, as speakers, ideologues, movement communicators, etc., but they are not 'created' by the movement. In the case of the Charter, participant media intellectuals could re-interpret their intellectual existence by movement discourse. It, however, was not created at that time, thus it was not exclusively bound to the movement. One of the reasons why the Charter declined was that a government coalition took over that was emotionally closer to Charter activists. The other reason, however, was that their identity was not bound to the Charter alone, so they did not need to hold on to it at any price. Charter spokespersons, temporarily in a movement intellectual position, returned to the media in 1994 or they became much more accepted, newly established intellectuals.

Another conclusion can also be drawn from the history of the Democratic Charter. A politics of principles is an advantage to political intellectuals compared to party politicians, since the language used is more familiar to them. A political discourse is their true field. The terminology, however, slowed down a demystification of politics, the process described by Max Weber as the creation of politics as vocation. The terminology of normative politics was used in reference to civil society, therefore it was transformed into a means of self-expression of political intellectuals. On the other hand, a sociologist spokesperson of the Charter emphasized the necessity of directly democratic forms and a social acceptance of democracy. He said that a 'self-therapy' of civil society rather than the new political élite could be expected to achieve that goal.[37]

Debates of the form above concerning intellectuals were really about democracy. The most important condition for the stabilization of a new democracy might be the establishment and operation of democratic institutions, a professionalism of the new political élite. Considerations about a substantive, idealized concept of democracy being a threat to the new set of institutions based on representation seemed to be well founded. The intellectuals of the Democratic Charter, on the other hand, were also right to believe that a new system, borne out of a radical political change, demands not only institutional, but also moral legitimacy. Social movements are just as much an integral part of democracy as political parties or legislative, executive and legal power. On the one hand debates around the Charter were, then, theoretical between different interpretations (representative versus participatory) of democracy. On the other hand, there was a political debate on what action would threaten or strengthen democracy in a given political situation. There were some who denied the necessity of making politics in the streets in a given situation, although they accepted it in general. There were others who generally denied the necessity of direct participation in the operations of a democracy, but in the given situation (with reference to an exceptional threat) supported the policy of mass demonstrations. Last, there were some, who failed to agree with movement politics either in general, or in actual cases and some others, who agreed in both cases. The debates were further motivated by differences in interpretation. They revolved around whether the parties considered the intellectual or mass movement character of the Charter more emphasized, or whether its dependence or independence of political parties was considered more desirable.

General hypotheses by Alvin Gouldner and others on an expected increase of intellectuals' class power made a great impact when they were published.[38] The feverish months of the changes in 1989 went on to confirm that feeling on the face of it. Nevertheless, the ideas represented by Fehér and Heller have proved to be more founded, 'the time has come for mass democracy rather than the class power of intellectuals'.[39] Regarding the whole Central and Eastern European region, this statement may sound overoptimistic or normative even today. Until there is an unquestioned consensus in society that democracy has no alternative, intellectuals in Central and Eastern Europe will have a chance to play a last tune as 'civil magicians' of democracy or as a nationalistic counter-point to it. The paradox of the Democratic Charter was in the fact that it was a kind of pro-democracy, civil rights movement whose slogans and terms were compiled by a hierarchical group of intellectuals who had had a privileged position, but were gradually losing their political influence. In the movement a confusion of roles by intellectuals, which could be interpreted as a 'counter-attack by the Estates of the Realm' against an institutionalized world of politics, was running side by side with a movement intellectual identity based on continuous critical discourse and maintaining a demand of civilian control over the institutions of politics.

Abbreviations

FIDESZ	Federation of Young Democrats
FSZDL	Democratic League of Independent Trade Unions (in short: The League)
FÜGE	Association of Independent Thinkers
MDF	Hungarian Democratic Forum
MSZMP	Hungarian Socialist Worker's Party
MSZOSZ	National Alliance of Hungarian Trade Unions
MSZP	Hungarian Socialist Party
SZDSZ	Alliance of Free Democrats
SZKH	Network of Free Initiatives
TDDSZ	Democratic Trade Union of Researchers

Notes and references

1. Bozóki, András (1994), 'Intellectuals and Democratization in Hungary' in Rootes, Chris and Davis, Howard (eds), *A New Europe? Social Change and Political Transformation*, UCL Press, London, pp. 149-175.
2. Böröcz, József (1992), 'Vanguard of the Construction of Capitalism: The Hungarian Intellectuals Trip to Power', *Critical Sociology*, vol. 18, no. 1, pp. 111-116.
3. Garton Ash, Timothy (1989), *The Uses of Adversity*, Granta, Cambridge.
4. Commisso, Ellen, Dubb, Stephen and McTigue, Judy (1992), 'The Illusion of Populism in Latin America and East-Central Europe', in Szoboszlai, Gy (ed), *Flying Blind; Emerging Democracy in East-Central Europe*, HPSA, Budapest, pp. 79-80.
5. Konrád, György and Szelényi, Iván (1979), *Intellectuals on the Road to Class Power*, Harcourt, Brace and Janovich, New York.
6. Kornis, Mihály, 'The Democratic Card', *Magyar Narancs*, January 11, 1992, p. 2.
7. Konrád, György, Interview with the author, November 23rd, 1992.
8. Bauer, Tamás and Kis, János, 'In Defence of Hungarian Democracy', *Magyar Hirlap*, September 9th, 1991, p. 7.
9. Ibid, p. 7.
10. Ibid, p. 7.
11. Róna-Tas, Akos (1992), 'The Selected and the Elected: The making of the New Parliamentary Elite in Hungary', *East European Politics and Societies*, vol. 5, no. 3. Autumn, pp. 357-393.
12. Bauer and Kis, 'In Defence', p. 8.
13. Farkas, Attila, 'Democratic Charter in the Next Week', interview with Ivan Peto, *Magyar Hírlap*, September, 1991.
14. *Democratic Charter*, 1991.
15. Farkasházy, Tivadar, 'The Unpoliteness of Hope', interview with Kisbali, László, *Beszelo*, November, 1991, p. 42.
16. Antall, József, 'He had to be Dismissed', *Magyar Hírlap*, December 2nd, 1991.
17. Csurka, István, Interview in *Magyar Hírlap*, December 2nd, 1991.
18. Konrád, Geörgy, Interview, *Reggeli Kurir*, December 3rd, 1991.
19. Megalakulas, 'The Foundation of the Charter', reported in *Magyar Nemzet* and *Magyar Hírlap*, December 9th, 1991.
20. Horányi, Geörgy, 'The Documentation of the Charter', MTA, Budapest, 1992.

21. Bánó, Atilla, 'Whose Charter', *Uj Magyarorszag*, December 12th, 1991.
22. FIDESZ, 'A Memorandum of the FIDESZ Faction', *Magyar Hírlap*, December 9th, 1991.
23. Bossányi, Katalin, Interview with the author, September 28th, 1992.
24. Solt, Ottília,'New March Fronts', *Beszelo*, March, 1992, pp. 9-12.
25. Tamás, Gáspár, Speech reported in *Magyar Hírlap*, March 16th, 1992.
26. Machos, Csilla (1991), 'Demokratischen Charta 91: Von der "alter" zur "neuen" Ungarischen Opposition', *Berliner Debatte INITIAL*, no. 4, pp. 57-68.
27. Nyilatkozat, 'Declaration', *Magyar Hirlap*, May 27th, 1992.
28. Konrád, György, 'An Examination of a Gesture', Magyar Hírlap, March, 15th, 1992.
29. Csurka, István, 'Some Thoughts about the Past Two years of the Regime Change and the New Programme of the MDF', *Magyar Forum*, August 20, 1992.
30. Felhívás, 'Manifesto', *Magyar Hirlap*, September, 24, 1992.
31. Konrád, György, 'Ladies and Gentlemen', *Magyar Hírlap*, September 25, 1992, p. 7.
32. Charta-day, *Magyar Hírlap*, February 8, 1993, pp. 1-4.
33. Konrád, György, 'What is the Democratic Charter', *Magyar Hirlap*, 24, February 7, 1993, p. 7.
34. Antall, Jószef, 'A letter to Arpad Goncz', *Magyar Hirlap*, November 9, 1993.
35. Színészek, 'A Letter of 162 Actors to the Prime Minister', *Magyar Hirlap*, November 26, 1993.
36. Eyerman, Ron and Jamison, Andrew, (1991), *Social Movements : A Cognitive Approach*, Polity Press, Cambridge, 1991, p. 98.
37. Miszivetz Ferenc (1993), 'The Crisis of Hungarian Democracy after 1989', *Kritika*, April, pp. 14-17.
38. Gouldner, Alvin (1979), *The future of Intellectuals and the Rise of the New Class*, Oxford University Press, New York.
39. Fehér, Ferenc and Heller, Agnes (1992), *The Glorious Revolutions of Eastern Europe*, T-Twins, Budapest, p. 7.

7. Vaclav Havel: a Case Study of the Intellectual as Politician

AVIZIER TUCKER

The Origins of Havel's Apolitical Politics

Vaclav Havel's anti-politics originated in his Heideggerian anti-modernism. During the sixties, Havel and his generation of Czech intellectuals developed their thought in the phenomenological tradition, as developed by Jan Patocka (1907-1977), who was a student of Husserl in Freiburg, and was influenced heavily by Heidegger. Later, Patocka wrote the text of Charter 77 of human rights and was, with Havel and Hajek, its first spokesperson.[1] After Patocka's death, Havel became the leader of the Charter 77 movement and dissent in Czechoslovakia until the 1989 Velvet Revolution. This intellectual milieu was fiercely anti-modernist and anti-technological. Heidegger's analysis of modernism was accepted blindly and uncritically. Yet, Havel and his contemporaries interpreted Heidegger in terms of their immediate totalitarian-modern environment.

For Havel, and Vaclav Belohradsky (b.1944), another student of Patocka who taught in exile in Genoa until 1989, with whose *The crisis of the eschatology of the impersonal* Havel was 'extraordinarily taken' (DIS 165),[2] the automatism and autonomy of the technological metaphysics of our age dominate the relations between modern socio-bureaucratic systems and humanity. Belohradsky expanded on Heidegger's theme of cybernetics as replacing philosophy and applied it to his political analysis. He conceived the modern state as a cybernetic entity, governed by anonymous, faceless bureaucrats who rule a multitude of atomized and alienated individuals living an inauthentic existence. However, the nameless, depersonalized bureaucrats are not controlling the system to whose survival they contribute because the system, like Spengler and Heidegger's 'technology', has acquired a 'self-momentum' of itself, an autonomous automatism (DIS 166). Manipulation by the system and alienation from our roots in authentic Being are universal

121

ills of modern-technological society for Belohradsky and Havel, of technology going amuck and controlling and manipulating humanity. Havel romanticized about a past when the rulers had been idiosyncratic persons rather than anonymous apparatchiks, innocent tools of anonymous power, built on the evils of science, technology, cybernetics, abstraction, and objectivity. Following Patocka and Belohradsky, Havel traced the inception of the spirit of scientific rationalism in science to Galileo, and in politics to Machiavelli (PAC 143).[3]

Havel conceived the totalitarian system as a convex mirror reflection of modern civilization, a warning to the West calling it to understand itself as it is being reflected in the Communist world (PAC 141-146). Havel's objection to Czechoslovak totalitarianism was merely an aspect of his greater and more thorough anti-modernism. The automatism of modern systems, their anonymity, leads to a loss of personal responsibility, moral responsibility, and the ethical dimension of society. Responsibility becomes another 'subjective illusion' to be destroyed by objective science (PAC 142).

Following Alexandr Solzhenitsyn, Havel conceived of Western democracies as different in means rather than in their moral essence from post-totalitarianism, they too are the victims of the automatism of technological civilization and its loss of moral responsibility (POP 116).[4] Lack of moral responsibility, alienation and inauthentic 'living in a lie' are not exclusive to the post-totalitarian world of communist East Europe, which Havel characterized as 'built on foundations laid by the historical encounter between dictatorship and the consumerist society' (POP 54). The culprit for the overall important moral disintegration of modern civilization as a whole is consumerism. Consumerism tempts modern humanity to choose material goods over moral values. This selling off of moral values for materialism occurred on both sides of the iron curtain. This crisis of the modern technological world is even more acute in the Western world, since it is better hidden than in the East, through the manipulation of people by professionally run political parties, secret and sophisticated methods of capital accumulation, consumption, production, and advertisement. Western methods of manipulation are far more subtle and refined, and therefore dangerous, than in the East (POP 116-118).

Havel's conclusion was that the West, like the East requires an *existential revolution*. Democracy, at most, could serve as a transition period for the countries of the Eastern bloc between totalitarianism, and the existential revolution, a restoration of authentic relations of the 'human order,' new experience of Being, rootedness in the universe and responsibility, a return to values like 'trust, openness, responsibility, solidarity and love' (POP 118).

Havel wanted to bring about Heidegger's existential revolution, an authentic relation to Being, as more than 'standing-reserve,' a respect of Being by 'letting things be'; a new epistemology based on disclosing Being, rather than on anthropomorphist correspondence conceptions of truth. Havel, like Heidegger, has not got a clue how this new way of thinking, a departure from Western metaphysics, and consequently a new world might look like. Heidegger did claim that this new way of penetrating the truth might resemble poetry, especially that of Holderlin, but Havel, surprisingly, since he himself is an artist, did not go into that. Like Heidegger, Havel claimed that he could only prepare expectation for this new authentic post-technological world. That solution would not be technological because technology cannot remedy itself, or political, but existential, down to the very basic and profoundest level of human consciousness (POP 114-115). Solzhenitsyn too, anticipated such a turn in civilization, 'a spiritual blaze ... a new height of vision ... the next anthropological stage'.[5]

Havel cited past solutions to the crisis of modernity, oriental thought or farming communities, but dismissed them because they are not universal. He saw the only hope in the ecological movement, though he perceived its vision as limited to the use of technology to oppose the dictatorship of technology (POP 114-115). Havel disapproved of the Green parties in Western Europe, because they were not radical enough.

In 1978, Havel saw the restoration of Western style parliamentary democracy as merely an appropriate transitional solution, to restore a sense of civic awareness, renew democratic discussion, allow political plurality, and basic expression of the aims of life. But, Havel also claimed that clinging to tried and tested parliamentary democracy is 'shortsighted' (POP 116-117). Havel wished to go beyond parliamentary democracy. Following multi-party parliamentary democracy Havel anticipated an existential revolution and a restoration of a relation between human beings and the 'order of being.' The political meaning of this 'existential revolution' would be the restructuring of society. New social structures would be held together by a feeling of communality rather than by expansionist mentality directed outward. The new structures can and must be 'open, dynamic and small', so that their members would not lose the dimension of personal responsibility. The new structures 'would be ... not in the sense of organizations or institutions, but like a community' whose authority is not based on tradition or power, but on its relevance for the solution of a certain problem. Havel wanted social organizations to appear and disappear spontaneously according to the needs of the moment (POP 118). The value underlying such organizations should be 'mutual confidence', not the mistrust of the 'collective irresponsibility' characterizing the 'classic impotence' of traditional democratic organizations (POP 117-119). The most anathematized organization for Havel was the parliamentary political party. Instead of political parties, Havel preferred unaffiliated individuals as candidates, to preserve the responsibility of public officials from creeping totalitarianism. Parties should not participate directly in politics because they are bound to become bureaucratic, corrupt, and undemocratic. Instead of parties, he wanted independent clubs or associations of free individuals for a specific cause, like the associations of dissidents (DIS 16-17). Havel, like Marx, left most of the details of the post revolutionary period out of his analysis since 'the essence of such a "post-democracy" is also that it can only develop *via facti*, as a process deriving directly from *life*, from a new atmosphere and a new "spirit"' (POP 119-120).

Havel's analysis of modernism is hopelessly unsophisticated. To be sure, there is something in his criticism of loss of responsibility in mass societies and loss of non-materialistic values in consumerist societies. But surely things in the West are more sophisticated than the way Havel put it. In pluralist societies, several metaphysical systems and ways of life co-exist. While there is some loss of responsibility, in democratic societies there are checks and balances (the Press, civic organizations, watch-dog groups, etc.) to guard against it. While consumerism has its negative side-effects, it has also partly cured the West of nationalism and belligerency, thereby making the life of everybody, including those with non-consumerist value systems, safer. Still, Havel's analysis of his own environment in POP is insightful and far more sophisticated. Though, Havel's alternative to Western-style democracy is vague and utopian.

The Attempt to Create Apolitical Politics

Havel perceived the main problem with Western-style multi-party parliamentary democracy as the destruction of personal responsibility, by alienating automatic political parties. Havel the dissident perceived all political parties as resembling the communist party. Having no familiarity with Western-style parliamentary democracy, Havel could not recognize that although political parties are less than ideal, they do not give absolute protection to their leaders from personal responsibility, as much as the Communist party used to protect its apparatchiks, especially in the presence of free press and other checks and balances.

As president, Havel did not change his views, favouring 'Politics Without Politicians.' Havel wanted citizens to vote directly for individual candidates. Havel's suggested solution abstracts one aspect of politics without political parties, a relative increase of responsibility, from its other aspects. Since, irrespective of Havel's existential revolution, the creation of political parties seems to be a universal phenomenon in free societies, the only way to stop their participation in elections is by governmental intervention, to curb the civil right for free association. Further problems arise in forming a government with a defined positive reform policy that has to negotiate with each individual member who can at any moment leave the governing coalition. Political parties also assist those candidates with less power and financial resources than others to participate in the political process. These problems soon arose in Czechoslovakia and rendered Havel's non-political politics obsolete.

Soon after the revolution, Czechs and Slovaks celebrated their newly found freedom for political association. By April 1990 there were 46 political parties in Czechoslovakia, including the party of 'the erotic initiative', and 'the party of the friends of beer'. Some 23 of these parties managed to obtain the 10,000 necessary signatures to be able to run for parliament. Havel and his supporters had to choose between discarding their vision of existential revolution in politics through non-political politics, and abolishing the basic human right of free political association. Unable to enjoy both worlds, Havel and his supporters gave up.

Accordingly, the first election programme of Civic Forum called for a Czechoslovakia that would be similar to other European countries, supporting explicitly a constitutionally based multi-party parliamentary democracy, modelled after Western Europe:

> The democratic political system is considered by us as an essential condition for the legislation of the results of the November Revolution. By acquiring legal status these results will no longer depend solely on the goodwill of individual political personalities. In this respect we want to realise the idea of a legal state in which political power is subordinate to laws; we want to realise the ideas of a parliamentary multi-party democracy with a balance of the executive, legislative and judicial powers ...[6]

Sasa Vondra, initially President Havel's adviser for foreign affairs, and a former Charter 77 spokesperson, analysed perceptively, in an interview he gave in the first part of 1990, the political situation in Czechoslovakia: as long as the main political issue was the struggle against totalitarianism, Civic Forum, a loose organization of dissidents of various political convictions had an important function to play in the struggle against, and the negotiations with, the communists. But after the victory of Civic Forum, its former

125

source of strength, its representation of widely differing views, 'has now become a relative disadvantage'.[7]

On 23 February 1991, Civic Forum dissolved itself. Two competing political bodies emerged to dominate the Czech political scene until the June 1992 election: The Civic Movement (OH) led by Foreign Minister, Jiri Dienstbier and Czech Prime Minister Petr Pithart; and the 'Thatcherite' Civic Democratic Party (ODS), led by then Finance Minister and today's Prime Minister Vaclav Klaus.[8] The Civic Movement in its insistence on calling itself 'movement' rather than 'party', upheld Havel's objection to political parties, only as an ideology; in practice it has been a political party composed of some of Havel's dissident-friends who attempted to maintain the philosophical-political tradition of the dissidents. The Civic Movement began its platform by referring to the old Civic Forum: 'The Civic Movement wishes to pursue the basic aims of Civic Forum....' The Civic Democratic Party began its platform by claiming that it 'aims to transform Czechoslovakia into a modern European state based on civil society.' The Civic Movement attempted to continue Charter 77 and Havel's tradition of politics without politicians, of non-ideological politics. 'Politics is not understood by the Civic Movement as a technocratic mechanism of power. Politics is not only the art of making decisions, but also the art of listening. The Civic Movement calls for dialogue and cooperation with the democratic right and the democratic left.'

It had been predictable that politics without politicians would not work, even before it actually failed.[9] Havel's personal refusal to lead or join a political party led to his eventual, at least since the June 1992 elections, political impotence. Without a political party to represent him in parliament, Havel has been unable to influence the decisions of the legislative body and the policy of the government. OH and the more conservative ODA (currently in coalition with ODS) have been close to Havel and are composed more than other parties of ex-dissidents. But none of these parties are directed or led by Havel, nor are they able (or at times willing) to pass legislation on his behalf. When executive, rather than symbolic, presidents wish to pass legislation, they have a presumption of support from their parties in the legislative bodies, and representatives in those bodies to attempt and pass the legislation, e.g. in France. Havel's legislative suggestions have been rejected out of hand. Havel pushed for a presidential regime without accepting the means of presidential democracy.[10]

But events revealed that much was wrong in Havel's assessment of these issues. By the summer of 1991, when he wrote his *Summer Meditations*, Havel had to revise his opinions and his intellectual positions. This fundamental turnaround was achieved by radically redefining key concepts. In *Summer Meditations*, Havel claimed that:

> There may be some who won't believe me, but in my second term as president in a land full of problems that presidents in stable countries never even dream of, I can safely say that I have not been compelled to recant anything of what I wrote earlier, or change my mind about anything. It may seem incredible, but it is so: not only have I not had to change my mind, but my opinions have been confirmed. (SM, p. 10)[11]

Havel's self misunderstanding apart, he moderated, adapted, and changed his ideas. Now, of all the Heideggerian anti-modernist and anti-technological rhetoric, there is only a brief and very mild vestige in Havel's current characterization of the 'existential revolution:'

> All my observations and all my experience have, with remarkable consistency, convinced me that, if today's planetary civilization has any hope of survival, that hope lies chiefly in what we understand as the human spirit. If we don't wish to destroy ourselves in national, religious, or political discord; if we don't wish to find our world with twice its current population, half of it dying of hunger; if we don't wish to kill ourselves with ballistic missiles armed with atomic warheads or eliminate ourselves with bacteria specially cultivated for the purpose; if we don't wish to suffocate in the global greenhouse we are heating up for ourselves or to be burned by radiation leaking through holes we have made in the ozone; if we don't wish to exhaust the non-renewable, mineral resources of this planet, without which we cannot survive; if, in short, we don't wish any of this to happen, then we must - as humanity, as people, as conscious beings with spirit, mind, and a sense of responsibility - somehow come to our senses.
> I once called this coming to our senses an existential revolution. I meant a kind of general mobilization of human consciousness, of the human mind and spirit, human responsibility, human reason. (SM, pp. 115-116)

It is striking to notice that although the ecological and political problems that the existential revolution is supposed to solve remain the same, Havel's 1991 version of the existential revolution surprisingly includes human reason. As a Heideggerian dissident, Havel blamed all the evils of the world, existential, political, ecological, and economic on human rationality, science and objectivity.[12]

In *Summer Meditations* 24 'anti-political politics', like the 'existential revolution', are redefined, and consequently lose their radical character. Now, Havel rewrites his history by claiming that:

> The political parties occasionally accuse me of being against political parties. That of course is nonsense.... One of the most sophisticated kinds of association - and at the same time an integral part of modern democracy and an expression of its plurality of opinion - is association in political parties. It would be difficult to imagine a democratic society working without them.
> So-obviously-I am not against political parties; if I were, I would be against democracy itself. I am simply against the dictatorship of partisanship... (SM, p. 53)

Instead of his earlier aversion to all political parties, Havel suggested in 1991 to merely limit their loyalty to party interests on the expense of the public interest, by adopting a new electoral system. Havel preferred a majority electoral system (similar to the American one) to the current proportional representation system, according to which citizens vote for parties that get represented in parliament according to the *national* percentage of the votes they get. In a majority system people would vote for a specific person, as in the United States, rather than for a party list where beyond the first names of the list, most of the candidates are unknowns. To prevent the total elimination of small parties from parliament, Havel suggested that two thirds of the parliament would be elected according to a majority system, while the other third would be elected proportionally. (SM pp. 53-59) In 1995 Havel suggested another parliamentary reform creating a higher house of parliament for the Czech Republic. However, without political party to represent Havel, Prime Minister Klaus can advise Havel 'to concentrate on things he understands like history and morality, and not talk about things he does not understand like economics and politics'. Still, Havel's 'reinterpretation' of his 'anti-political politics' is far more reasonable and realistic than the original one.

Without Havel's leadership, the Civic Movement, the political party whose policy is probably the most similar to Havel's, and whose members are Havel's old dissident-friends, suffered total defeat in the 6 June 1992 elections. This was partially a result of their administrative incompetence and indecisive policies about free market reforms and the split with Slovakia. But the absence of Havel's leadership and shared responsibility certainly contributed to their failure both on the executive branch of government and eventually in the elections. In effect, these elections and the following resignation of Havel and his aides in the presidential Hradcany castle completed a process of 'de-dissidentization' of Czech politics. One by one, the dissidents who carried on the struggle against communism since 1968, and who lead the 1989 Velvet Revolution, have been pushed out of political life.

Without political allies, Havel had no direct influence over the 1993 constitution of the Czech Republic that determined his presidential responsibilities. In effect, Havel's philosophy proved detrimental for the possibility of its realization through political means. In today's Czech Republic and Slovakia one can be in politics, or out of politics, but never above politics. By trying to be above politics, Havel threw himself out of them.

Personal Moral Responsibility

Havel's original incentive for developing non-political politics was a desire for increased personal responsibility in politics. As president, Havel has had the chance to set personal example of moral behaviour. In his speech to the joint session of the US Congress in February 1990 Havel perceived his vocation as president in listening to the call of conscience, and sounding it in politics:

> If I subordinate my political behavior to this imperative mediated to me by my conscience, I can't go far wrong. If on the contrary I were not guided by this voice, not even 10 presidential schools with 2000 of the best political scientists in the world could help me.
> This is why I ultimately decided - after resisting for a long time - to accept the burden of political responsibility. [13]

Havel perceives the role of the intellectual in politics, his vocation, as an intermediary consciousness, between the Heideggerian call of conscience to return to authenticity, and social being. The responsibility of the intellectual for the world, the hope of this world, is to represent human conscience. Havel in effect has a theory of 'trickle down conscience,' that runs something like: Being-> Conscience-> Consciousness of the philosopher-politician -> Authentic social being. Havel perceives his (the philosopher's) role in politics as representing conscience in society, leading it back to authenticity. Still, it is not clear what the content of that authenticity is, or how Havel the politician can be any more effective in leading the way to authenticity than Havel the dissident.

129

How to lead (in the pedagogical sense of the word) humanity to authenticity is one of the most difficult problems in phenomenology and existentialism. Heidegger claimed that there is no answer and we can only hope. Patocka discovered and practiced sacrifice as a road to authenticity.[14] President Havel can help destroy the negative, alienating elements: dismantle the automatic communist alienating system and deconstruct its ideology. Positively, he can tell the truth and exhort and inspire his citizens to behave according to his absolute and universalist system of values. Still, all these measures have little to do with Havel's position of political power. After the Velvet Revolution, all democratically elected governments would have dismantled the old regime and its ideology. Havel's role as 'the conscience of the nation' has nothing to do with actual political power. It only means that Havel can use the presidency as a platform to ensure that the media and the people would pay more careful attention to what he has to say, and even that, only in case they understand him. Still, there are specific cases where Havel had a clear choice between authentic moral or immoral inauthentic decisions. Karl Jaspers, following Max Weber, differentiated between 'ethics of moral conviction', and 'ethics of social responsibility'. The practitioner of ethics of moral conviction neither morally evaluates his actions according to their consequences, nor takes responsibility for the consequences of his actions. The practitioner of ethics of social responsibility takes responsibility for the foreseeable consequences of her actions, and demands that others do the same. When it comes to politics, ethics of social responsibility is far superior, in Jaspers's view, to ethics of moral conviction because:

> When the practitioner of the ethics of moral conviction wants to act, he founders because he must disavow altogether the justification of the means by the end. Since political action is bound to the specific means of force, he must be consistent and reject all action that makes use of this morally dangerous means.[15]

Yet, intellectuals, have a natural tendency toward ethics of conviction:

> ... the intellectual, the involved generalist, in contrast to the specialized and neutral expert, always opts for the ethics of conviction over the ethics of responsibility. It is choosing this ethics of conviction that for many people he or she symbolizes 'courage' and 'generosity' compared to the presumed cynicism of the ethics of responsibility--which is why 'it's better to be wrong with Sartre than right with Raymond Aron'....[16]

130

In the Czech and Slovak context, nobody would agree to be wrong with Sartre. So, this should be rephrased as 'it is better to be wrong with Patocka and Havel than be right with Klaus'. As a dissident, Vaclav Havel and his fellow dissidents had neither the chance, nor the need, to practice the ethics of social responsibility. With no political power, Havel could not use means of political force for his ends. He was responsible only for himself, and the consequences of his actions hardly changed the lives of most Czechs and Slovaks. As a dissident Havel attempted to preserve his human authenticity, his 'life in truth'. As a president with political power, there is a sudden need to differentiate means from ends, and practice consequentialist ethics (the view that the correctness of moral conduct is judged in terms of its results) of social responsibility.

As a Heideggerian, Havel regarded the political crisis that led him to power as based on a deeper crisis in the history of being. In his 1990 new year speech, Havel blames the identification of being and men with production tools and forces on the communist regime:

> The previous regime, armed with its arrogant and intolerant ideology, denigrated man into a production force and nature into a production tool. In this way they attacked their very essence and the relationship between them. It made talented people who were capable of managing their own affairs... into cogs in some kind of monstrous, ramshackle, smelly machine whose purpose no one can understand. It can do nothing more than slowly but surely wear itself down, along with all the cogs in it.[17]

This mechanization of man leads to loss of moral responsibility, as described in Havel's 1978 essay 'The Power of the Powerless' and his 1990 new year's presidential address to the Czech and Slovak people. Following Heidegger's discussion of 'everydayness' in *Being and Time* Havel claimed that in modern society, no one can be singled out for blame, while everybody is obliged to search his own soul and confront those aspects of his personality that led him to cooperate with a system that victimized him and forced him to 'live in a lie', to deny true and authentic moral identity.

> When I talk about a decayed moral environment... I mean all of us, because all of us have become accustomed to the totalitarian system, accepted it as an inalterable fact and thereby kept it running. In other words, all of us are responsible, each to a different degree, for keeping the totalitarian machine running. None of us is merely a victim of it, because all of us helped to create it together.

Why do I mention this? It would be very unwise to see the sad legacy of the past 40 years as something alien, handed down to us by some distant relatives. On the contrary, we must accept this legacy as something which we have brought upon ourselves. If we can accept this, then we will understand that it is up to all of us to do something about it. We cannot lay all the blame on those who ruled us before, not only because this would not be true but also because it would detract from the responsibility each of us now faces - the responsibility to act on our own initiative, freely, sensibly and quickly....[18]

Future Civic Forum's theoretician and Prime Minister of the Czech Republic from OH until 1992, Petr Pithart (currently an academic), while still a dissident agreed with Havel in his analysis of the broad power basis of the totalitarian regime in Czechoslovakia, of the alienating-alienated existence of most ordinary citizens, and the loss of responsibility:

> ... the Czechoslovak situation is particularly complex because it is the result of a status quo maintained by the power wielders as well as ordinary citizens. Ordinary citizens are victims of the status quo, yet they are forced to uphold it by their actions. It is now beside the point that initially, many people did not willingly support the status quo.

Pithart, like Havel, bemoaned the loss of responsibility:

> Today's nationwide decline may very well be described as consequence of people's loss of their sense of duty toward themselves, their fellow human beings, their community, their nation, their customers and partners, and (if you will) towards God.[19]

The important practical implication of this analysis is that those who cooperated with the communist authorities in Czechoslovakia should not be held responsible for their actions, should not be prosecuted, since nobody in Czechoslovakia was responsible for the totalitarianism system, while everybody contributed to a greater or lesser degree to its creation and perpetuation.

Yet, liberated Czechs (more than Slovaks) sought vengeance against those who cooperated with the communist authorities. In the case of the quislings who ran Czechoslovakia for the Soviets publicly, it is easy to determine their guilt. But most of the informers cooperated clandestinely, and since they do not admit their relationship with the communist security services, the only evidence for their co-operation is the secret files, left by the former regime.

These files are naturally less than reliable, since they may record false information when operatives may have 'invented' agents (as in Graham Greene's *Our Man in Havana*), or can be forged. For Havel, the people who cooperated with the communist authorities were alienated and alienating at the same time, and hence cannot be held responsible for their pre-Velvet Revolution actions.

Still, the Czechoslovak federal parliament adopted in early 1991 a resolution to appoint a committee to investigate the files of the communist secret service (StB) in order to find whether any of the members of parliament, and the higher echelons of the executive branches, collaborated with the totalitarian authorities. The committee operated without Western-style due process of investigation, rules of evidence, impartial judicial process, or possibility for appeal. Liberal critics of the law pointed that the accused, as in Kafka's book, can neither confront their accusers, nor know the secret evidence against them. It is impossible to observe 'due process' in judgments based on secret files where the accused can neither confront their accusers, nor examine the evidence. Supporters of the law pointed out that the law did not create a new category of criminal offence, but merely required of people holding high political office to be beyond suspicion of cooperation with the communists. Even if losing office, such a person could re-apply within five years, and meanwhile could not be penalized in any other way. Supporters of the law regard it as designed to create public confidence in the new political and legal systems. In this process of 'lustration' ten members of parliament were named as being mentioned in the files as collaborators.

Civic Movement (OH), the splinter of Civic Forum whose agenda was the most similar to Havel's held that,

> Czechoslovak society cannot be made whole if the guilt of the representatives of the Communist regime is not punished. Those who have committed crimes must be put on trial, if there are no legal obstacles. Those who bear political responsibility must accept moral judgment. However, the cleansing of Czechoslovak society must have a firm legal framework. No purges must take place. The Civic Movement disagrees with the principle of collective guilt.[20]

Havel himself, as expected, expressed his objection to lustration. In an interview he gave to the Czech magazine *Mlady Svet*, Havel claims that the new existential fear from the future, from finding one's name in the files of the secret police, can form a dramatically exciting subject for a play:

Just imagine someone who was importuned all his life by the secret police, and has learned how to take evasive action, to prevaricate and equivocate. At last, he thinks he has just about escaped their clutches, that he has successfully deceived them. After the revolution, this person feels an enormous sense of relief; now he can breathe easily because they, the secret police, can no longer bother him.... And now, suddenly, there is a new fear: he hears how, one after another, people who were marked as secret collaborators swore that they had never been collaborators, that someone had put them on a list without their knowledge, that on the basis of a single meeting in a cafe they were entered on a list of 'candidates' for secret collaboration or something worse, just so some cop would get to chalk up the credit.[21]

Havel recalls an incident when he was presented with an envelope labelled 'Vaclav Havel, born October 5, 1936... 1965-CANDIDATE... 1967-ACCEPTED,' and feeling that fear about what turned out to be his file in the Writers Union...

As president, one of Havel's functions is to sign all bills into effect. Despite his objection to the law of lustration, Havel did sign it into effect. In a lecture he gave at New York University, Havel attempted to excuse his behaviour: Had he not signed the bill, it would have gone into effect anyway, and he would have thrown his country into a destabilizing political crisis. 'It would have been a typically dissident-like, morally clean yet immensely risky act of civil disobedience.' Havel finally expressed doubts about his decision, concluding that 'history' will be the judge of the consequences of his action.

It is interesting to note the ethical shift from the ethics of conviction of Havel the dissident, toward consequentialist ethics of responsibility in Havel the president. As a dissident, Havel did not have to take into consideration the circumstances or the consequences of his actions because he hardly has the power to change either. Havel the president acquired power and accordingly, changed his philosophy and hoped that the consequences of signing the unjust bill would be better than those of not signing it.

It is hard to accept Havel's consequentialist calculation. The late Alexander Dubcek, the former reform-communist leader of the Prague Spring, at the time, speaker of the federal parliament, refused to sign this bill of lustration, and no major constitutional crisis ensued. Yet, from a philosophical perspective, the actual reason for Havel's miscalculation is not as important as the conscious shift from Kantian ethics of conviction, to consequentialist ethics of social responsibility, and the confused inexperienced way Havel practiced it. Similar examples can be brought from the cases of arms sales.

Today, Havel, the powerless president, shifts back to ethics of conviction, because his pronouncements do not influence political decisions.

Conclusion

I do not think it is warranted to conclude from the Czech experience that morality and politics cannot mix. Rather, it is important to attempt to practice the right kind of sophisticated and responsible morality. The Heideggerian inspired misinterpretation of modernity did not matter for the ethical behaviour and sacrifice of the dissidents. As politicians the Heideggerian perspective (though valuable in phenomenology) misled the dissidents to misunderstand the Western modern alternative to totalitarianism. Havel's alternative to modernity was as vague as Heidegger and as utopian as non-political-politics (in its original formulation).

Still, politics-without-morality is no superior alternative to Havel's non-political-politics. Politicians may have the technique of holding on to power, but without the correct moral compass, they may misuse this technique. Politics and politicians need philosophy and philosophers. But if philosophers are to have a positive and effective influence over politics as politicians, they must have the right kind of philosophy, and adopt ethics of responsibility. Havel and his generation of non-political politicians had the right moral principles, derived from Patocka's Charter 77 of human rights, but the incorrect philosophy of modernity and a lack of experience in the practice of ethics of social responsibility. Therefore their branch of non-political politics failed.

Notes and references

1. On Patocka and Charter 77 see: Tucker, Aviezer (1992), 'Patocka Vs. Heidegger: The Humanistic Difference', *Telos*, no. 92, pp. 85-98.
2. Havel, Vaclav (1990), *Disturbing the Peace, A conversation with Karel Hvizdala*, trans Paul Wilson, New York.
3. Havel, Vaclav (1986) 'Politics and Conscience', trans. Kohak, E and Scruton, R. in Vladislav, J. (ed), *Vaclav Havel or Living In Truth*, London: Erasmus Foundation.
4. Havel, Vaclav (1986), 'The power of the powerless' trans. P. Wilson, in *Vaclav Havel or Living In Truth*.
5. Solzhenitsyn, Alexandr, *A World Split Apart*, Commencement Address Delivered at Harvard University, June 8 1978, trans. Irina Ilovayskaya Alberti, New York, pp. 58-61. Patocka, however, did characterize this post-metaphysical age of Harmony, Being, and Love, through a Heideggerian ontic interpretation of Dostoyevsky's *Brothers Karamazov*. See the second of his two Studies on Masaryk (1976) in Patocka, Jan, *La Crise du Sens*, trans. Erica Abrams, Ousia, Brussels.
6. 'Accepting Responsibility for Our Own Future: The Election Programme of Civic Forum' (1990), in *East European Reporter*, vol. 4, no. 2.
7. 'View from the Castle' (1990), (an interview with Sasa Vondra by Jan Kavan) in *East European Reporter*, vol. 4, no. 2.
8. 'Thatcherite' in quotation marks because its rhetoric aside, it has a policy of full employment and assured protected housing.
9. Writing in the summer of 1990, I claimed that: 'Since the creation of political parties is a universal phenomenon in free societies, it is reasonable to assume that such parties will spring up in Czechoslovakia as well. In such a situation Havel and his supporters will have to choose between discarding their vision of an existential revolution in politics or abolish the right of free association'. Tucker, Aviezer, 'Vaclav Havel's Heideggerianism', *Telos*, 85, p. 76.
10. In the summer of 1990, I predicted that in the case of Civic Forum splits, the political parties 'may either keep Havel as a figure-head without real power, or abandon him as the leader of a small Green party. The least likely scenario is that Havel will succeed in implementing his reactionary policies', Ibid, p. 78.
11. Havel, Vaclav (1992), *Summer Meditation*, trans. Paul Wilson, New York. Cf. my review (1992), of *Summer Meditations* in *Telos*, no. 91, pp. 179-184.
12. See especially, Havel, Vaclav (1992), 'Politics and Conscience', trans. Erazim Kohak and Roger Scruton, in *Open Letters: Selected Writings*

1965-1990, Vintage Books, New York, pp. 249-271. Havel's Heideggerian positions about rationality, technology, and science, were influenced by those of his teacher, and the author of Charter 77, Jan Patocka.

13. Havel, Vaclav (1991), 'Address to a Joint Session of the United States Congress', Whipple, Tim, *After the Velvet Revolution: Vaclav Havel and the New Leaders of Czechoslovakia Speak Out*, New York, pp. 69-80. For a fuller analysis of Havel's address, see, Tucker, Aviezer (1992-3), 'Waiting for Meciar,' *Telos*, no. 94, pp. 167-182.

14. Patocka, Jan (1990), *Kacirske Eseje O Filosofii Dejin*, Praha, (Heretical Essays on the Philosophy of History). Cf, Tucker, Aviezer (1992) 'Sacrifice: From Isaac to Patocka', *Telos*, no. 91, pp. 117-124.

15. Erlich, Edith et.al. (1986), *Karl Jaspers: Basic Philosophical Writings*, (from Die Atombombe und die Zukunft des Menschen) trans. E. B. Ashton, Athens, Ohio, p. 418.

16. Ferry, Luc and Renaut, Alain (1990), *Heidegger and Modernity*, trans. Franklin Philip, Chicago, p. 10.

17. Havel, Vaclav, 'New Year's Address', in Wilson, Paul (ed), and trans. (1992), *Open Letters: Selected Writings 1965-1990*, New York, p. 391.

18. Ibid.

19. Pithart, Petr (1990), 'Social and Economic Developments in Czechoslovakia in the 1980's - Part 2', in *East European Reporter*, vol. 4, no. 2.

20. 'Radical but not Ruthless: Programme of the Civic Movement (abridged)' in *East European Reporter*, vol. 4, no. 4.

21. 'Uncertain Strength': (1991) An Interview with Vaclav Havel, conducted by Dana Emingerova and Lubos Beniak, trans. Paul Wilson, *The New York Review of Books*, pp. 6-8.

8. Art over Politics: European Intellectuals and the Cultural Cold War

STEVEN LONGSTAFF

The decade following World War Two was profoundly demoralizing for many European intellectuals, especially those on the non-communist left. As socialists and social democrats were confronted with the extension of Soviet power into the heart of Europe, many found themselves uneasy in their traditional anti-capitalist and anti-militarist convictions. Moreover, the new and major role of the United States in the defence of Western Europe and in its economic revival left many Europeans with a diminished sense of their own significance.

This chapter examines the efforts of the Paris-based Congress for Cultural Freedom (CCF) to capitalize on the malaise of European intellectuals in its mobilization of European scholars, writers, journalists, artists and scientists for 'Atlantacist' Cold War positions. The central proposition advanced here is that the Cold War must be seen, not just as a military-diplomatic struggle, but as a contest between cultures. In this contest intellectuals were at the forefront of the West's mobilization of anti-Soviet ideology. The centrepiece in the cultural offensive against the Soviet Union was the CCF which was secretly organized and funded by the the Central Intelligence Agency. The Congress was part of what came to be a vast network of trade unions, political parties, student organizations, news services, publishing houses, research organizations, foundations, and other philanthropic institutions either funded or penetrated, to some degree, by the CIA, but even within this empire, the Congress for Cultural Freedom must be reckoned an extraordinary initiative in Kulturpolitik: extraordinary not so much in the prestige and celebrity of its collaborators (the communists too had famous writers, painters and scientists who supported their aims), but rather in its undeniable success in realizing its goals, especially where Europe was concerned.[1]

One mission of the Congress, which became more important as Cold War tensions eased after Stalin's death in 1953, was to publish and circulate the writings of dissident intellectuals in the East, and in this and other ways to provide material and moral support for them. Concerning these programmes, which have been assessed in detail in two recent studies of the Congress,[2] it is sufficient here to acknowledge that they were carried out with scrupulous regard for the precarious existence of those who were affected. Indeed, the fact that they were largely humane in their consequences is the best available justification for the CIA's post-war cloak and dagger intervention into Europe's intellectual affairs. But these outreach operations, significant though they became, were never the primary concern of the CCF. From its beginnings in 1948 a rather more complex and elusive task presented itself to the CIA and State Department patrons of the Congress: the aim of overcoming resistance to the US dominated alliance that the Truman administration was determined to bring about.[3]

Wooing left-wing and liberal intellectuals away from Marxist views and pro-Soviet sympathies, defusing resistance to American definitions of collective security, convincing educated Europeans (despite McCarthyism) of the unique fitness of the United States to lead the West: these were the daunting objectives of the CCF. In the early years organizational and policy confusion made these aims hopelessly over ambitious. Problems and disputes within the Congress at this time mirrored fundamental disagreements within the US national security establishment. At issue was the very nature of the enemy. Was any form of peaceful coexistence possible in light of the messianic aims of the Stalinist totalitarianism? Was not the West sealing its own defeat by allowing the USSR to consolidate control over its newly acquired territories?

The clearest way to frame this debate is to see it as one between containment and liberation; the terms used by CIA advisor and Congress founder, James Burnham, who advocated an East-European strategy to break up the Soviet bloc.[4] But not everyone was willing to embrace Burnham's roll-back strategy with its exlicit threat to the USSR of nuclear annihilation. Nevertheless his ideas were widely discussed at this time within national security circles. For a time the State Department and the CIA, after its creation in 1948, were very eager to mount 'resistance-building' operations in Russia's own back yard. Indeed, shaking one or more of the satellite countries loose from the Kremlin's control seemed an enticing prospect in the late 1940s, especially after Tito's defection. Even the moderate George F. Kennan, Burnham's rival as a strategist and the author of the containment policy, made numerous speeches to this effect in 1948.[5]

Meanwhile, the Berlin blockade, the Zhdanovist cultural purges in Russia, and the outbreak in 1948 of a new round of show trials in Eastern Europe were contributing to the volatile atmosphere. Add to this the success of the

Comintern's 'peace' offensive in Western Europe and elsewhere, the rampant pro-Soviet and anti-American views of the French intellectual mainstream,[6] and it is plain to see why Burnham, and other ex-Stalinist or ex-Trotskyist intellectuals (Sidney Hook, Arthur Koestler, Irving Brown, Bertram Wolfe and Melvin J. Laskey) were called upon by the State Department and the CIA to serve as advisers in the late 1940s.

It is this contingent, at any rate, that, beginning in 1948 began organizing the West's Kampfergruppen (Fighting squads). 'Give me a hundred million dollars', Hook suggested with typical ebullience in 1949, 'and a thousand dedicated people, and I will guarantee to generate such a wave of democratic unrest among the masses - yes, even among the soldiers of Stalin's own empire, that all his problems for a long time will be internal. I can find the people'.[7]

Hook was fresh from a stint of advising the American military government in Berlin when he made this statement. To him, as well as to the others mentioned above, every possible effort had to be directed towards spreading the message of cultural and political freedom to the 'enslaved' populations of the East. Essentially, the US national-security managers and their intellectual advisers and operatives were of one mind in their mistaken beliefs about Soviet vulnerability. Hence the vehemence with which the Congress founders (Hook, Burnham, Lasky Koestler, et.al.) issued their warnings against 'coexistence' and 'neutralism' in the West.

Neutralism in this view (the acceptance of a divided Europe with communists controlling the East) was tantamount to capitulation. It was also an affliction to which British labourites and Scandinavian social democrats (groups with little experience of communism) were believed to be particularly susceptible. Such was the rallying cry of the CIA's ex-communists and ex-Trotksyists. In the short term their credibility was in doubt, but in the period 1948-50, after three years of Western pasivity in the face of the Cominterm's Kulturraegertum (carrying the banner of culture) in Germany and elsewhere their position seemed compelling.

Their initial efforts at mobilization were quite successful. The most important initiative was the launching, at the height of the Berlin blockade in 1948, of an international monthly, *Der Monat*, under Melvin Laskey's editorial direction.[8] (The youthful Lasky, a former US Army captain, with ties to *Partisan Review* and the New York literary avante-garde, was discretely funded by the US military government.) With contributions from Bertrand Russell, Arnold Toynbee, Arthur Koestler, Jean Paul Sartre, Rebecca West, Clement Greenberg and numerous other non-German notables, *Der Monat* was an overnight sensation. In 1949-50 it devoted over half its space, '230 densely packed pages in all',[9] to translations of George Orwell's *Animal Farm* and *1984*.

After this high-impact response to Germany's Lesehunger (book hunger), Lasky's notoriety knew no bounds. In Soviet circles he was frequently vilified as the 'the father of the cold war'.[10] Meanwhile there was a well attended and well publicised 'counter-rally' in New York, which was organized by Hook as a response to the Waldorf Peace Conference that American Stalinists staged in March 1949. The state department was impressed by these events and it was decided that the time had come for a more sustained drive towards cultural mobilization. Not surprisingly it fell to the enterprising Lasky to organize it.[11] The project which resulted was the founding event of the CCF; an elaborate series of open air speeches, panel discussions and press conferences staged in Berlin in June 1950.

Berlin Inaugural

Invitations were issued in the name of the esteemed mayor of Berlin, Ernst Reuter. People would be invited on an individual basis, Lasky had earlier explained, and the host would be pleased to pay for the travel, hotel and other expenses of the invited guests out of 'counterpart' funds.[12]

In the event, some 117 Americans and Europeans and one Asian (from 119 different countries) heeded the call. As the delegates assembled on June the 25th and 26th, 1950, news of the North Korean invasion of the South reached the divided city and reinforced the martial air of the proceedings. The conference prospectus informed delegates that they had been invited as 'the intelligentsia of the free world'. The Berlin event would be a first attempt at, 'openly discussing and formulating an independent program for the defense of their democratic ideals'. But in a keynote address Arthur Koestler declared that the time for discussion had passed. Not debate but action was the order of the day. 'You don't argue in the front line. Let your communication be Yea, Yea, Nay, Nay' Koestler intoned, quoting Mathew to an audience of cheering Berliners. Anything else, any attempt at compromise with communism, would be suicidal.

Berliners, who flocked in their thousands to the main sessions, were given plenty to cheer about over the five day event. There were dramatic appearances by intellectual refugees from the East bloc, elaborate denunciations of the 'total unfreedom' existing beyond the Brandenburg Gate, messages of solidarity for the artists and writers in the satellite countries and ringing endorsement of the American intervention in Korea. What had been billed as a series of productive discussions was turning out

141

to be another Wroclaw, the Wroclaw of the ex-communists, or so it appeared to many of the French, Scandinavian, and British participants, whose restiveness increased with every declamatory challenge to the Kremlin.[13]

'Yes we are converts from communism, and proud of it', Austrian writer Franz Borkenau shouted towards the end of a panel discussion on 'The Defence of Peace and Freedom'. Earlier Borkenau had delivered a stinging rebuke to liberals and social democrats, arguing that communism was a dialectical outgrowth of liberalism's utopian emphasis on individual freedom. Gesticulating wildly he went on to declare that past guilt must be atoned for; that ex-communists alone understood communism and ways of combatting it, even if liberals might disapprove of their methods. Communism, he concluded, meant 'war and war and war and civil war and civil war and civil war'. It could only be destroyed by uncompromising frontal attack.

Borkenau's seemingly wild statements captured the adversarial dichotomy the Congress planners sought to project, while the moderate tones of liberals and social democrats were seen as a liability. As another Congress insider, Ignazio Silone, put it: 'the final battle would be between communists and ex-communists'. Prior to Borkenau's outburst, which was applauded deliriously by the mostly German audience, Burnham and Koestler had also been expiatiating on this theme, with Burnham using the occasion to excoriate the British and other West Europeans for clinging to the old battle cries of the left. Socialism versus capitalism and left versus right were redundant categories, argued Burnham. The only issue now was that of 'relative freedom versus total tyranny'. He believed the British to be so wedded to outmoded conceptions as to be constitutionally incapable of responding to Stalinist realities.[14]

Burnham believed that a well disciplined organization was necessary to combat the Soviet threat. He advocated a United Front in which all the anti-communist elements would take their orders from a leadership dominated by former Marxists and communists; those who understood the true nature of the struggle. In the same spirit Burnham also castigated those non-communists who had expressed reservations about the atomic bomb. There were 'good' as well as 'bad' bombs, 'white' as well as 'black'. Moreover, it happened to be the case that the 'good' American bombs had been Europe's sole defence for the past five years. Yes, he concluded, let us have peace. But there was only one way to peace: through freedom. And that would only be assured through total victory over communism.[15]

As at the Soviet sponsored Wroclaw Peace Conference in 1948, where a few westerners led by Julian Huxley and A.J.P.Taylor were finally moved to protest against the regimented lying and viciousness of the communist speakers, so the verbal pyrotyechnics of Burnham, Koestler, and Borkenau finally proved too much for some of the Berlin delegates, whose indignation over the illiberal and warlike tone of the proceedings now hardened into outright revolt. When the managers of the Congress presented a 'Manifesto on Freedom', drafted by Koestler, which stated that totalitarianism had 'no right to citizenship in the republic of Spirit', the British made a formal protest. Led by A. J. Ayer and Hugh Trevor-Roper, this group was defeated in the special committee charged with considering the manifesto, but carried their protest to a plenary session. There, according to Trevor-Roper, the Danish and Norwegian delegates threatened to leave the conference if the 'English amendment' were voted down. Also French and Italian delegates rallied to the recalcitrants side. In the face of this concerted opposition, the offending passage was withdrawn, but despite this Hook and Burnham protested to the bitter end. Some other passages, offered by Trevor-Roper and Ayer with the intention of lending the document a less self-satisfied and complacent air regarding civil liberties in the West, were added to Koestler's draft. Thus revamped, the manifesto won the support of all the delegates; an achievement trumpeted in subsequent Congress literature.

The Wroclawe Manifesto, significantly enough, had failed to receive unanimous support. But the concessions at Berlin to the 'incorrigible liberalism' of the West Europeans were only partly successful in clearing the air. Later, when it was time to select a standing committee to oversee the establishment of a permanent Congress for Cultural Freedom, no further risks were taken with democracy. The members of this continuation committee, stated Trevor-Roper, 'were not elected in the normal way, but nominated by the managers of the Congress'. Not surprisingly Ayer and Trevor-Roper were excluded, despite the obvious support for their views, and despite the fact that they were the only two English delegates who had taken a consistent part in the proceedings.[16]

The Berlin meeting thus broke up on a note of rancour, which took the organizers by surprise. The negative reaction also led to an abrupt change of direction, especially after reports of the meeting appeared in the French, Italian and British press, focusing on the exaggerated flamboyance of the ex-communist stars of the proceedings, even the most staunchly Atlanticist of these papers - le Monde, The Manchester Guardian and Rome's II Mondo - gave the meeting a lukewarm reception.[17] But if a frontal assault on the West European drift towards co-existence, (i.e. acceptance of the East-West stalemate) had proved ineffective, then how was such 'neutralism' to be opposed, especially among European elites? By the same token, how was America's leadership of the 'Free world' to be promoted and justified? Certainly not by a rallying call for liberation of the East at the cost of peace.

143

Nor by insisting, a la Hook and Burnham, on the curtailment of the democratic rights of Western communists and fellow travellers.

The identity of the CIA officer who ordered the tactical volte-face which followed in the wake of the Berlin meeting remains a mystery. In any event, Koestler and Burnham, whose names by this time had become bywords for anti-Soviet bellicosity in Western Europe,[18] soon found themselves isolated within the fledgling organization, and then permanently sidelined.[19] Brown, the American Federation of Labour's representative in Europe, and the initial conduit between the CCF and the CIA, was soon replaced in this capacity by a more plausible benefactor. Both he and Sidney Hook, though they continued to serve on the organization's executive committee, saw their influence diminish. As for Lasky, a disciple of Burnham's, as editor of *Der Monat* and later *Encounter*, he did continue to play a major role in the Congress, but only after undergoing a quiet change of heart.

Meanwhile, and to the disgust of the hardliners, plans for another Berlin-style rally to be held in Paris were shelved, and individuals with a less conspicuous cold war aura, such as Stephen Spender the poet and the composer Nicholas Nabokov, were appointed to key positions.

At Berlin, artists had been conspicuous by their absence. 'Besides myself,' Nabokov tartly recalled, 'There wasn't a single musician, painter, sculptor or even a poet.'[20] This was to change abruptly when the Congress established itself as a permanent organization, with headquarters not in Berlin, as originally mooted, but in Paris.

Art Over Politics

Nabokov was soon to become an important instrument of this change. Named Secretary General of the Congress's 'International Secretariat' in the Autumn of 1950, he took up his position the next spring and, together with Julius 'Junkie' Fleischmann, set about organizing a spectacular festival of music, painting, sculpture and literature. Fleischman, a scion of the famous yeast and gin family, had a genuine philanthropic interest in the arts and was thus a very plausible conduit for CIA funds.[21] Entitled 'Masterpieces of the Twentieth Century', the festival opened in Paris in April 1952, with a truly staggering lineup of events and performers. There were new and specially commissioned ballets and operas; a selection of works by 65 modern composers, with special emphasis on those forbidden in the USSR; a special exhibition of art, from Matisse to Henry Moore, with panel discussions chaired by the Director of the Paris Museum of Modern Art on 'The Spirit of Painting in the 20th Century'. Also there were six literary forums bringing together 75 leading writers from all corners of the globe and special American attractions, such as the Boston Symphony Orchestra and the New York City Ballet. Finally, there were the great celebrities, including Stravinsky, Menahin, Ballanchine and William Faulkner. 'My dream Festival', as Nabokov called it privately.[22] Publicly he depicted it as an answer to communist claims about Western civilization; that it was corrupt, culturally bankrupt and incapable of anything more than cheap commercialism or parasitic snobbery in the arts.

> We will take up the challenge ...; we shall appear at the trial of Western civilization and show, with concrete evidence, that our civilizaton is alive and, indeed, more vigorous and creative than ever. We shall mobilize in the face of the totalitarian empires - which have reduced art and thought to slavery and can now produce little more than massive postcards, busts of generals, and military marches - all the artistic and intellectual riches produced by the societies of the West through free research and spontaneous creation: the Masterpieces of the 20th Century![23]

For all the sententiousness of this curtain-raising speech, the organizers had the wisdom to let the performances and art works speak for themselves, with only the subtlest, most ingratiating reminders of the communist regimes' hostility to the explicit modernism of the month long programme. Missing was the call to arms that had marked the Berlin inaugural. Despite some carping in the French press over the size and lavishness of the American cultural 'invasion', the Parisian cultural elite were clearly impressed. Elle, the fashion magazine, devoted a whole issue to 'How to Dress for the Festival of the 20th Century', and the French government even made Fleischman a *Chevalier de la legion d'honneur* in recognition of his role as patron. As for the real patrons they too were impressed. The point after all, was not so much to put Western culture on display as show off the best of American art and artists, 'in the teeth of European contempt for us as uncultivated', as one State department official put it.[24] On that score US foreign-policy managers reckoned they got their money's worth.

The image of boorish and uncultivated America was only one concern, however. The point was also 'to lure European intellectuals into some contact with Congress attitudes'.[25] Hence the art exhibits, symphony tours, music conferences, painting competitions, commemorative literary events and scientific meetings that followed in the wake of the festival's success. Lecture tours to the Far East and other distant places by various 'Ambassadors of Letters' were likewise arranged.[26] Typically these were undertaken by celebrated, but mostly superannuated poets, such as Spender, James T. Farrell and John Dos Passos. Nabokov's role at these events was that of the 'attendant lord'. He officiated and oversaw proceedings.

> ...one that will do
> To swell a progress, start a scene or two,
> Advise the prince; no doubt an easy tool,
> Deferential, glad to be of use,
> Politic, cautious, and meticulous,
> Full of high sentence, but a bit obtuse;[27]

Obtuse at any rate in thinking that his pose   as head of the International Secretariat of the Congress, or master strategist of its 'rational, ice-cold, determinedly intellectual war against Stalinism' was likely to convince anyone with more than a passing knowledge of the CCF's affairs.[28]

W.H. Auden once described his friend 'Nicky' (with whom he had collaborated on an opera of *Love's Labour's Lost)*, as too sociable a person to do justice to his musical talent.[29] An affable 'flaneur', who, by his own admission had taken thirteen years to 'worm' his way back to New York from the 'bleak American provinces', Nabokov was no strategist, but he was the ideal front man for the CIA's most important instrument in the war of culture. Born into an aristocratic family that had fled Russia at the time of the revolution, Nabokov had collaborated with Diaghilev in his youth. He was an associate of Stravinsky, Prokofiev and Koussevitsky. His 'small but firm reputation'[30] was chiefly the result of works commissioned in the forties by the Boston Symphony and Philadelphia orchestras. He had also served as a 'chief cultural assistant' in Berlin after the War and for six months on the voice of America. In short he had credentials and connections to exploit, especially in the State department, and he knew how to take orders. Giving the orders in this particular instance was a shadowy figure out of US military intelligence named Michael Josselson, who some months after the Berlin fiasco was installed at the centre of the stymied organization, assuming the title of Administrative Secretary of the Congress.

In a manoeuvre that clearly indicated the delicate nature of Josselson's position, the names of some 25 international office holders and executive committeee members appeared on the Congress's stationery, but not that of its all-powerful Administrative Secretary. Born in 1908 in Estonia, into a middle-class Jewish family, Josselson had attended a gymnasium in Berlin during the 1920s, had fled Hitler's Germany in the 1930s and gone to Paris, where he worked as a representative for American department stores. He then moved on to the United States, where he served in the army and later

146

joined the Office of Strategic Services (OSS), operating at first in a propaganda unit and then as an enemy interrogator. After the war he supervised the American licensed press in Berlin as well as helping in the rehabilitation of prominent NAZI figures in the Arts.

Josselson also joined the CIA. Probably this was the key reason why he hid behind Nabokov and titular president Denis de Rougement at the CCF. But Josselson had the decision-making power, he had the last word about magazine projects, editorial appointments, lecture tours, conference participants and, of course, funding issues. A superb linguist, with an excellent command of German, French and fluency in other languages, including Russian, he was by all accounts a man of wide-ranging interests and considerable charm. Stephen Spender, spoke of his 'real culture, imagination and humanity', while to Daniel Bell, who spent a year in Paris working under him, Josselson was an 'absolutely extraordinary human being'.[31] But the key to his success in orchestrating so many talents, personalities and influences was hardly his interest, his charm, nor his interest in culture, much less in cultural freedom. It was his extraordinary canniness about intellectual motives and susceptibilities; coupled with his willingness to have others coin the phrases, write the articles, deliver the interviews and travel to exotic parts of the globe as defenders of Western culture.

Josselson's cool professionalism was thoroughly tested in the first years of the CCF's existence, most notably by the disgruntled hard-liners, loosely grouped around Sydney Hook in New York, who dominated the American Committee for Cultural Freedom (ACCF). 'The main activity of the Congress must be to make demonstrations, to take principled stands and to involve European Intellectuals - not to mobilize the work of artists', fumed *Commentary* editor Elliot Cohen in June, 1951, when news of Nabokov's 'dream festival' reached New York. Hook for his part, felt that the Parisians were far from lacking opportunities to hear modern music and see modern art. He would favour such an event only if it were expanded into a 'Festival of Arts, Letters and Politics'. This idea was unanimously adopted by the ACCF's executive committee, who also proposed that a smaller, 'unpretentious' conference be convened in Paris in the Autumn of 1951. It should deal with such 'political' topics as 'Religion and the Struggle for Survival of Western Civilization' and the 'New European Resistance'. The American Committee was greatly concerned with the issue of French neutralism; it had to be dealt with immediately and head on. So the ACCF stated in a communique to Paris.[32] But none of these alarms and proposals had any effect on the CCF's International Secretariat, which continued to

147

forge blithely ahead with 'Masterpieces of the 20th Century' and related projects.

What the CCF leadership correctly grasped was that the political climate in America was already too extreme for European sensitivities. With McCarthyism, the McCarran Act, the trial of the Rosenbergs and the pledges by Eisenhower, during the 1952 residential campaign, that the Republicans would roll back the USSR in Eastern Europe. The last thing Josselson and Nabokov wanted to hear was the fundamentalist diatribe of former communists and Trotskyists on the American Committee. After all, the point was to highlight the deficiencies of the USSR, not to emulate them. Thus the American Committee were informed that the hostility of the European press and public opinion dictated a non-polemical approach. Even the uncompromising cold-warrior Irving Brown was of the opinion that political activity in Europe was 'almost impossible'.[33]

What the American Committee wasn't told, however, was that one after another of the CIA's 'resistance building' operations in Eastern Europe had been rolled up by Soviet security forces, leaving the United States little hope it 'might contest the (the Russians) on their own territory'. Necessarily after 1951: 'the battlegrounds of the Cold War ... were to lie elsewhere'.[34] For the CCF under Josselson, elsewhere chiefly meant Latin America, India, Japan and other parts of the Far-East. At Berlin the Congress had presented itself to the world as a movement of Europeans and Americans dedicated to overcoming the great 'Ausseinandersetzung' (sundering) of Eastern and Western Europe. But as early as March 1951 a large international meeting of Asians, Europeans and Americans was held in Bombay. Thereafter an increasingly substantial part of the Congress's budget was devoted to bombarding elites in Asia and elsewhere in the Third World with Western cultural propaganda. The great ideological contest had begun.[35]

Notes and references

1. For an account of the role of the CIA in the CCF see Braden, Thomas, A. 'I'm glad the CIA is Immoral', *The Saturday Evening Post*, May 20, 1967, p. 10.
2. Gremion, Pierre (1988), *Le congres pour le liberte de la culture en Europe, 1957-1967,* Centre national de le research scientifique, Paris. Also Coleman, Peter (1989), *The Liberal Conspiracy: The Congress for Cultural Freedom and the Struggle for the Mind of Postwar Europe*, Collier Macmillan, London.
3. For an account of the unity of economic and military policy for Europe in the Truman administration see Leffler, M. P. (1993), *A Preponderance of Power: National Security, the Truman Administration and the Cold War*, Stanford University Press, Stanford, CA, p. 235.
4. Burnham, James (1952), *Containment or Liberation*, John Day, New York.
5. Leffler, *Preponderance of Power*, pp. 235-236.
6. Cf. Judt, Tony, *Past Imperfect: French Intellectuals, 1944-1956*, University of Caliornia Press, Berkeley, pp. 187-204.
7. *Politics*, VI, (Winter, 1949), p. 36.
8. See, Longstaff, S. A. (1993), 'Missionary in a Dark Continent': Der Monat and Germany's Intellectual Regeneration', *History of European Ideas*, XXI, no. 1, pp. 93-99.
9. Rodden, John (1989), *The Politics of Literary Reputation: the Making of 'St George' Orwell*, Oxford University Press, New York.
10. Interview with Melvin Lasky, June 14, 1990.
11. Nabokov, Nicholas (1975), *Bagazh: Memoirs of a Russian Cosmopolitan,* Atheneum, New York, p. 239. In fact the claim that the monies came from Marshall plan funds is probably fraudulent. More likely the source was the CIA via the American Federation of Labour.
12. Koestler, Arthur (1955), *The Trail of the Dinosaur*, Collins, London, p. 183.
13. Trevor-Roper, H. R., 'The Berlin Congress', *Manchester Guardian*, (July 10, 1950), p. 10.
14. Ibid.
15. Quoted in Mendelssohn, Peter (1950), 'Berlin Congress', *New Statesman and Nation*, July 15, p. 62.
16. Trevor-Roper, 'Berlin Congress'.
17. See Arnold, G. L. (1950), 'The German Reviews', *Nineteenth Century*, CXLVIII, Nov, p. 247.

18. Diggins, J.P. (1975), *Up From Communism: Conservative Odysseys in American Intellectual History*, Harper Row, New York, p. 251.
19. According to Kevin J. Smant, Burnham's ties to the CIA ended in 1952. See, Smant, K. J. (1992), *How Great the Triumph: James Burnham, Anticommunism and the Conservative Movement*, Maryland University Press, Lanham.
20. Nabokov, *Bagazah*, p. 240.
21. CIA funds for the CCF and other organizations were channelled through dummy foundations such as the Farfield Foundation, which was created in 1952 with Fleischamn as president.
22. Nabokov, *Bagazah*, p. 243.
23. Luethy, Herbert (1952), 'Selling Paris on Western Culture', *Commentary*, XIV, p. 71.
24. Donnelly, Albert, J. Jr. memo to Julius Fleischman, (Nov. 6, 1951), *American Commmittee for Cultural Freedom Papers*, Taminent Institute, New York University.
25. Braden, 'I'm Glad the CIA is Immoral', p. 11.
26. ACCF Executive Committee Minutes, (15/2/52).
27. Elliot, T. S. (1962), 'The Love Song of J. Alfred Prufrock', in *The Waste Land and Other Poems*, Harcourt Brace and World, New York, p. 8.
28. Nabokov, *Bagazah*, p. 242.
29. See Carpenter, Humphrey (1981), *W. H. Auden: A Biography*, Houghton Miffin, Boston, p. 428.
30. Ibid, p. 428.
31. Spender, Stephen (1978), *The Thirties and After*, Random House, New York, p. 128.
32. ACCF Executive Committee Minutes, (6/6/51).
33. Ibid, (12/3/52).
34. Powers, Thomas (1979), *The Man Who Kept the Secrets: Richard Helms and the CIA*, Alfred Knopf, New York, pp. 57-58.
35. See, Lasch, Christopher (1967), 'The Cultural Cold War', *Nation* (Sept 11), p. 202.

9. Intellectuals and the American Security State

PHILIP K. LAWRENCE

In 1945 the United States emerged as the undisputed, one great power of the post-World War Two era. This power was manifest in numerous resources at America's disposal. The 20 billion dollar gold reserves, the 12m men/women in uniform, the fact that the US produced 50% of the world's manufactured goods and owned half the world's shipping.[1] However, amongst this inventory of global might there was a technology which made previous military instruments seem insignificant. Through the efforts of scientists and administrators, working on the largest engineering project in history, the US possessed the atomic bomb. Initially justified as a counter to a possible NAZI weapon the bomb brought the war to a dramatic end in August 1945. Its awesome power was revealed in the attack on Hiroshima where in a matter of minutes 68,000 individuals perished, while another 76,000 were seriously injured.[2] The casualty statistics, though, were not really the point. The issue was that one weapon could destroy a whole city. Immediately, then, it was necessary to speculate on the possible effects of the use of 50 or perhaps a hundred of such devices. More specifically, in the United States, a debate began amongst military planners concerning the impact that atomic weapons would and should exert on military doctrine and real defence policy.

While the technology itself was unique so too was the US's geo-strategic position and its need to develop a grand strategy, virtually from scratch. In the following decades this was achieved with remarkable speed. What was extraordinary about this process was the degree of involvement of intellectuals in it. Thus a distinctive feature of American thinking on defence in the post 1945 period has been the power and influence it has accorded to intellectuals. As William Kincade notes, 'What stands out, however, in contrast to the strategy-making of other powers and times, is the role of the civilian or 'scientific' American strategists and the influence of their theories

...'.[3] My aim in this chapter is to reflect on the causes and consequences of this process and to chart and illustrate some aspects of its evolution.

Knowledge and Power

It is not usually supposed that intellectuals are close to the apex of political power. However, special circumstances concerning the atomic bomb and the American state have given specific academics and intellectuals more power than is usually recognized. In the first place the bomb was an intellectual project. Its very feasibility was suggested to Roosevelt by Einstein as counter to a possible Nazi bomb. Subsequently, a scientist became head of the Manhattan Project and Oppenheimer and others then attained enormous power through the aegis of the Atomic Energy Commission. But what is even more unusual is that social scientists accrued significant power within the US state. According to Rothstein intellectuals of a Realist orientation filled a gap within the American state which resulted from the US not having a long standing foreign policy-making elite. Many of these were European emigres whose experience of totalitarian regimes in Europe gave them strong reasons to support the ideological slant of US style liberalism.[4] In addition the new global responsibilities of the US and the security dilemmas created by the bomb gave a quantum leap to the required amount of intellectual work needed in the area of policy advice and guidance.

In military circles the use of intellectual expertise was already established by the practise of recruiting special services operatives from universities. The whole image and career of the academic/intellectual in the US in the post-War period has been different from that in Europe. In Germany the role of universities in supporting the Nazis in the twenties and thirties undercut their potential as agents of the state. In other European states the strength of communism in the twenties and thirties in academia led to similar problems of trust. But the post-war American experience was that there was a significant residue of loyalty that could be tapped. In International Relations the trust in intellectuals was enhanced because scholars were committed to the very tenets of Cold-War practice which embodied their theoretical horizons. As Michael Banks notes, 'So confident were many of the authors of their understanding of the basic political structures of the world and the forces that moved them, that they permitted the discipline to become the handmaiden of superpower rivalry'.[5]

Another important reason why certain academics and intellectuals attained power is that the decision making in the sphere of nuclear weapons planning was highly secretive. The general population had some idea of what nuclear policy entailed, but the detail was utterly secret. The secrecy also entailed a degree of conspiracy between certain agencies as in some cases it presupposed deception. A recent BBC Panorama of 9/3/94 revealed a series of covert nuclear experiments in the US where citizens were exposed to radiation without their knowledge or consent. It was done with the conivance of a handful of scientists and it was successfully kept dark. In the apocalyptic confrontation with the USSR it was believed in some quarters that such steps were justified. In January 1950 when the decision was made to build the H-bomb no more than a hundred individuals knew of this epochal move.[6] Throughout the 1950s the establishment remained suspicious of any processes that would widen the base of informed opinion. In the early 1950s attempts by Scientific American to publish critical articles were prevented by the AEC which had thousands of copies burned.[7]

In academic debate on strategy the key institution was the RAND Corporation. Here scientists and social scientists were pondering the question of nuclear war. But there was no sense of needing to contribute to public opinion. RAND, originally part of Douglas Aircraft, was working for the Airforce. As Fred Kaplan explains, '... there was the elitist assumption, pervasive at RAND, that influencing military officers and Pentagon officials was what really counted, that airing views to the general public served no purpose and might, in fact, be seen as displaying disloyalty to RAND's sponsor the US Air Force'.[8] In this climate there was no concern for any ethical problems that might be created by secrecy. Through think-tanks, such as RAND, individual academics could be recruited when it was clear that they were completely loyal. Other colleagues would often not know what work was being undertaken. Thus the whole process was under very strict control, a situation which persisted until the mid-1960s when Vietnam split US campuses and ended bipartisanship on issues of foreign policy.

Strategy and Legitimacy

The significance of the work of the planners in the 50s was that it created a taxonomy; a framework through which nuclear issues came to be grasped. The concepts developed disclosed the world of nuclear planning in a language which was acceptable to the political elite and also useful in the sphere of political justifications. As I shall argue this was the critical contribution that intellectuals could make. The potential for concern and agitation over nuclear issues was immense. In elite circles there was often anxiety, as when Eisenhower screened the top secret film Operation Ivy (1953) in the White House. In the film an entire atoll disappears in the wake of an H-bomb test; according to Spencer Weart, Eisenhower and others present, were visibly shaken by the scale of the destruction.[9] Hence I shall contend that there was a need for a mode of discourse which removed the neurosis and anxiety from nuclear speculation. As I have argued elsewhere a key reason why this was possible is that nuclear strategic theory lacks empirical data. There has been no concrete realm of lived experience to contradict the extrapolations of the theorists of Armageddon. Also the theorists were spreading a message that was attractive. If there was to be nuclear war then we would hope that it could be controlled, that we could recover, that civilian targets could be avoided and that perhaps, in some bizarre sense, the West could win. The last point was very significant in military circles as motivating the armed forces to merely enact suicide, when the loss of their own society was certain, would not be easy. It is not surprising, then, that USAF and SAC found the doctrine of Mutual Assured Destruction distasteful. Nor is it surprising that in the late 1970s and the 80s intellectuals, such as Colin Gray, were recruited to help find a route away from strategic stalemate.

The growth of state power in the sphere of defence had the potential to raise enormous problems. In the US traditional values tend against big government and permanent and large military institutions. Moreover, with nuclear weapons the problems were amplified in a number of respects. Atomic weapons raised the spectre of global destruction and were likely to frighten the domestic population. Thus, as Michael Howard pointed out some years ago, reassurance is a vital component of nuclear deterrence. In addition nuclear weapons necessitate secrecy and heightened internal security to prevent theft, sabotage and contamination. Their presence in society is, in itself, a cause of tension and anxiety. Because of this the nuclear state must appear 'in control' of its nuclear operations. Policies which include the possibility of nuclear confrontation need to be seen as rational and credible.

Anxieties about nuclear security are not just a question for the general population; as I indicated above they pervade political elites as well. Ever since America has had nuclear weapons some political leaders, scientists and strategists have contested their legitimacy and morality. Scientists, in particular, have been ambivalent about their own creations. In order to fashion hegemony the state has thus faced conflicts, division and naked anxiety. However, the nuclear state in the United States did secure a consensus on nuclear security. The means and style of achieving this have varied, with overt coercion an ingredient in the 1950s. However, a key element in the articulation of nuclear security has been the discourse of the civilian intellectuals who fashioned a cohesive ideology of nuclear rationality. Michael MccGwire sees it thus: ' ...in America, a significant

154

proportion of government officials and consultants in the fields of defense and foreign policy have been drawn from those who have taught or studied these theories at university. It was these theories that defined the agenda and provided the strategic discourse throughout NATO'.[10] Particularly in the 1950s and 1960s a liberal and technocratic colonization of the public space of defence was achieved in the United States. From the mid 1960s the academic community was split, but not those advising on the issues of nuclear weapons. As Colin Gray has recently affirmed in *Political Studies* the community of advisers remained committed to a consensus even in the turbulent 1980s.[11]

The significance of the earlier nuclear discourse arises from the particular problematic of nuclear security. With conventional war it is necessary in domestic society to present the 'face of the enemy'. Propaganda discourse justifies the fate of the adversary through the articulation of powerful negative images. In the Gulf war the US public was subjected to prolonged propaganda about the Iraqis and, in particular, Saddam Hussein. Above all else this propaganda inserted a genuine sense of threat and hostility in the public space where the war was debated and justified. But the Gulf war was always going to be won, there was no risk of nuclear escalation and the USSR was sidelined. By way of contrast this approach could never work with nuclear conflict. A nuclear showdown always needed to be a step away from reality. It was necessary to dramatize a threat; but this was geo-strategic not personal. Nuclear diplomacy was not typically an exchange of insults and overt threats. My thesis is that the strongest hegemony over nuclear issues was attained by a liberal/technocratica; a fusion of 'reasonableness' with scientism and instrumental rationality. In other words a clear attempt to fashion a modernist interpretation of nuclear policy. In the US ready made discourses existed concerning a modernist understanding of American destiny and the role of science in that destiny. The discourse of nuclear control sat comfortably on prepared ground.

Traditional Concerns

From a traditional liberal viewpoint the role of intellectuals in defence planning raises difficult questions about the relationship between the state and universities and also the moral responsibilities of intellectuals. In Hitler's Germany two contradictory trends in this area had both appeared equally disastrous. On the one hand scholarship for its own sake and ascetic aloofness insulated academics from the effects of state brutalism; on the other obedience to the legitimate authorities and the belief in the state as the ultimate arbiter of ends incorporated German universities into the NAZI's grotesque plans for extermination, slavery and eugenics. As the intellectual exile Franz Neumann revealed, his career at Breslau, Leipzig, Rostock and Frankfurt was blighted by anti-semitism and other manifestations of restoration and nationalist ideologies. But Neumann explains how the arrival of the totalitarian state made impossible a situation that was already difficult for intellectuals because of nationalism. In the nation-state we see, 'the bureaucratization of modern society and, with it, the trend to transform the intellectual into a functionary of society'.[12] But in totalitarian systems there exists a need to, 'completely control man's thoughts, and ... thus transform culture into propaganda'.[13]

In certain respects Neumann's comments go to the heart of the major dillemma I wish to highlight in this chapter. Post-War reflection on the issue of the role of intellectuals has tended to see any problem as existing in the totalitarian context. But in principle the Nuremburg trials highlighted legal criteria which transcended the jurisdiction of the nation-state. However, intellectuals in the US mainstream, who offered their services to the containment, warfare state seemed oblivious to reflection on some of the inherent problems this posed. One reason for this is an inherent narcissism which seems implicit in Enlightenment narratives concerning the West. But the Enlightenment model of the university and of the intellectual was already outmoded. The dominant understanding of what the purpose of universities was in the twentieth century had changed dramatically. A century or more earlier American universities had often celebrated an Enlightenment yearning for critical self reflection and open debate which corresponds to the classical liberal view of intellectual life. In his plans for the University of Virginia, Jefferson believed the academy should, 'unmask their usurpation, and monopolies of honours, wealth and power'.[14] But by the 1900s the twin aims of higher education had become scholarship and service. As regards the latter Socrates had posed the dilemma as one between the inclination to combat or to cater. By 1945 it was clear which of these was the guiding light in the US. As Roszak remarked, '... service came to mean the indiscriminate adaptation of the university to every demand that monied interests and the general public could make.'[15] According to the same author this has culminated in a situation where, '... the ideal of service has matured into a collaboration between the universities, the corporate world and the government.'[16]

During World War II the links between the state, business and academia were both necessary and uncontroversial. However, for some scientists, disquieting signs were apparent before 1945. In 1944, as US troops occupied Stuttgart, the failure of the Germans to get close to production of atomic weaponry became clear. In consequence scientists on the Manhattan Project began to argue that the bomb need not be used in anger. The scientists, though, were quickly rebutted and in some cases doubts about state policy began to emerge. What should have been clear was that traditional understandings of the role of science in society no longer applied. In the interwar years the greatest natural scientists had worked together with little regard for national interests and state power. The scientists comprised a community committed only to truth. But the rise of the NAZIs and the persecution of Jewish and other scientists brought state power brutally into the world of intellectual enquiry. At the beginning of World War Two American and British atomic scientists could no longer risk the open discussion of their work. Particularly with the military promise of nuclear fission the state moved to colonize the terrain of intellectual endeavour.

In World War Two the justification for this was an obvious expediency. But the temporary measures meant to harness intellectual power became a way of life. The institutionalization of a security threat in the form of the Cold War created an enduring legitimacy for 'patriotic' scientific endeavour. Clearly, I regard this as controversial, but let us look at another point of view. In his book *Strategic Studies* Colin Gray takes up the precise issue that we are dealing with here.[17] Gray declares immediately and honestly that the strategic analyst seeks political influence: 'In addition, he has always sought to balance scholarly professional work with public policy advocacy'.[18] The brief of the analyst is to, '...discover ways in which the US can preserve vital interests and function in the international order as a global superpower'.[19] Gray also concedes the epistemic weakness of strategy; 'Unlike many other fields of inquiry, strategy does not entail a quest after truth'.[20] Following Bernard Brodie Gray takes the line that the issue in strategy is practical: simply, will the idea work?

Some of these ideas were reiterated in a recent review article by Gray in *Political Studies*. In my view he rightly chastized some of the more bizarre and idealistic claims that have recently made about international peace and order.[21] However, the problems evident in his earlier work remain. Realists such as Gray are, in my belief, too closely tied up with the practices of the state. What I fail to see is how the analytical procedures of intellectual investigation lead to the normative commitment, in this case, to support the US state in its practices of securing particular advantages for one polity. Why is the policy expert loyal to the US state? This question never arises and reveals a residue of unconsciousness concerning normative aspects of the project. The ideological decision to be loyal is simply incorporated into the technical endeavours of the policy expert. It may be that the US state is actually pursuing policies which are disastrous for the rest of the world. I am not suggesting this for one minute, the point is that Gray is tying his endeavours as a scholar to a specific and particular interest. In Gray's work this arises because certain central features of political life are immutable. The key concept is force, the central datum is conflict and in the international arena rivalry and nuclear weapons are facts of life.[22] According to Gray critics wrongly see defence analysts as warmongers because they do not invent the reality they describe or theorize. There is an immutable datum that defines international relations: 'Deplorable though it may be, the fact remains that the world of international politics is a jungle wherein the strong and ruthless devour the weak'.[23]

But these are not 'facts', this view characterizes one paradigm in International Relations which Gray is assuming is the only tenable position by according it ontological primacy. By downplaying theory in this way he can also present his discourse as the 'world'. However, the field of international politics is not an obvious datum that can be read off mechanically. It is a terrain of interpretation. Whether Nicaragua was a threat to the USA is not a factual question, but rather an issue laced with interpretive and ideological elements. Similarly there can be no obvious rendering of an issue such as the US embargo against Cuba or US behaviour towards Vietnam after the end of the Vietnam War. More generally the question of the former central balance; the conflict with the USSR, was also never a datum. A passage in the earlier book shows how the contentious can be reduced to the obvious: 'The general military fact underlying this book is the appreciation that the United States must endure, through much of the 1980s, a condition of multi-level weakness vis-à-vis the USSR'.[24] An alternative view is that because of the views of analysts such as Gray the US spent around one thousand million dollars contending with an adversary that was imploding. The technical advice, the policy advocacy, was not some value-free expertise which came from a substantive body of theory and data characterized by epistemic rigour. This advice; advice actually given to the Reagan administration, represented the opinion of strategists such as Gray that the US had been too soft with the USSR and that a tougher line was indicated. It is essential to realize that the policy advocacy of the nuclear was deeply embedded within ideology. Certain intellectuals were providing rationalizations for what were often highly contentious policies. Looking back Gray believes the policies that were advocated were an outstanding success: 'As statecraft, the US defence programmes of the 1980s were politically successful beyond the wildest dreams of their most enthusiastic supporters'.[25] I would suggest that the jury is still out on this issue. With the criminalization of Russian society, the outbreak of numerous civil wars and the prospect of widespread

158

disintegration in the former USSR there is still much to play for. Also it is far from clear that the social costs imposed on the US in order to pay for the Reagan strategic vision will not have harmful and lasting consequenses. Nor should we forget that some Realists in the US, notably John Mearsheimer, see the end of the Cold War as a trigger to political disharmony amongst the Western Alliance. The point is that this is really all just opinion. But in all this conjecture what has happened to truth? For Gray scholarly truth and the truths of statecraft are not synonymous: '...scholarly truth can differ from truth in the realm of statecraft'.[26] The truth of state policy lies in its effects, but these cannot be read off as though they are obvious. The consequences of the end of the Cold War are a matter of contestability; they demand interpretation and they reside within the framework of theoretical investigation.

As the treatment given by Gray indicates, few policy advisers seemed to grasp that ethical and epistemological issues were raised by advocacy. Thus the incorporation of the endeavours of social scientists into the domain of military policy planning seems to have emerged in a fairly unconscious fashion. The crisis of the Second World War was permanently replicated in the Cold War and reinforced by the McCarthyte 1950s. As Irene Gendzier has shown collaboration extended to the creation of a paradigm of political development where US foreign policy goals and the fate of developing countries were seen as identical. As she demonstrates this collusion was exposed by Vietnam: 'The alleged neutrality of social science research was exploded before the evidence of complicity between well known scholars of Development and political change, and the policy planners in charge of military operations in Southeast Asia'.[27]

In the Humanities and Social Sciences the forging of links between academia and defence and intelligence agencies developed during World War II through the activities of the Office of Strategic Services. This organization scoured universities in order to locate experts in special areas and in particular highlighted the skills of political scientists and International Relations scholars. In 1965 John Gange, then President of the International Studies Association, remembered that, 'The Office of Strategic Services was like a big university faculty in many respects - sometimes staff meetings were just like faculty meetings'.[28] The relationship also worked in the opposite direction as well. One time director of the CIA, William Raborn, revealed that, 'in actual numbers we could easily staff the faculty of a university with our experts. In a way, we do. Many of those who leave us join the faculties of universities and colleges'.[29]

The RAND Corporation

Given these linkages it is entirely unsurprising that in the post-1945 period academics were drawn into the world of nuclear target planning and more general speculation about nuclear war. The key institution in this respect was the RAND corporation which, as noted above, emerged from the connection between Douglas Aircraft and the United States Airforce. The historical significance of RAND and was explored in the 1980s in two seminal studies by Fred Kaplan and Gregg Herken.[30] More recently some defects in RAND thinking have been explored by Manuel de Landa.[31] He reveals how RAND's original mathematical orientation determined the social science perspective which was later developed. According to de Landa RAND thinking reduced the question of the Soviet threat to a mathematical simulation based on a zero-sum game. To begin with this was an intellectual exercise, but as I argue below the Kennedy Administration institutionalized RAND theorizing. As de Landa notes, 'Although born at RAND during the 1950s, Systems Analysis did not become an institution until Robert McNamara became Secretary of Defense for the Kennedy Administration. He brought with him an army of "whiz kids" from RAND, and used them to limit the power of military decision-makers ...'[32]

In the 1950s RAND gradually became a centre of fusion between the world of academia and formal government service. Although RAND had a permanent staff it was typical for the corporation to recruit from universities. A famous example was Bernard Brodie who came to RAND via the Centre for International Studies at Yale and the Air Targets division of the Airforce. In 1945 Brodie and other colleagues at Yale sketched an intelligent and perceptive theory of deterrence in a study called the Absolute Weapon.[33] However, this study did not become relevant to US nuclear doctrine until the declaratory policy of assured destruction was enunciated in the 1960s. In the early days at RAND work on nuclear planning was concerned with speculation about nuclear war and the Airforce's confusion over a new strategy. Key questions concerned the potency of the bomb, the likely casualties if the weapon were used and the number of bombs needed.[34] This was novel and worrying for some social scientists and Brodie's colleague Jim Lipp dropped out because of moral anxieties. As Fred Kaplan observed, 'Nobody had ever killed 35 million people on a piece of paper before'.[35] As this process unfolded it became increasingly unclear where the boundary between the state and universities could be drawn. The traditional liberal arts view of intellectual work no longer explained the role of intellectuals in

160

society, but no alternative notion was forthcoming. As I have suggested, in the context of the Cold War a residue of unconsciousness clouded the issue. The state had articulated a new code for scientists and intellectuals which had barely been noticed, because the ends to which the endeavour was geared seemed legitimate. In the 1960s and 70s the issue exploded on US campuses because of Vietnam, but by then the incorporation of the university was irreversible. In general Western liberal states have continually expanded the role of state organs without any explicit forms of justification for increased public power. In the US a critical ingredient in this process has been the creation of an intellectual, military and industrial triangle motivated and sustained by the Cold War. As Campbell has argued the articulation of the modalities of the Cold War has been central to the project of securing America's identity in the contested terrain of domestic society.[36] In particular the invocation of danger has functioned as a highly consensual force. At the beginning of the Cold War a sustained effort was needed to convey the message of peril, threat and danger. But at the same time the dangers of nuclear armaments needed to be displaced and neutralized. Events in Europe in 1948 gave the Americans a clearer image of an enemy and also gave Truman much needed leverage in his battle with Congress for larger appropriations. Behind closed doors there were fundamental anxieties about the atomic strategy, but the deteriorating international situation militated against open discussion. In January 1950 Truman gave the go-ahead for construction of a hydrogen bomb and America's commitment to an atomic strategy of actual or threatened mass destruction was sealed. Fundamental questions, though, remained to be answered. Should the US strike first or second? Was the bomb a means of deterring or winning wars? Were US strategic bases vulnerable to surprise attack? How could atomic bombs best be delivered to their targets?

These questions and many others were posed and answered by scientists and social scientists working at RAND and American Universities in the 1950s. Their efforts were central in the sphere of policy discourse. As Herken reveals, 'Since 1945, American policy on nuclear weapons has been sometimes determined - and always influenced - by a small "nucleus" of civilian experts whose profession it has been to consider the fearful prospect of nuclear war'.[37] Their efforts led to a debate which framed a limited public airing of questions which has since been dubbed a 'golden age' of strategic thinking. From 1960 the defence intellectuals were actually brought into government. Thus what began as indirect policy prescription became real guiding principles of US strategic policy.

The process which galvanized intellectual interest in defence policy in the 1950s was the Eisenhower administration's 'New Look'. At the heart of the new policy there was an increased reliance on nuclear weapons, created by fiscal restraint and the new specific notion of extended deterrence, called by Secretary of State, Dulles, massive retaliation. The policy, while popular with the Strategic Air Command, aroused bitter controversy elsewhere and sparked a contest where the administration was pitted against all other participants. The policy was regarded by RAND strategists as crude and inflexible and likely to lack credibility. Also leading defence writers in universities turned their critical talents against the new doctrine.

At RAND Bernard Brodie highlighted the lack of refinement in nuclear planning. In the Strategic Air Command the aim was to maximize damage to Soviet urban industrial targets. As one writer put it the plan was to leave Russia, 'a smoking, radiating ruin at the end of two hours'.[38] Brodie, in contrast, was postulating the use of smaller, tactical nuclear weapons, against Soviet ground forces. However, a grim prospect now haunted these speculations. The United States's original plans for atomic weapons had reactivated the doctrines of strategic bombing. However, these ideas presupposed an American nuclear monopoly which had ended in 1949. But even worse, from a United States perspective, the USSR had developed the hydrogen bomb in 1953 and would soon possess the means to deliver it to the continental United States.

This new reality lay at the back of a whole tradition in strategic theory which had to grapple with novel circumstances. The threat of nuclear apocalypse had to be incorporated into a discourse of scientific control and rationality. What mattered here was not that the theories were coherent, factually corroborated or credible. The point was to have an edifice of scientific rationality; to sustain the myth that apocalyptic military power was under control. The myths were important for the public because of the issue of political order and anxiety; the potential risks of a doomsday military policy for domestic society were enormous. However, the rigour of nuclear discourse was also necessary for planners and political elites. The implementors had to believe in their own project. Critically, from the horizons of American culture, the enterprise had to be under control and the military artifacts compatible with a vision of scientific process.

This hyper-modernist project was centred on the RAND corporation where exponents of maths, physics, games theory and econometrics developed a technocratic categorial framework of nuclear war. This framework disguised the fact that the dialectical relationship of destruction between the superpowers was not amenable to an overarching system of management. The US could only influence the process indirectly. The concepts developed by defence intellectuals in response to this issue were counterforce theory, graduated deterrence, limited war, intra-war deterrence, escalation

162

dominance, crisis management and game theory. Klein argues that the effect of this work was to colonize dissent and legitimize nuclear planning, 'the effect of their work is to co-opt critique by enframing strategy within a techno-logic of deterrence...'[39] As I have indicated underlying this is a powerful ideology which is pivotal in the US self image. The ideology is best understood as a technocratic representation of liberal progressivism. It focuses on ideas of abstract reasoning as a problem solving tool where thought is a form of engineering device. In the American context it has led to the idea that science and technology can overcome any problems posed for humans and that the scope of modernism is unbounded.

In the case of weapons technology the application of this ideology is obvious. However, it is essential to realize that the social sciences have been viewed in this light as well. With the Soviets able to attack the US with atomic weaponry a whole new field of enquiry was disclosed. What were Soviet intentions? How did the leadership perceive the US? Which threats would frighten the USSR most? How would the public respond to defence policy which had created a doomsday machine? How could the US best signal its intentions? When crises developed how could they be controlled? In classical realism the 'ifs' and 'buts' of war and diplomacy had never been ironed out by any faith in scientific management. However, in the nuclear age the contingencies, the unforeseen, the accidental and the interpretive were unacceptable to US defence intellectuals. Thus at RAND the systems analysts, mathematicians, economists and political scientists were seeking to bring defence under scientific control. According to Spencer Weart the search for coherence and order was illusory. He writes of the enterprise in these terms, 'From the 1950s on, the sharpest analysts left ambiguities, internal contradictions, and blind leaps of logic in their writings. Most changed their position from one year to the next and sometimes, it seemed, from one page to the next.'[40]

In the mid 1950s a work which crystallized the intellectual crusade for nuclear rationality was William Kaufman's edited collection called, *The Requirements of Deterrence*.[41] Kaufman, a political scientist at the Princeton Centre for International Studies, was specifically responsible for the concepts of graduated deterrence, limited war and mutual restraint. In response to the policy of massive retaliation his overall critique emphasized the lack of credibility and flexibility of Dulles's plan. The major policy goal which Kaufman sought to put in place was a US capacity to deter communist aggression at every conceivable level, including a substantial conventional deterrent. Kaufman was one of the first strategists to seek to put the nuclear genie back in the bottle. The particular emphasis Kaufman put on conventional forces appealed to the army and his work was widely read by

163

army generals. However, this policy preference was never enacted, rather Kaufman's ideas were applied to a nuclear format where graduated deterrence was viewed as a scale of incremental uses of tactical nuclear weapons. The ideological significance of his views lay in their presumption that it would be possible to control warfare in a discriminate and subtle fashion. Hence Kaufman was a pathfinder for the Nato dogma of the 1960s and 1970s known as flexible response. The important political myth which was created was the idea that a nuclear war could be a finely tuned process which was always under political control. This was crucial in public debate about defence issues because the generalized anxiety of the layman could be offset by the cool and sober expertise of the defence specialist. Kaufman's policy relevance was rewarded in 1956 by a move to the RAND corporation and later by posts in the Kennedy Administration At RAND Kaufman found that many of his ideas were gaining credibility and that a consensus about counterforce was already in place.

Another RAND theorist who advocated counterforce was the redoubtable Herman Kahn. Kahn, a physicist, had originally worked on mathematical models of bomb design, but during the 1950s he addressed himself increasingly to issues of strategy. Always likely to shock his audience he once told airforce generals, 'Gentlemen, you don't have a war plan, you have a war orgasm.' Kahn's mission, as he saw it, was to bring precision and rationality to war doctrine and his ideas were widely aired. Prior to the publication of his magnum opus *On Thermonuclear War* in 1960 he did hundreds of talks and briefings and was heard by thousands of people.[42] Kahn's undoubted influence was enhanced by the fact that he was a noted futurologist and, thanks to Kubrick's Dr Strangelove (1964), where the central character was based on Kahn, a national figure. It should be noted that Kahn's ideas were at the more bizarre end of the continuum of strategic thinking. However, it would be naive to assume that his theories have lacked policy relevance. Kahn proposed deterrence based on a doomsday machine which was very controversial, but Kaplan notes, 'Yet the Doomsday Machine was only a slightly absurd extension of existing American and Nato policy'.[43] In order for the US to obtain political utility from its nuclear arsenal Kahn believed that it must have the capability and the will to initiate nuclear war or to threaten to do so. In light of this he was an enthusiast for extensive civil defence programmes and he had a clear commitment to the idea that the US could recover after a nuclear war. Although some of his ideas are freakish, such as the need to have radiation meters in shelters in order to distinguish the ill from those who were faking, other ideas percolated into the strategic grammar of the early 1980s. Escalation dominance, intra-war deterrence and fighting a protracted nuclear war were cornerstones of recent

Pentagon policy and were all evident in his 1960 publication. At the time fellow scientists were divided about Kahn's ideas, but their power came from the appearance of scientific rigour which characterized the work. Stuart Hughes described On Thermonuclear War as, '... one of the great works of our time'.[44] A different view was taken by Noam Chomsky: 'Kahn proposes no theories, no explanations, no factual assumptions that can be tested against their consequences, as do the sciences he is attempting to mimic. He simply suggests a terminology and provides a facade of rationality'.[45]

In contrast to Kahn, whose eccentric and apocalyptic theories were regarded as provocative, Kaufman exerted a real influence on defence planning and the emerging strategic grammar of the late 1950s. Indeed, Kaufman's career reveals the fusion of the university and the national security apparatus rather neatly. In the late 1950s Kaufman did a series of briefings for airforce generals which sought to sell the strengths of counterforce, limited war and mutual restraint. In the airforce counterforce was already in vogue as the Strategic Air Command was the vehicle which would strike at 'time urgent' targets in the USSR.[46] However, the 50s plans amounted to the unrestricted obliteration of Russia and, as later in the British case, a fixation about destroying Moscow. In consequence airforce generals were unhappy about the intellectual niceties of Kaufman's theories. At an infamous briefing at SAC headquarters in December, 1960 the new CIC Thomas Power made the following point to the political scientist, 'Why do we want to restrain ourselves ... Restraint! Why are you so concerned with saving their lives. The whole idea is to kill the bastards.'[47] Nevertheless the Airforce was, in fact, in accord with Kaufmann's views. The reason was that counterforce was a mechanism for articulating a vision of strategy which undercut the appropriations of the other services. Also, while purple language could be used in the privacy of briefings this was not the lingua franca of political legitimacy. The RAND taxonomy helped to neutralize anxiety about the Strategic Air Command. A process endorsed by a significant and loyal Hollywood output in the 1950s around the theme of the bomber. As Franklin notes, 'By the mid-1950s the strategic bomber had become a major icon of American culture'.[48]

Although William Kaufman's ideas appealed specifically to SAC, the truth was that ideas coming from RAND, Princeton, MIT and Harvard offered new justifications for increased numbers of weapons across the board. Eisenhower set up the Science Advisory Committee in 1957 and again academics from MIT and Harvard figured prominently, especially Kissinger, Schelling and Halperin. At RAND Albert Wohlstetter's concern over vulnerability, expressed in the R290 study on SAC basing, fed directly into the Gaither panel report, *Deterrence and Survival in the Nuclear Age*. This report handed to Eisenhower in November 1957, was highly pessimistic and recommended the spending of an extra $44 billion on defence over the next five years. Another significant contribution was Kissinger's *Nuclear Weapons and Foreign Policy*,[49] which was commissioned by the Council on Foreign Relations while the author was a junior academic at Harvard. The book, which was widely read, was especially popular in army circles as it supported their drive for increase deployment of tactical nuclear weapons as a counter to Soviet power. The essential message of the work was that US military technology would only have utility if politicians were prepared to use it.[50]

The climate in which these ideas were expressed was one of acute anxiety on defence matters. The defence intellectuals, writing in universities and think-tanks, reflected this anxiety and concentrated their attack on the seeming complacency of the Eisenhower administration. On specific matters of policy some intellectuals were close to real centres of power, especially if their departments were doing work directly for the CIA, as the Centre of International Studies at MIT was.[51] However, as regards the central questions of defence policy, the contribution of academics as they shuttled between university and think-tank was, as I suggested above, to create a taxonomy; a grammar and semantics of strategic analysis. The concepts they developed disclosed the reality of weapons and defence planning and set the terms of debate for the next three decades. This is not, then, a disinterested account of a pre-existing state of affairs. The facts of strategic planning were enclosed in concepts of deterrence, counterforce, limited war, first and second strikes and escalation dominance. This, in itself, is a major contribution to the politics of defence. In particular these ideas set the boundaries for legitimate and illegitimate criticism; they distinguished between friend and foe. But after 1960 defence intellectuals actually saw real war plans and, in the case of Vietnam, provided both operational concepts and policy initiatives.

From Rhetoric to Policy

The arrival of the Kennedy administration in Washington in 1960 brought academia into the White House, the State Department and the Pentagon. Indeed, the number of Cambridge men and Rhodes scholars in the government was a constant source of pride to the President and his close advisers. At the Pentagon, the new Secretary of Defence, Robert McNamara had been president of Ford America. However, this background in business did not dispose him against intellectuals. On the contrary McNamara brought in a large number of analysts from RAND who had previously worked at

MIT, Princeton and Harvard. McNamara's goal was to bring defence under rational and scientific control; to organize the budget more effectively and, in particular, to maintain political control over nuclear weapons. In order to achieve this he believed the skills of mathematicians, political scientists, economists and systems analysts would be crucial and such specialists were duly put into key roles in the national security machine. Above all, in the early days, the new secretary sought to rationalize nuclear strategy. To this end the new administration put in effect the SIOP which Secretary Gates had initiated at the end of the Eisenhower period.

The first SIOP was finished in December 1960 and was dominated by SAC. The plan envisaged an attack with immediately available munitions which would mean the detonation of 1459 warheads with an explosive power equivalent to 2,164 megatons against 654 targets in Russia, Eastern Europe and China. In this optimum mix strategy estimated fatalities were 175 million.[52] If the entire force available were to be used then 3,423 weapons would be delivered with a yield of 7,847 megatons. Here fatalities would be 285 million with a further 40 million injured.[53] Airforce Chief of Staff, Tommy White thought the plan excellent. But SAC commander Thomas Power was concerned about a point of detail, he asked White what would happen if China was not involved? White replied, '... I hope nobody thinks of it because it would really screw up the plan'.[54]

The atavism and crudity of the view cited above could have no place in the discourse of rational strategic policy. McNamara was briefed on the SIOP in February 1961 and immediately decided that it must be reworked. The intellectual put in charge of reworking the SIOP was Daniel Ellsberg who had come into the government via RAND and Harvard. Ellsberg was in a unique position to tackle the problem because he had actually seen the real war plans. Quite by accident Ellsberg had stumbled across a document called JSCAP Annex C which had never been viewed by any civilian, including the President. While the document was shocking in itself, as it called for the obliteration of the USSR, what particularly disturbed Ellsberg was the realization that planning and discussions at RAND had borne little relation to operational realities. The Airforce and SAC had been happy to bounce ideas around in RAND briefings, but the analysts had not been given access to real plans. RAND theorizing in the 1950s can thus be seen as a vivid form of textuality. The intellectual agenda, the strategic grammar and the tactical niceties of deterrence created a lucid framework of legitimacy for policies which actually connoted nihilism: SAC simply intended to bomb the USSR into obliteration. RAND thinking had been premised on growing US vulnerability and on the need to find a rationale for SAC. However, the intelligence estimates made available to RAND personnel had been false.

There was no bomber gap, no missile gap and SAC had a rationale which was massive superiority.

The myth of US vulnerability had been at the centre of the Kennedy critique of the Eisenhower defence policy. Within days of coming to office Kennedy was briefed on the nature of the myth by his scientific adviser Jerome Wiesner who had come into the government from MIT. In the meantime Ellsberg had gone back to RAND to deliver a sensational briefing on the missile gap. He told an astonished audience that there was a gap and that the ratio was 10:1; then he added that it was in the US's favour.[55]

The revision of the SIOP undertaken by Ellsberg was known as Project One. Project One again reveals the overwhelming presence of the ideology of control and instrumental rationality which pervaded the RAND corporation. The likely brute facts of confrontation, which only films and novels have attempted to depict honestly, disappeared beneath a veneer of precision, calculation and cold analysis. RAND thus established a counter-factual rhetoric which articulated a value-neutral framework for nuclear war. Thomas Power was once asked what happens when nuclear war begins. He replied, 'My mind just stops there'.[56] The RAND revision of the SIOP reveals how and why this is possible. The language of strategic discourse left no space for real death and destruction. Hence its practitioners could enter a conceptual world where the horrors of nuclear war had been eliminated. Project One left 'invulnerable forces in reserve', it effected, 'targeting discrimination', it tightened, 'command and control', it regretted,'collateral damage' and it culminated in the policy of, 'second - strike counterforce'. The SIOP revision concluded a period when there had been intense intellectual interest in nuclear strategy. But, after Cuba concern moved elsewhere. In intellectual circles interest in strategy now shifted to another domain. To put it simply the concepts of limited war, intra-war deterrence and escalation dominance were now applied to the escalating conflict in Vietnam.

Intellectuals and Counter Insurgency

The historical and intellectual roots of US involvement in Vietnam lay in Truman's containment doctrine and in the domino theory. Truman's aim had been to contain communist expansion on a worldwide level and he was willing to commit conventional forces in order to achieve this goal. In comparison the Eisenhower years saw a reliance on nuclear weapons and a geo-strategic focus on Europe. As a presidential candidate Kennedy had attacked this policy and, upon entering office, he was committed to responding to communist aggression everywhere and at every level. Moreover, after Cuba, Kennedy and his advisers perceived the main threat to be insurgency in the Third World and, particularly, Chinese support for wars of national liberation. As Ambrose notes, 'There was also universal agreement on the need to prove to the Chinese that wars of national liberation did not work and to show the Third World that America stood by her commitments. These views were held most strongly by JFK's personal advisers, led by Walt Rostow and McGeorge Bundy'.[57] An important reason why intellectuals were so significant in the Kennedy years was the President's habit of setting up ad hoc committees which often bypassed the usual agencies. As Ambrose indicates two of the key intellectual advisers in the Kennedy administration were McGeorge Bundy and Walt Whitman Rostow.[58] According to Halberstam the former, who sat on the committee which managed the Cuban missile crisis, was arguably the brightest star in the Kennedy constellation; a man of high intellectual attainment and impeccable upper class credentials. Bundy, the son of Harvey Bundy who had been a friend of and aid to Henry Stimson, had been educated at Groton and Yale and had gone from Yale to teach political science at Harvard. Kennedy appointed him as Special Assistant for National Security Affairs which gave him a leading role in Vietnam. Bundy's deputy, Walt Rostow, who acted as Chief of the State Department's Policy Planning Staff, was also a leading intellectual, but he was from a radically different background. He was born in New York in 1916, the son of a Russian, Jewish immigrant.[59] He graduated from Yale, was a young Rhodes scholar and while in his twenties was recruited for the Office of Strategic Services. In 1950, at the age of 34, Rostow founded the MIT centre for International Studies with money provided by the CIA.[60] In 1953 he and colleagues produced a CIA funded book, *The Dynamics of Soviet Society*, which was only available to the public in an abridged version. However, the loss of academic freedom did not bother Rostow. For him the highest goal of academic work was to serve the nation-state.

Rostow's impact on policy can be seen in the report he submitted to Kennedy after a fact finding mission to Vietnam undertaken with General Maxwell Taylor in October 1961. Following an earlier expedition headed by Lyndon Johnson, Rostow and Taylor endorsed the advice which the Vice President had brought back. They recommended an increased military presence. He further advised Kennedy that North Vietnam should be bombed in a graduated escalation which should match Hanoi's support for the Viet Cong. Kennedy accepted the recommendations, apart from the one to bomb the North.[61] At the time of the Rostow mission there were 1,364 US advisers in Vietnam, by November 1963 there were 15,000.[62] In 1961 another critical academic input came from economist Eugene Staley of Stanford -

home of the army's think. In the summer Staley visited Saigon and made a series of suggestions to the Diem government. Of these the Strategic Hamlet's programme was the most significant. The original idea was to bring peasants into protected Havens to isolate them from the VC, prevent recruitment and to stop VC hiding in villages.[63] The reality was rather different. The villagers were coerced off their land at gun point in order to create free-fire zones for the ARVN and later American forces. The programme was instituted in 1962/63 and involved the movement of 8,700,000 people into Hamlets. Bernard Fall described it as, 'the most mammoth example of "social engineering" in the non-communist world'.[64] As to methods it was described by Marine Colonel William Corson as, 'forced resettlement, physical oppression, coercion and political "persuasion" by the club'.[65]

In the Kennedy years Bundy's contribution was essentially to be the intellectual arbiter. He would weigh the advice the President was receiving and then point up the pros and cons of particular paths. At this time, and throughout, the major advocates of using increased force were Taylor and Rostow. However, by 1965 the situation had changed. As the Pentagon Papers illustrate a major concern of the Johnson administration was the question of American credibility. Despite intelligence reports which were sometimes plain lies the truth was known; the war was going badly. The ARVN were performing poorly, morale was low and there were massive defections to the communists. For Bundy, who was not especially interested in Asia, this was an important issue, as it was for Johnson. Credibility involved demonstrating to allies that US security guarantees meant something. For the administration it meant not retreating in ignominious defeat. After a year's very uneasy relationship with Johnson, Bundy and the President began to see eye to eye on the issue of credibility.[66] In January 1965 Bundy suggested to Johnson that he make a trip to Saigon to check, first hand, the situation on the ground. By early February he was in Vietnam. On the 7th the VC launched a mortar attack on the US base at Pleiku; killing eight American soldiers. Bundy visited the injured and was outraged; the cool intellectual exterior cracked. The result was a memo to Johnson urging instant retaliation and a graduated series of bombing raids against the North.[67]

Back in Washington the Bundy memo was significant in pushing Johnson towards the decision for wholesale bombing, known as operation 'Rolling Thunder'. From this time on the US incrementally increased the firepower unleashed on Vietnam and the number of combat troops, ultimately to 500,000. In intellectual terms this was limited war, graduated deterrence and escalation dominance. In human terms it was something else. The destruction of Vietnam was unprecedented. By 1970 more bombs had been dropped than in the whole of human history. By 1973 the tonnage of explosives used was 8 million and there were 21 million bomb craters in South Vietnam. As well as bombs the airforce also used Agent Orange to defoliate the countryside. At the end of the war 1/2 of Vietnam's coastal mangroves had been destroyed, 1/3 of its hardwood forests and 6 million acres of farmland was poisoned by chemicals. As to casualties there are no definite figures, but one estimate is 2.6 million dead.[68]

This carnage was enacted by a government racked by doubts, but convinced of the truth of certain intellectual ideas about power and the use of military force. The role of intellectuals though, was not just a case of Harvard and Yale men giving advice inside the government. During the Vietnam years connections between academia and the Pentagon extended to the national level and many universities were embroiled in scandals as the scale of research for security agencies became apparent. But let me be clear the cosy relationship between academia and the state had changed. Academics were still serving the security state, but there was now concerted opposition in universities.

The interface between the state and academia widened in the 1960s because of the government's need of experts in development and modernization. As the US surveyed its relations with the Third World it became critical to plot a trajectory for the relationship. In other words rather than fight governments which had instituted communism it would be easier to 'manage' Third World developments towards liberalism and capitalism. Just as intellectual capital had brought nuclear strategy under control so it could engineer social development.

This new tactic, though, was much more difficult. Nuclear strategy was written in documents and programmed into computers. There were no real word counterfactuals to contend with. Moreover, the small number of academics who really counted in the nuclear field could be given exhaustive security checks. However, by moving into the intellectual terrain of development and modernization the state was engaging universities in areas where there was widespread controversy and debate. Departments of Sociology and Social anthropology proved less tractable than those of economics and political science and the state patronage sparked by Vietnam produced a reaction against development. Gendzier notes:

If Political Development Studies were sparked by postwar U.S. foreign policy and the need for a cadre of domestic experts, the war in Vietnam generated the conditions that opened the door to widespread support for counter-development studies...[69]

171

The most notorious case was the army's project Camelot, conceived in 1963 by the Army Office of Research and Development. The plan was to spend $4-6 million channelled through the American University's Special Operations Research Office. The project was headed by the sociologist Rex Hopper, who by 1965 had acquired the services of 33 leading US behavioural scientists. The research aimed to isolate the causes of social and political breakdown in Latin America, Africa, Asia and the Middle East and to recommend strategies to forestall such breakdown. The orthodox view of this was that it was part of a development strategy; to ensure that Third World countries trod the path of economic liberalization. However, it must be observed that the project was launched during a period of revolutionary change in the Third World. Thus, it is possible to view Camelot as an anthropological strategy for counter insurgency.

Project Camelot was aborted in 1965 by McNamara, but as Robert Nisbet has shown, this was not because of the domestic dispute in American academia, it was the result of an international scandal.[70] In 1963 a Professor of Anthropology travelled to Chile to make contact with Chilean social scientists. He sounded out his contacts to see if they would collaborate in a US army project to study political unrest. The Chilean academics failed to see the attractions of working as agents for the US army in their own country and shortly afterwards a diplomatic storm broke out between the two countries.[71]

Camelot was a well known example, but it was the tip of an iceberg. Building on contacts established by OSS, the CIA and the State Department after 1945 there was an extensive network of University-Intelligence contacts by the 1960s. Academics at Michigan State University were working on a project for the CIA to train South Vietnamese policemen.[72] In 1967 it was discovered that the Executive Director and the Treasurer of APSA were respectively the President and Vice President of Policy Research Incorporated, which was a CIA front.[73] This led to some scandal in US political science circles, but the International Relations establishment was not unduly abashed probably because American International Relations Departments were receiving substantial funding from Defence and Foreign Policy agencies. In 1966, William Crochet, of the State Department commented:

The colleges and Universities provide us with a rich body of information about many subjects, countries and people through special research studies prepared for many clients and purposes. For example, the United States Government is spending $30m this year on foreign affairs studies in American Universities.[74]

Reasons and Motives

One could list links between universities and Security organizations ad infinitum, but here let us turn now to their causes and consequences. In an important article, entitled, 'Lying in Politics' Hannah Arendt gives illuminating insights into the Pentagon Papers (McNamara's 47 volume history of US policy in Vietnam).[75] Throughout the documents Arendt observes the impetus to retain credibility to save face and to maintain certain images for domestic consumption. As the prosecution of the war became simultaneously more destructive and less effective the need to cover up the truth and to ignore dissenting voices - such as George Ball's - increased. In this respect the behaviour of the defence intellectuals became more and more an act of bad faith. By late 1966 many in the Administration such as McNamara, Ellsberg and McNaughton (a former Harvard Law Professor) had lost faith in the policy. However, the ubiquity of deception continued. While Rostow still believed that victory was imminent and that the bombing was working, those around him were playing damage limitation. In Arendt's view the Pentagon Papers reveal that image making, rather than containment, was the ultimate policy and as she comments the intellectuals, 'played the game of deception and falsehoods'.[76] Collectively the self deception which abounded concerned the myths that furnished the policy from the beginning. That communism was a monolith, that there were two states, that the North had attacked the South and that the war was against the North. As individuals the civilian advisers had doubts about these particular assumptions, but as a collective intelligence unit the doubts were submerged under the ideological front of the policy and the image making. As to the reasons for failure Arendt regards them as remarkably simple: '... the wilful, deliberate disregard of all facts, historical, political, geographical for more than 25 years'.[77]

The acquiesence of the intellectuals in deception points to a fusion of personal motives and general ideological factors. In a commentary on Project Camelot Irving Louis Horrowitz listed some of the motives that drove the 'consultants'. There was first the excitement of a big project; of transcending what C. Wright-Mills had demeaned as 'abstract empiricism'. There was the exhilaration of power; of rising above the humdrum ordinariness of the campus and the classroom. There was the Platonic arrogance inherent in advising and educating an elite. There was an enlightenment zeal about using social science as a vehicle for humanization and finally a sense of dizzy excitement; of becoming a doer, rather than a thinker.[78]

Part and parcel of the process was thus the basic desire for social advancement. The top advisers were clearly members of an elite, their establishment credentials were unambiguous. Moreover, their careers indicated that there were glittering prizes. After government service it was quite typical for these men to go on to be presidents of the largest foundations or universities. Thus in the lower echelons of academia there was a clear perception of a career ladder that culminated in endorsement by the state.

In the whole of this process there was a fundamental unconsciousness about the politics of these developments. After 1945 there was virtually no oppositional intellectual culture in the US. In the 1950s Macarthyism moved academic debate to the right, while the syndrome Daniel Bell called the 'end of ideology' robbed intellectual life of fundamental political reflection. The mainstream of American politics - understood as pluralism - was seen as a neutral political ground devoid of the patent absurdities of the left and the right. Under the sway of behaviouralist commitment to ethical neutrality US political science should have realized that all purposes were contestable, subjective and lacking foundations. However, this reflection was never applied to core US values. The two party-system, capitalism, materialism and the belief in science were simply unquestioned as the foundation for all academic purpose. In consequence to serve the state, to bring their values into being on a worldwide stage was completely non-controversial. In Rostow's modernization theory all nations were heading towards a rational, productive and affluent future. In assisting the American state social science was just promoting - at a faster rate - a historical process which was inevitable.

These aspects of American intellectual life explain, I believe, why intellectuals were prepared to be closely associated with policies which caused untold misery and suffering. The core values, the theory and the instrumental rationality preordained the idealism of the American way. Thus Kennedy's idealism, which was wrapped up in the semantics of universalism, was really the universalization of particular American beliefs. On the day that Che Guevara was killed Rostow called a staff meeting. He announced, 'The Bolivians have executed Che ... They finally got the son of a bitch. The last of the romantic guerillas'.[79] For Rostow men like Che were deluded opponents of progress, to liquidate them was an act of liberation. The theory, then, could legitimize any cruelty because it was correct. Numerous examples can be found of this form of logic, but the following is an archetypical case. In testimony to the House Committee on Foreign Affairs, Professor David Rowe, Director of Graduate Studies in International Relations at Yale proposed a policy of mass starvation against China. He said: 'Mind you, I am not talking about this as a weapon against the Chinese people. It will be. But that is only incidental. The weapon will be against the government because the internal stability of that country cannot be sustained by an unfriendly government in the face of general starvation'.[80]

Conclusions

The role of intellectuals in supporting, designing and implementing state security policy is both significant and controversial. Robert Engler exposes some of the contradictions that were apparent in the Vietnam years:

> Working directly for the military is commonplace, and classified social science projects are widespread. It is reported that MIT has awarded a number of higher degrees for classified theses. One loses the capacity to distinguish between satire and reality when an applicant for a university position in political science, currently employed by the Rand Corporation, explains modestly on his vita, under the heading of publications, that many of his writings are classified and hence not available for listing or inspection.[81]

In the United States the prerequisites for an intellectual branch of the security state were first, a general atrophy of the idea of the critical and independent university and second, the concrete institutional links forged in World War II by the OSS. In the Cold War the independence of security relevant knowledge was no longer tolerated and natural science succumbed to the state's embrace. But at the same time the politically dangerous business of nuclear strategy required a legitimizing discourse; a mode of persuasion which would secure consent. My view is that traditional forms of military-cultural discourse could not engineer legitimacy in the nuclear sphere because America was vulnerable to obliteration. The inevitable defeat of the adversary because of Yankee ingenuity was no longer assured. Security had become dialectical and symmetrical. Accordingly the world of nuclear confrontation became disclosed as an area of calculation, management, prediction and rationality. The elites managing the nuclear apparatus could thus believe that they were involved in a credible and rational process. Even after a nuclear war images conveyed the notion of a still functioning state apparatus, albeit in a wasteland.

The impetus to cooperation with the state was enhanced by the McCarthy years when neutrality was suspect. Moreover, predominant theories in American political science such as value-neutrality, the end of ideology and modernization insinuated a sense of unconsciousness about collaborations. The security state was a force for the very values which underwrote academic endeavour.

175

In the late 1960s the problems of collusion were exposed by Vietnam and a left-liberal reaction set in. However, the fragile liberal consensus of the 1970s was undercut by economic failure and the ferocious assault of the new right. But, a new nuclear consensus was not created. The rhetoric and policy of the Reagan administration created an inevitable fissure in the wider strategic community which remained until the end of the Cold War. However, the lure of state patronage has not dried up. As the terrorism industry and the Gulf War reveals there is still plenty of scope for the purveyor of expertise. As Edward Said notes:

> So pervasive has the professionalisation of intellectual life become that the sense of vocation ... has been almost swallowed up. Policy oriented intellectuals have internalised the norms of the state.[82]

Notes and References

* An earlier version of this chapter appeared as (1996), 'Strategy, Hegemony and Ideology: the Role of Intellectuals', Political Studies, 44, No. 1, pp. 44-59.

1. Kennedy, P. (1988), *The Rise and Fall of the Great Powers*, Unwin Hyman, London, p. 358.
2. Blair, B. (1985), *Strategic Command and Control*, Brookings, Washington, p. 24.
3. Kincade, W. (1990), 'American National Style and Strategic Culture', in Jacobsen, C. (ed), *Strategic Power: USA/USSR*, Macmillan, London, p. 13.
4. Rothstein, Robert (1972), 'On the Costs of Realism', *Political Science Quarterly*, vol. LXXXV11, no. 3, pp. 347-62.
5. Banks, M. (1988), 'The Evolution of International Relations Theory' in Banks, M. (ed) *Conflict in World Society*, Harvester, Brighton, p. 9.
6. Lawrence, Philip, K. (1988), *Preparing for Armageddon*, Harvester, Brighton, p. 35.
7. Spencer Weart (1988), *Nuclear Fear*, Harvard University Press, Cambridge. Mass, p. 234.
8. Kaplan, Fred (1983), *The Wizards of Armageddon*, Simon & Schuster, New York, p. 170.
9. Weart, *Nuclear Fear*, p. 157.
10. MccGwire, M. C. (1984), 'The Dilemmas and Delusions of Deterrence', in Prins, G. (ed), *The Choice: Nuclear Weapons versus Security*, Chatto and Windus, London, pp. 81-82.
11. Gray, Colin (1993), 'Through a Missile Tube Darkly: New Thinking about Nuclear Strategy', *Political Studies*, vol. XL1, no. 4, p. 668.
12. Neumann, Franz (1976), 'The Intelligentsia in Exile' in Connerton, P. (ed), *Critical Sociology*, Penguin, Harmondsworth, p. 429.
13. Ibid. p. 429.
14. Quoted in Roszak, T. (1969), 'On Academic Delinquency' in Roszak, T. (ed), *The Dissenting Academy*, Penguin, Harmondsworth, p. 12.
15. Ibid, p. 5.
16. Ibid, p. 17
17. Gray, Colin (1982), *Strategic Studies*, Greenwood Press, New York.
18. Ibid. p. iii.
19. Ibid. p. 9.
20. Ibid. p. 7.
21. Gray, 'Through a Missile Tube', p. 661.
22. Gray, Strategic Studies, p. 8.

23. Ibid. p. 28.
24. Ibid. p. 21.
25. Gray,'Through a Missile Tube' p. 664.
26. Ibid. p. 664.
27. Gendzier, I. (1985) *Managing Social Change: Social Scientists and the Third World*, Westview, Boulder, p. 9.
28. Quoted in Windmuller, M. (1969),'The New American Mandarins', in Roszak (ed), *Dissenting Academy*, p. 112.
29. Quoted in ibid, p. 112.
30. See Kaplan, *Wizards of Armageddon* and Herken, Gregg (1985), *Counsels of War*, Alfred Knopf, New York.
31. de Landa, Manuel (1991), *War in the Age of Intelligent Machines*, Zone, New York.
32. Ibid. p. 102.
33. Brodie, B. (1946), *The Absolute Weapon*, Harcourt Brace, New York.
34. Herken, *Counsels of War*, p. 6.
35. Kaplan, *Wizards of Armageddon*, p. 78.
36. Campbell, D. (1992), *Writing Security*, Manchester University Press, Manchester, Ch. 1.
37. Herken, *Counsels of War*, p. xiv.
38. Quoted in ibid. p. 83.
39. Klein, B. (1988), 'Hegemony and Strategic Culture', *Review of International Studies*, vol. 14. no. 2, p. 139.
40. Weart, *Nuclear Fear*, p. 234.
41. Published as Kaufman, W. (ed) (1956), *Military Policy and National Security*, Princeton University Press, Princeton.
42. Kaplan, *Wizards of Armageddon*, p. 226.
43. Ibid. p. 223.
44. Quoted in N. Chomsky, 'The Responsibility of Intellectuals' in T. Roszak (ed), 'Dissenting' p. 241.
45. Ibid, pp. 241-242.
46. Bracken, P. (1983), *Command and Control of Nuclear Forces*, Yale University Press, New Haven, pp. 78-81.
47. Quoted in Kaplan, 'Wizards' p. 226.
48. Franklin, Bruce (1988), *War Stars*, Oxford University Press, New York, p. 116.
49. Kissinger, Henry, (1957) *Nuclear Weapons and Foreign Policy*, Harper, New York.
50. Ibid, p. 114.
51. Wise, D. and Ross, T. B. (1974), *Invisible Government*, New York, p. 244.

52. Kaplan, *Wizards of Armageddon*, p. 256.
53. Ibid, p. 269.
54. Quoted in ibid, p. 270.
55. Ibid, p. 255.
56. Quoted in Weart, *Nuclear Fear*, p. 235.
57. Ambrose, Stephen, (1978), *American Foreign Policy: the Rise to Globalism*, Penguin, Harmondsworth, p. 205.
58. See also Halberstam, D. (1972), *The Best and the Brightest*, Random House, New York, p. 193.
59. Ibid. p. 193.
60. Wise and Ross, *Invisible Government*, p. 244.
61. Ambrose, *American Foreign Policy*, p. 208.
62. Ibid, p. 208.
63. Ibid, p. 207.
64. Fall, B. (1963), *The Two Vietnams*, Pall Mall Press, London, p. 373.
65. Corson, W. (1969), *The Betrayal*, Norton, New York, p. 48.
66. Halberstam, *Best and Brightest*, pp. 628-640.
67. Ambrose, *American Foreign Policy*, p. 215.
68. Franklin, *War Stars*, p. 118.
69. Gendzier, *Managing Social Change*, p. 15.
70. Nisbet, R. (1970), *Tradition and Revolt*, Vintage Books, New York, pp. 250-253.
71. Ibid. p. 252.
72. Engler, R. (1969), 'Social Science and Social Consciousness', in Roszak (ed), *Dissenting Academy*, p. 181.
73. Windmuller, *New Mandarins*, p. 113.
74. Crockett, W. J. (1966), 'Two-Way Communication with the Educational Community', *Department of State Bulletin*, vol. 55, pp. 73-74.
75. Arendt, H. (1973), 'Lying in Politics', in Arendt, *Crisis of the Republic*, Penguin, Harmondsworth.
76. Ibid, p. 15.
77. Ibid, p. 38.
78. Cited in R. Nisbet, *Tradition and Revolt*, p. 250.
79. Quoted in Halberstam, *Best and Brightest*, p. 197.
80. Quoted in Chomsky 'Responsibility of Intellectuals', p. 240.
81. Engler,'Social Science and Social Consciousness', p. 111-112.
82. Said, Edward (1992), *Culture and Imperialism*, Chatto, London, p. 366.